Inclusion or Exclusion in the Sacred Texts and Human Contexts

Muhammad Shafiq • Thomas Donlin-Smith
Editors

Inclusion or Exclusion in the Sacred Texts and Human Contexts

palgrave
macmillan

Editors
Muhammad Shafiq
Hickey Center & IIIT Chair for
Interfaith Studies and Dialogue
Nazareth University
Rochester, NY, USA

Thomas Donlin-Smith
Department of Religious Studies
Nazareth University
Rochester, NY, USA

ISBN 978-3-031-70179-5   ISBN 978-3-031-70180-1   (eBook)
https://doi.org/10.1007/978-3-031-70180-1

© The Editor(s) (if applicable) and The Author(s), under exclusive license to Springer Nature Switzerland AG 2024

This work is subject to copyright. All rights are solely and exclusively licensed by the Publisher, whether the whole or part of the material is concerned, specifically the rights of translation, reprinting, reuse of illustrations, recitation, broadcasting, reproduction on microfilms or in any other physical way, and transmission or information storage and retrieval, electronic adaptation, computer software, or by similar or dissimilar methodology now known or hereafter developed.
The use of general descriptive names, registered names, trademarks, service marks, etc. in this publication does not imply, even in the absence of a specific statement, that such names are exempt from the relevant protective laws and regulations and therefore free for general use.
The publisher, the authors and the editors are safe to assume that the advice and information in this book are believed to be true and accurate at the date of publication. Neither the publisher nor the authors or the editors give a warranty, expressed or implied, with respect to the material contained herein or for any errors or omissions that may have been made. The publisher remains neutral with regard to jurisdictional claims in published maps and institutional affiliations.

This Palgrave Macmillan imprint is published by the registered company Springer Nature Switzerland AG
The registered company address is: Gewerbestrasse 11, 6330 Cham, Switzerland

If disposing of this product, please recycle the paper.

Dedicated to all those organizations, supporters, and individuals in public and private institutions who work wholeheartedly to promote interfaith dialogue and peaceful coexistence.

Preface

My fellowship during my graduate studies at the Ecumenical Library at Temple University, Department of Religion, was a blessing in disguise. It was a great learning opportunity for me reading articles on ecumenism and understanding how the Protestant community had struggled through to overcome their divisive differences. I learned about the significance of dialogue, a gateway to overcome differences, build bridges, reconcile, and cooperate for the better cause of humanity.

This exposure led me to participate in ecumenical meetings and conferences. But the discussion and papers presented there were about Christian theology and denominational differences. Jews, Muslims, and others had little space. When I enquired about this with my Jewish professor, the late Dr. Zalman Schachter-Shalomi, in 1978 upon returning from a conference, I was told that it was still good to participate. When Jewish, Muslims and members of other faiths increase in number in these conferences, the doors will open.

The doors opened during the middle of 1980s. We had witnessed before that the World Parliament of Religions Congress in Chicago in 1893 had come up with the ambitious agenda of tolerance and peaceful coexistence. But the First World War in 1914–1918 and then the Second World War in 1939–1945 along with the Holocaust plunged the world into deep darkness. Consequently, the United Nations was formed in 1945 to restore peace in the world. Just as nations were at war, world faiths were also divisive and hostile toward one other. Also, the Protestants and Catholic missionaries in Africa and Asia faced tremendous obstacles to continue their work in the face of the nationalist movements seeking freedom from the European colonialism. It was time for change. To build religious bridges among faiths, the World Council of Churches was created in Amsterdam in 1948. While the World Council of Churches was contemplating this change, the Vatican at Rome came up with Nostra Aetate during Vatican Council II, recognizing the Protestant Christian Community as fellow Christians and Jews and Muslims as monotheists, paving the way for dialogue among faiths. Gradually, the word *interfaith* dialogue became more known in communities, replacing ecumenical dialogue.

As educational institutions responded to the Civil Rights Movement by emphasizing the teachings of African and African American studies as well as women and gender studies on college/university campuses, the same was essential to expand it to global and interfaith studies to meet the challenges of our contemporary world. Nazareth College, now Nazareth University, was perhaps the first in the academic world to establish the Center for Interfaith Studies and Dialogue (CISD) on November 28, 2001, shortly after the September 11 tragedies. In 2004, the Center was integrated academically and, in 2011, was renamed the Brian and Jean Hickey Center for Interfaith Studies and Dialogue in honor of two of the Center's most dedicated long-time supporters. At the same time, the Islamic and Interfaith Studies Chair was created through the generous support of the International Institute of Islamic Thought at Herndon, Virginia.

In fulfilling the goals associated with the Hickey Center and IIIT Chair, we began the Sacred Texts and Human Contexts series of conferences on issues of Social Justice and its publications in 2013. The purpose was to bring together experts in interpreting the traditions of the world's religions and cultures to examine common issues. The series provides a source for new ideas and critical reflection on old ideas to stimulate the intellectual life of interfaith dialogue in our global world. The conferences are open to all, and the peer-reviewed publications are a result of these conferences. We had our first conference in June 2013 at Nazareth University which dealt with those sacred texts that divided and united humanity. Two hundred and fifty religious studies professors and religious professionals participated and more than seventy academic papers were presented. The peer-reviewed papers resulted in a book of twenty-six chapters, titled *Sacred Texts and Human Contexts: A North American Response to a Common Word Between Us and You*. Our second international conference, on the topic of wealth and poverty, was held at Fatih University in Istanbul, Turkey, in 2014 and the peer-reviewed papers were published in a book titled *Poverty and Wealth in Judaism, Christianity and Islam* by Palgrave Macmillan in 2016.

The Conference Committee then decided to include all faiths in future conferences. Therefore, our third international conference was on nature and the environment in religions and it was held in May 2016, and the peer-reviewed papers were published in *Nature and the Environment in Contemporary Religious Contexts* in

2018 by Cambridge Scholars Publishing. Our 2017 international conference focused on women and gender in religions, and selected papers were published in *Making Gender in the Intersection of the Human and the Divine* by Cambridge Scholars publishing in February 2019. Our next conference was in 2018 on religions and (de)legitimization of violence, and the peer-reviewed papers were published in *Religions and (De)Legitimization of Violence* by Palgrave Macmillan in 2021. Our conference on Mystical Traditions: Approaches to Peaceful Coexistence was held virtually on May 23–25, 2021. Selected papers were published in *Mystical Traditions: Approaches to Peaceful Coexistence* by Palgrave Macmillan in 2023. Our conference on Inclusion or Exclusion: The Self and the Other in Sacred Texts and Human Contexts was held at Nazareth College of Rochester on May 22–24, 2023, and Palgrave Macmillan has accepted the manuscript for publication. We are planning to have our next conference on Race in Sacred Texts and Human Contexts in May 2025.

Institutions can not thrive without collegial and financial support. The Hickey Center and IIIT Chair is blessed with such support by Nazareth University's President Beth Paul, Dean of the College of Arts and Sciences, Thomas Lappas, University administration, faculty, and staff. Special thanks go to the Religious Studies Department, particularly Chair Corinne Dempsey, Susan Nowak, Thomas Donlin-Smith, and Bishal Karna. We also extend our gratitude to our generous donors, most importantly Brian and Jean Hickey and the International Institute of Islamic though (IIIT) at Herndon, VA.

The challenge of discerning the scholarly needs of the interfaith movement and designing the programs to fulfill these needs would not have been possible without a team of committed religious leaders, professionals, and academics, all dedicated to the common cause of respectful tolerance and peaceful coexistence in our diverse world. The Hickey Center and IIIT Chair is thankful to all members of the Conference Committee, including David Hill, Mustafa Gokcek, Richard Salter, Etin Anwar, Matthew Temple, Michael Dobkowski, Shalahudin Kafrawi, and, of course, Thomas Donlin-Smith, an advisor and a co-editor of this scholarly endeavor.

In addition to all those mentioned above, I must mention my family: their forbearance is amazing especially that of my grandchildren, who are so often disappointed that their grandpa is busy with college work at home and can hardly spare enough time to play with them. I am thankful to my family for their patience and understanding of the importance of this work of interfaith. I must thank Dr. Angela Herrald and the students of the Hickey Center for their hard work on this project.

The Hickey Center and the IIIT Chair is indebted to its founders, and many community leaders and individuals who continue to give us hope for future and support to continue in our mutual quest for respectful interfaith and cultural dialogue and peaceful coexistence.

Thank you,

Rochester, NY, USA   Muhammad Shafiq

Acknowledgements

We acknowledge Dr. Angela Herrald for assisting in the editing of the manuscript and our dedicated Hickey Center and IIIT Chair student workers for their tireless support of the Sacred Texts and Human Contexts Conference held at Nazareth University in May 2023.

Introduction

Inclusion or Exclusion in Sacred Texts and Human Contexts is the sixth in a series of volumes flowing from the "Sacred Texts and Human Contexts" conferences held by the Hickey Center for Interfaith Studies and Dialogue at Nazareth University and its partner institutions. Previous conferences and essay volumes have brought an interfaith lens to examine topics such as wealth and poverty, the environmental crisis, sex and gender, violence, and mysticism. While the previous volumes tended to address specific social controversies dividing contemporary societies, in this book, contributors dive deep into the fundamental issue of otherness itself. The authors of these essays explore the range of human stances toward the other—our openness to difference—as seen in the sacred texts and communal experience of some of the world's religious traditions.

There are profound psychological, theological, sociological, anthropological, and ethical dimensions to experiencing the other, and this complex experience is richly expressed within the religious traditions. While the title of this volume adopts the dyad of "inclusion" and "exclusion" to summarize our responses to those we see as different than ourselves, the religious sources analyzed by the authors reflect a wide and nuanced range of emotions and critical considerations arising from this experience. Boundaries that distinguish one from another are crucial at every level of human life, from the walls of our cells to our formation of individual identity, to our construction of families, to our sense of communal belonging, but boundaries are not simple matters. Endless questions arise about the wisdom and justifications of our boundaries, the hospitable openings that perforate our walls, and how to relate to those who remain outside. "Exclusion," in its most hateful, violent, xenophobic forms, is easy to condemn (but sadly not always avoided in religious history), but many of our questions about relating to others across our boundaries are subtle and complicated.

The book is organized into three parts: "Exclusion or Inclusion in the Sacred Texts Traditions," "Comparative Studies of Exclusion or Inclusion in Religious Traditions," and "Contemporary Approaches to Exclusion or Inclusion in Religious Traditions," although individual essays often have connections to more than one of these broad headings. The arrangement is intended to focus attention on critical analysis of religious texts relevant to our theme, the beneficial insights provided by careful comparison of religious sources, and examples of current issues of religious inclusion and exclusion.

The essays of Part 1 examine our topic through selected texts of Judaism, Mahayana Buddhism, Evangelical Christianity, Islam, and Confucianism, underscoring the broad range of spiritual traditions represented in this book. Saundra Sterling Epstein, in "A Framework for Inclusion and Exclusion in Jewish Law and Practice," confronts the difficult realities of community boundaries and explains some Jewish methods for negotiating those boundaries. John M. Thompson asks the question "Does *Everyone* Get to Ride the 'Great Vehicle'?" and in doing so raises critical questions about radical inclusion in religious ideals. The issues for Thompson are quite different than those addressed by Jason Okrzynski, who is examining a religious tradition that gravitates toward an exclusivist soteriology. Okrzynski accepts the challenge of developing an "Ontology of Inclusion in Evangelical Christian Traditions." Muneer Kuttiyani Muhammad, in "Revisiting the Madinah Pact: Towards Rebuilding an Ideal Inclusive Society," looks carefully at how the early Islamic community handled the diversity of its social situation in order to glean lessons for contemporary practice. Finally, Mathew A. Foust raises issues of inclusion that are very old within Confucianism yet also very timely for us with his essay, "Confucian Exclusivism: A Challenge to Confucian Exemplarist Morality."

The essays of Part 2, "Comparative Studies of Exclusion and Inclusion in Religious Traditions," create a fascinating interfaith kaleidoscope as Christian, Muslim, Hindu, and Jewish sources are arranged alongside one another for critical comparison. John W. Fadden takes a fresh look at a famous twentieth-century example of interreligious influence in his "Legitimating the Other's Wisdom for Common Cause: Rev. Dr. Martin Luther King's Palm Sunday Sermon on Mohandas K. Gandhi." Like Fadden, Hans A. Harmakaputra demonstrates a Christian reading of a source from another religion: in this case, Islam. His "Encountering God's Grace in Islam: A Christian Reading of the Forty Hadith of Nawawī" shows us the creative possibilities of bringing a hospitable spirit to others' sacred texts. "From Exodus to Hizmet: Redefining Other and Self in Thought and Action," by Ori Z. Soltes, compares Jewish and Islamic sources to examine the powerful influence that religious myths and movements can have on our self-understanding and our relationships with others. "All Lovers Are Welcome: Rumi and the Spirituality of Hospitality in Fihi Ma Fihi," by June-Ann Greeley, concludes this section of the book on an inspiring and poetic note by exploring the emphasis on love and hospitality in the writings of Jajaluddin Rumi.

In Part 3, "Contemporary Approaches to Exclusion and Inclusion in Religious Traditions," the emphasis is on current struggles for more inclusive human relations within and among religious communities. José-David Padilla, OP, leads the way with his "Search for Belongingness: A Social Rhetorical Reading on Migration in the Bible." Considering the large-scale displacements and migrations of humans across the face of the planet at this moment, hardly any topic of inclusion and exclusion could be more timely. We have been saddened by the recent death of our friend and Nazareth University colleague, Abdoul Aziz Gaye, yet we are grateful for having experienced his personal warmth and careful scholarship. His work "Al-Walā' Wa-Al-Barā': The Principle of Loyalty to Muslims and Disavowal of Non-Muslims" Theorized by Ibn Taymiyya, Adopted and Developed by Early Wahhabism, provides a critical examination of boundary construction in Wahhabi Islam. Ahmet Celik also focuses on Islam, demonstrating the presence of "Multiple Political Discourse in the Islamic Tradition," with his insightful analysis of three major Islamic political thinkers. Etin Anwar brings us to the current moment in American culture with "The Hateful Rhetoric Against Muslims and the Authority-making of Islamic Identity," an analysis of an American myth of Islam as inherently violent and a proposal for an "Ijtihadi-feminist" construction of a counternarrative of nonviolent Islam.

The final essay of the book, "Religious Identity in a Pluralistic Age: The Paradox of Being Simultaneously Rooted and Open," by Mark King, is an apt conclusion to the volume. In both its statement of the issue and its method of analysis, it reminds us of the key elements seen in other essays as well. A general issue underlying this book is to use King's opening sentence, "how to remain rooted yet open: rooted in the practices and beliefs of their tradition, yet open to the wisdom and truth of others outside their faith tradition." Each of us is rooted in, and draws meaning from, our particularities, yet our well-being and the common good require stepping out into hospitable inclusion of others. King's method is to consult a deep and diverse pool of exemplars, not only from the Catholic faith where he is rooted but from Buddhism as well. As seen repeatedly in this book, the method is the message. When we employ the methods of interfaith study, considering and honoring wisdom from diverse sources, we exemplify in our scholarly method the humane inclusion we wish to see lived more fully in all dimensions of our communal lives.

Department of Religious Studies   Thomas Donlin-Smith
Nazareth University
Rochester, NY, USA
tdonlin1@naz.edu

Contents

Part I Inclusion or Exclusion in the Sacred Texts Traditions 1

1 A Framework for Inclusion and Exclusion in Jewish Law and Practice 3
   Saundra Sterling Epstein

2 Does *Everyone* Get to Ride the "Great Vehicle"?: Exclusive Inclusivism in the Lotus Sūtra 27
   John M. Thompson

3 Inclusive Evangelicalism? Toward An Ontology of Inclusion in Evangelical Christian Traditions 43
   Jason Okrzynski

4 Revisiting Madinah Pact: Towards Rebuilding an Ideal Inclusive Society 59
   Muneer Kuttiyani Muhammad and Muhammad Mumtaz Ali

5 Confucian Exclusivism: A Challenge to Confucian Exemplarist Morality 75
   Mathew A. Foust

Part II Comparative Studies of Inclusion or Exclusion
         in Religious Traditions   91

6   Legitimating the Other's Wisdom for Common Cause:
    Rev. Dr. Martin Luther King's Palm Sunday Sermon
    on Mohandas K. Gandhi 93
    John W. Fadden

7   Encountering God's Grace in Islam: A Christian Reading
    of the Forty Hadith of Nawawī 107
    Hans A. Harmakaputra

8   From Exodus to Hizmet: Redefining Other and Self
    in Thought and Action 123
    Ori Z. Soltes

9   All Lovers Are Welcome: Rumi and the Spirituality of Hospitality
    in Fihi Ma Fihi 139
    June-Ann Greeley

Part III Contemporary Approaches to Inclusion or Exclusion
         in Religious Traditions   153

10 Searching for Belongingness: A Social Rhetorical Reading
    on Migration in the Bible 155
    José-David Padilla

11 Al-Walā' Wa-Al-Barā': The Principle of Loyalty to Muslims
    and Disavowal of Non-Muslims 167
    Abdoul Aziz Gaye

12 Multiple Political Discourses in the Islamic Tradition 183
    Ahmet Celik

13 The Hateful Rhetoric Against Muslims
    and the Authority-Making of Islamic Identity 201
    Etin Anwar

14 Religious Identity in a Pluralistic Age: The Paradox
    of Being Simultaneously Rooted and Open 225
    Mark King

Concluding Remarks 241

Index 245

Notes on Contributors

Thomas Donlin-Smith Professor of Religious Studies at Nazareth University, teaches comparative and biomedical ethics, religion and politics. His research analyzes religious ethics, science, and politics. He is an advisory board of the Hickey Center and serves on institutional research ethics committees. He received his M.Div. from Wesley Theological Seminary and Ph.D. from the University of Virginia.

Muhammad Shafiq Professor of Religious Studies at Nazareth University, directs the Hickey Center for Interfaith Studies and holds the IIIT Chair for Islamic and Interfaith Studies. He teaches Islam, interfaith studies, and comparative religion. He received his M.A./Ph.D./Fulbright Fellowship from Temple University. His research has culminated in 50+ articles, 9 books and multiple national/international conferences.

List of Figures

Fig. 8.1　Finding Home: Lilith by Siona Banjamin.................. 136
Fig. 8.2　Finding Home: Tikkun ha-Olam by Siona Banjamin.......... 137

Part I

Inclusion or Exclusion in the Sacred Texts Traditions

A Framework for Inclusion and Exclusion in Jewish Law and Practice

Saundra Sterling Epstein

Introduction: Every Human Being Is Created in the Image of God (Genesis 1.27)

Central to Jewish belief, every being is included in the family of humanity. The beginning of the Torah cites the first relationship as between G-d and human beings and the earth, before we consider religious belief. Adhering to this foundational teaching, it seems intuitive that all are part of the Jewish communal collective, as everyone is included by The Creator God. However, this inclusion is limited in terms of Jewish law as it is often articulated.

> For my house shall be a house of prayer for all people. (Isaiah 56:5)

As Jewish Law defines various categories of people in terms of who are obligated (*Mechayavim*) in various dictated actions (*Mitzvot*), who are exempt (*Peturim*), and who are forbidden (*Asurim*), this ideal of "for all people" is lost. Most often, the correlation of who is required to perform a dictated action and who is exempt or

---

S. S. Epstein (✉)
Department of Religion, Syracuse University, Syracuse, NY, USA

© The Author(s), under exclusive license to Springer Nature Switzerland AG 2024
M. Shafiq, T. Donlin-Smith (eds.), *Inclusion or Exclusion in the Sacred Texts and Human Contexts*, https://doi.org/10.1007/978-3-031-70180-1_1

forbidden has to do with the specificity of language in the Torah itself, the authoritative text for these determinations.[1]

Unfortunately, in much of the collective historical journey, these categorical groupings have been misunderstood and too often, when people are exempt from a certain action, this has devolved into their being excluded by authorities and communities in the name of Jewish law, but often due to other influences. These exclusions continue to proliferate at a lightning speed, causing more people in our contemporary world to feel that they and their very lives are at odds with Jewish law.

Our present cultural and political conservatism has fueled this dynamic, requiring Rabbinic and Academic leaders to seriously consider how we continue to observe the texts of our law, both in letter and spirit; while not severely limiting the participation of various groupings in our larger collective, due to external factors, detached from the original law. This has caused a significant backward slide in parts of our more religiously defined communities regarding who is in and who is out. While proponents of such exclusion cite Jewish Law (Halacha) as their support, this is often erroneous.

While these determinations are based upon precision of language in the Torah, the definitive source of Jewish law and practice; the increased degree of exclusion is often connected to societal and culturally contextual factors. Rabbinic and other scholars work hard at trying to understand the actual intent of the language, which undoubtedly goes beyond the literal meaning of the words. In doing so, foundational elements of Jewish law and observance are used to expand and further ensure that implementation of Jewish practice accommodates both what the original language meant and what was not conveyed.

---

[1] In the literal understanding of Jewish practice and law, the degree of obligation is primary in determining various restrictions. These exclusions and inclusions are not about the value of the individual mentioned but rather, their place in the larger community. This is culturally defined, and it is this principle that is utilized when looking at what inclusion looks like in the Jewish legal world throughout history. This is exclusive of other lines of demarcation in the more liberal Jewish world, where for example, socio-economic or cultural divides may be defined. For a fuller discussion of this topic, see "Inclusion of Women and LGBTQ Persons in Orthodox Judaism," Dr. Saundra Sterling Epstein, in *Making Gender in the Intersection of the Human and the Divine*, Hickey Center for Interfaith Relations, Nazareth College, Rochester, New York, Winter 2019.

1 A Framework for Inclusion and Exclusion in Jewish Law and Practice

In this context, four groups who may be excluded will be discussed, using Biblical rooted texts, Rabbinic understanding and qualification, and contemporary examples of addressing and including these groups:

A. Women have often been a critical source of discussion as entire communities are based on the lack of presence of women in the public square, confined to the home, not to be outside of this private domain. This was not the intent of Jewish Law; yet, it is standard practice in some communities.
B. Race is not addressed in these texts, but later in commentaries. Cultural contexts with their inherent prejudices and judgments inform the original readings to make it appear such. The identity of Moses' wife in numbers is one example as is that of the Queen of Sheba.
C. Physical differences and mental capacity have been factors whereby individuals have been limited in their access to Jewish practice and involvement. There are exemptions from various required practices for specified categories of people due to their own limitations, as well as the understanding (or misunderstanding) of words. The rabbinic lens provides a better understanding of what was intended in the aspirational breadth and breath of who should be part of the community.
D. People who are different have always provided a challenge. Due to lack of knowledge, people are too quick to *prejudge,* the resulting *prejudice* creating suspicion and fear. This too is against Jewish Law. In Deuteronomy, Chapter 23, in Moses' final teachings as he prepares for death, he adjoins the Jewish nation to not hate the Edomite nor the Egyptian, for the former is their family and the latter gave them residence. While we understand that there would be reasons to exclude others we do not like, in so many instances, this is actually forbidden. This is also the case with those who convert and join the Jewish entity.

We speak of *Klal Yisrael*—the entirety of the Jewish People and claim that every person is created *Be'Tzelem Elokim*—in the image of God. In conforming to this fundamental principle, all members of our respective communities are to be included to the fullest degree possible. We can do this with reason, being obedient to the texts that formulate our law while ensuring that we do not sacrifice one element of the totality of this system for another.

Impact of Exclusion and Groups Working to Alter This Dynamic

In Deuteronomy, Chapter 29, we read as follows:

9	You are all standing this day before the Lord, your God the leaders of your tribes, your elders and your officers, every man of Israel,
10	your children, your women, your convert who is in your camp, and your woodcutters and water drawers,
11	that you may enter the covenant of the Lord, your God, and God's oath, which… God is making with you this day.[2]

Here as often in Torah, Talmud, and elsewhere in Jewish teachings, the inclusion of all members of the community of the Children of Israel is intended. While there may be accommodations regarding categories of people, these adjustments are intended to ensure the inclusion of all members of the community.

Before addressing the aforementioned groups, let us consider what research has confirmed regarding being ostracized from one's faith community and the impact on the excluded party. In one such study, Zamperini et al. examine the correlation between being excluded from religious belonging and one's well-being.

> Scientific literature has systematically shown that being ostracized constitutes an experience of psychological pain. In short, ostracism arouses social suffering because four basic needs are threatened, … Ostracism threatens our need to belong… [and] threatens the need to maintain high self-esteem because it carries with it the implicit or explicit accusation of having done something wrong. Third, ostracism can threaten the need for control over interactions with others. Fourth, ostracism can threaten the need to maintain our belief in leading a meaningful existence … induc[ing] a state of insignificance and increas[ing] cognitive accessibility to thoughts about death.[3]

---

[2] In most instances, texts will be cited and referenced within the body of the paper. All translations indicated here are from the original Hebrew text and are the result of the composite of several translations as well as the thinking of this author in being as true as possible to the accuracy of language and its intent while maintaining brevity. Any misrepresentation is the responsibility of the author.

[3] Zamperini, Ariano, Marialuisa Menegatto, Miriam Mostacchi, Simone Barbagallo, and Ines Testoni, "Loss of Close Relationships and Loss of Religious Belonging as Cumulative Ostracism: From Social Death to Social Resurrection," in Behavioral Science, June 2020 found at https://www.ncbi.nlm.nih.gov/pmc/articles/PMC7349362/

1 A Framework for Inclusion and Exclusion in Jewish Law and Practice

This is a particular problem in the Orthodox, observant Jewish world to be distinguished from more liberal iterations of Jewish community. As the ritually restricted world increasingly separates from the larger general population, its silo of acceptance continues to narrow and exclude too many.

A bright spot presently is the plethora of groups that have arisen with the goal of recapturing the essence of what it means to be an inclusive Jewish community. While many in Orthodoxy continue to amplify divisions and exclusionary behavior according to their understanding of Jewish Law, we are living in a time where these practices are increasingly being questioned within Orthodoxy at its largess. It should be noted that the presence of these groups includes those that have existed for 30 years to groups that are only a few years old. Here are a few examples.

Ohr Torah Stone (OTS) is a "Modern Orthodox movement committed to illuminating authentic Torah Judaism rooted in *halakha*, and relevant to contemporary life. OTS envisions a world in which every Jew has access to dynamic Jewish learning opportunities and vibrant, welcoming Jewish communities capable of engaging our children and inspiring our grandchildren." With 30 educational institutions, social projects, outreach programs and leadership development initiatives for men and women, OTS, founded in 1983, is transforming Jewish life, learning and leadership…[4]

Torat Chayim includes 350 Orthodox Rabbis and Rabbaniot (female clergy) committed to fostering a more pluralistic and progressive future, reflecting past generations and text-informed roots. Its members work towards Torah-rooted progress in the Jewish community and in society at large. "Torah is about rootedness and Chayim, meaning life, is about dynamism. We want a Torah that is strongly rooted in tradition and that is also responsive to—and pushing us forward in—our time. This Torah is about ethics, human dignity, and the perpetuation—and sanctification—of life. The goal is to work to ensure that Torah only adds to—and never detracts from—human dignity and the sanctity of life." This is an initiative of **Uri L'Tzedek** (the Orthodox Social Justice movement).[5]

Uri L'Zedek was founded to indicate that it is not in spite of Orthodoxy that we believe in the importance of social justice, [but] it is specifically Jewish Law that dictates we include the *ger*—the stranger, the vulnerable, and the marginalized in our lives and community. Viewing the world through a Torah lens means we have a social responsibility toward humanitarian issues. There is an obligation to stand together with all people of faith and in society at large to combat the suffering and oppression of all who are vulnerable and marginalized.[6]

People for Orthodox Renaissance and Torah [PORAT] is committed to a tolerant and inclusive Modern Orthodox community. PORAT … advocate[s] for thoughtful

---

[4] Ohr Torah Stone https://ots.org.il
[5] Torat Chayim http://www.toratchayimrabbis.org
[6] Uri LeTzedek https://utzedek.org/about-us/

halachic observance and progressive education by supporting organizations dedicated to these ideals and fosters open dialogue while advancing Torah values. These dialogues focus on marginalized groups unjustly excluded and advocate as well as provide legal bases from Jewish Law for their inclusion.[7]

Other initiatives will be cited within discussion of specific groupings. Clearly, there is recognition that while exclusive behaviors have developed and intensified, they are to be challenged as we regain our core identity as Jewish people dedicated to and founded upon Torah values.

Inclusion of Women in Religious Spaces

The full inclusion of women in religious, educational, and social life has been a fraught subject, with the obligation to participate publicly reserved for males in this society. While this is representative and normative for cultural mores throughout history, this is not the case today.[8] Given societal factors, women's place in the world today and educational and professional opportunities as well as expectations, it is relevant to look at the roots of our present dynamic.

With the Emancipation in our general world and the Jewish Emancipation (*Haskalah*) that accompanied it in the late eighteenth century, the democratization of education was prevalent in more countries and cultures. As women began to be included more in the general world and educated to a commensurate degree, it was clear that Jewish educational opportunities also had to be available.[9] At the beginning of the twentieth century, the Bais Yaakov schooling system for girls was founded to meet this need. Albeit the education was not on a par with that afforded males; yet,

---

[7] PORAT http://poratonline.org

[8] This differentiation is based on the distinction between those being obligated in communal life and worship and those who are not so. Jewish Law and its development have acknowledged changes in societal norms, levels of access and so many other factors that have resulted in increased participation, education and involvement of women in spheres in which they were previously not as present. While acknowledging that there are communities today that prefer this status of non-involvement, there have been thoughtful scholars who have extensively explored these changes. One such resource is *Hilchot Nashim,* at https://www.jofa.org/ta-shma-the-halakhic-source-guide The discussions in Volumes I and II focus on women making intentional choices instead of passively accepting exclusion. Edited by Rahel Berkowitz, Maggid Books, USA, 2018.

[9] While this discussion is focused on inclusion of women, it would be incomplete without the context of when such inclusion was not a priority. That being said, there are many women

1 A Framework for Inclusion and Exclusion in Jewish Law and Practice

this did open an important door, again as restricted by the mores of the time as much as Jewish sensibilities. As more opportunities became accessible to women, the religious Jewish community had to accommodate the demands of equality.[10]

There are many who will claim that this increased inclusion of women is the result of modernist political and cultural trends, a point that Tamar Ross makes in her book, *Expanding the Palace of Torah: Orthodoxy and Feminism*.[11] Nonetheless, historical precedents teach otherwise. Most certainly, we see powerful, public, and educated women throughout history. In terms of more recent historical context, the focus of this exploration, we have the Halakhic stance of Rabbi Israel Meir ha-Kohen (the Hafetz Haim 1838–1933) who references the Talmudic text of Sotah as follows:

> Rabbi Eliezer's opinion that "Everyone who teaches his daughter …" was relevant in different times. At a time when religion was weakening, women should be taught in order to strengthen their faith. Otherwise, they would leave the way of God.[12]

This is amplified as the years have gone on with the realization that as women are more and more present in the public arena, their voices and participation should reflect their education and experience. As public schooling for all was accessible, this was paralleled in the observant Jewish world with school systems being founded and expanded. Some advocated for minimalist education for women, looking at it as a mere defense against social changes, with the primary role of the women still confined to the home.

---

who did distinguish themselves through Biblical, Rabbinic and all times in our Jewish History. The Biblical Matriarchs, Miriam, Devorah, Beruriah in Talmudic times, businesswoman Gracia Mendes, the first female Rabbi, Osnat Barzani and so many others defied any stereotype of women not being important and consequential leaders in their own rights. For one source among many, go to https://jwa.org. For history of this development and many other resources, https://jwa.org/encyclopedia/article/torah-study#pid-16777.

[10] For a substantive and well-researched discussion of this development, Ross, Tamar, *Expanding the Palace of Torah: Orthodoxy and Feminism,* United States: Brandeis University Press, 2004 and 2021. Ross explains how in her youth in the 1940s and 1950s, her parents realized that as a female, she would not get a substantive education in any type of Jewish educational institution so they sent her to public school and her Jewish learning was through what we now call homeschooling.

[11] Ibid., p. 20.

[12] Rabbi Israel Meir ha-Kohen (the Hafez Hayyim, 1838–1933) (Halakhot on *Sotah*, 20, in a collection of his writings. Jerusalem: 1990. Similar opinions are to be found in many responsa, such as *Zion* by Rabbi Ben Zion Firer (vol. 3, p. 131, 1956) and Rabbi M. Malka, Responsa *Afikei Mayim* (Chapter 3, 10:21, 1995).

Voices in favor of more expansive roles and public presence increased significantly. Representative of this is Rabbi Samson Raphael Hirsch (1808–1888) who states as follows:

> Jewish women must study the Written Torah and the laws they have to follow, since Jewish women saved the spirit of Israel on many occasions. An understanding of Jewish literature and knowledge that would lead to true allegiance to Torah and to reverence are essential to the education of the minds and hearts of women, just as of men.[13]

Even in Modern Orthodoxy, there are those who would still impose limits on women's learning, such as Rabbi Abraham Kook, who advocates for individually motivated learning as opposed to formal educational involvement. By contrast, Rabbi Yoseph Dov Soloveitchik, with whom most in this modern iteration of classical Jewish practice agree, explains that women should be accorded equal status in all matters, learn in co-educational settings, and be honored with leadership roles in communities. It is this perspective that initiatives such as those cited here take on as their moniker.

There has been a specific push in this direction since the 1980s coming from women themselves, advocating on their own behalf instead of waiting for permission from their male counterparts. One cannot ignore that social and cultural influences as well as options available in other streams of Jewish experience influenced this.

While this has continued to be a challenge in much of the Orthodox world, note this statement from PORAT on February 5, 2018:

> In 2018, as these changes are making an impact, PORAT applauds the Orthodox Union's desire "to maximize the participation of women within ... synagogue professionals" while "[d]eveloping appropriate titles for women of significant accomplishment, holding professional positions within the synagogue, educational and communal structure, thereby acknowledging their achievement and status" (OU, 1/31/2018). We are pleased that the OU decided not to take action against the synagogues that employ women in clergy positions, but we are disappointed that this is not a permanent decision... PORAT hopes that the OU will continue its role as an organization open to the entire breadth of the Orthodox community and ... ensure this future by advocating ... a future in which women in clergy positions are respected and valued.[14]

---

[13] Rabbi Samson (ben) Raphael Hirsch (1808–1888), in *Horeb; A Philosophy of Jewish Laws and Observances*, Chapter 75, Translated from the German by Dayan Dr. Isador Grunfeld, London: Suncino Press, 1962, p. 341.

[14] From website of PORAT at http://poratonline.org

We note that there is some progress regarding inclusion of women in leadership roles, but this does not come without its hesitations and lack of conviction on many levels. This impetus has also led to leadership within the ranks of Orthodox Jewish women.

The **Jewish Orthodox Feminist Alliance** was founded in 1997. JOFA advocates for expanding women's rights and opportunities within the framework of *halakha* and to build a vibrant and equitable Orthodox community in which inclusion of women in all appropriate ways is a given.[15]

In 2009, another step forward was achieved with the founding of a seminary that ordains women to function in the religiously observant world. **Yeshivat Maharat** defines its vision as creating "a world in which Judaism is relevant, Jewish communities are educated, and diverse leaders guide individuals to live spiritually engaged lives." It aspires to achieve this by its mission "(t)o educate, ordain and invest in passionate and committed Orthodox women who model a dynamic Judaism to inspire and support individuals and communities."[16]

In addition to these ordained spiritual leaders, *Yoatzot*, female spiritual and Halachic advisors, are more prevalent in an increasing swath of the Modern and even Centrist Orthodox world. These women serve as Halachic decisors for the community, in general, and for women, particularly, especially in issues that are related to the reality of their lives as women.[17]

In parallel formation to leadership and visibility and presence in the Orthodox Jewish world, as women have stepped up to advocate for themselves, there are also organizations that have been founded to address domestic violence, the Halachic

---

[15] From website of https://www.jofa.org

[16] https://www.yeshivatmaharat.org While these advances and initiatives advocate for full inclusion of women in religiously observant spaces, there are differences according to Halacha, regarding how these female spiritual leaders function. This is not the same as in the more liberal iterations of Jewish observance where equality of function is practiced. Here while the fullness of the role of women is the goal, it is done so within a Halachic frame.

[17] Yoetzot are female advisors in various matters of Halacha/Jewish Law. They now function in many communities and provide a more reasonable avenue for women who have questions that are personal about their intimate lives, about trying to procure a divorce, family matters and other concerns that they will feel more comfortable sharing with a woman than a male Rabbi. The irony is that in many religiously pitched communities there is little if any social or casual connections or deep friendships between men and women. It is perplexing why it has taken so long to ascertain that there would be reluctance to go to a male Rabbi with a personal question. This was another way to ensure exclusion and disenfranchise too many women in these communities.

problem of women who cannot secure a divorce and other areas of advocacy and validation for all women.[18]

Clearly voices of women have become more prominent, leadership roles more present, and inclusion, for those who wish to access it, more available. There is still progress to be made, while these significant steps forward must be acknowledged in the inclusion, protection, and validation of women in the religious Jewish sphere.

Racial and Ethnic Differences

Racial identity is at no point a criterion for exclusion in the Jewish nation from a text-based perspective. While there are many thoughts regarding the actual racial composition of the Semitic peoples (sometimes identified as a race), it is not discussed as a construct of its own. Nonetheless, as Kevin Burrell indicates in his exhaustive research on the *Hebrew Bible and the Development of Racial Theories in the Nineteenth Century*,

> Racial ideas which developed in the modern west were forged with reference to a Christian worldview and informed by the Bible, particularly the Old Testament. Up until Darwin's scientific reframing of the origins debate, European and American race scientists were fundamentally Christian in their orientation.[19]

In other words, just as various religious communities reflected the dynamics, changes, pressures, and elements of the surrounding cultures in which they functioned, survived, and thrived; this influence and assimilation of ideas and trends worked in the opposite direction as well. Burrell continues:

---

[18] The abuse and violence against women was a silent subject for too many years. Many prefer to live the myth of "that does not happen here in our nice religious communities," and this is simply not the case. For discussion on this topic, see "Domestic Violence: The Secretive Suffering of Too Many Jewish Women," Dr. Saundra Sterling Epstein, published by Hickey Center for Interfaith Relations, Nazareth College, Rochester, New York. Winter, 2019. Some of the organizations that now exist to address this problem are Jewish Women International found at https://www.jwi.org/, Project S.A.R.A.H. at https://uwprojectsarah.org and to help Agunot, women who are "chained" in marriages of abuse due to the lack of recognition of women's rights to initiate Jewish divorce proceedings, there is the Organization for the Resolution of Agunot or ORA at https://www.getora.org. DINAH provides legal services to women at risk in the Jewish community.

[19] Burrell, Kevin, "Slavery, the Hebrew Bible and the Development of Racial Theories in the Nineteenth Century," Department of Religious Studies, Burman University, Lacombe, AB 6730, Canada, September 2021, Available at https://doi.org/10.3390/rel12090742

1 A Framework for Inclusion and Exclusion in Jewish Law and Practice

Racism, ... prejudice based on the premise of fundamental biological differences between human groups, is a phenomenon that developed only in the modern West (Montagu 1997; Braude 2011). European imperial expansion and colonialization of foreign territories ...in the latter half of fifteenth century were the most significant catalysts for the emergence of racial science (Mazzolini 2014; Horsman 1981). Ultimately, both the imperial prowess of Europe as well as human physical diversity found explanatory power in the concept of race. By the nineteenth century, race, both as a popular and a scientific concept, had come to dominate European and American thought. (Gould [1981] 1996; Kidd 2006)[20]

Burrell and others opine that as various European cultures wanted to identify themselves as superior, they used the construct of racial identity to do so. In distancing themselves from indigenous populations and claiming their privileged status, they used, or misused, the Old Testament as a "legitimizing totem for human malignity."[21]

In our contemporary world of polarization and anachronistic bases for erroneous theories about inherent differences among people for purposes of exclusion, this dynamic is so present. External prejudices and villainization of a plethora of groups, including religious identities, racial and ethnic identities, gender and sexuality, etc. has fomented a psychological climate in which each group that is maligned degrades another.

KAMOCHAH has gained significant traction in its advocacy for Jews of Color, deriving its name from the statement of Torah "and you shall love your neighbor as yourself, Ve'Ahavta *Lereacha Kamocha*." This group originally was incepted to achieve the following mission: "To advance racial equity in the U.S. Jewish community by centering the leadership of Jews of Color and ensuring that our communities and institutions reflect the multiracial reality of the Jewish people."[22]

After the George Floyd murder and other incidents against people of color, a small group of Black Orthodox Jews who had been gathering, celebrating, and observing for years were feeling the impact of increasing racial tensions in America. This small group needed more than their own gathering spaces. They were subjected to hatred outside of the Jewish and black communities as well as isolation within the Jewish community to which they belonged. As a result of this feeling of

---

[20] Ibid.

[21] https://jewsofcolorinitiative.org.

[22] https://jewsofcolorinitiative.org/newsletter/new-ways-of-growth-kamochahs-new-york-chapter-for-black-orthodox-jews/.

double alienation, the following explanation is offered regarding the genesis of this new entity by Maayan Zik:

> The discussion of how Black Jews are treated in the Jewish Orthodox space—and in the Jewish world at large—came up. Black Jews became a bit more visible, and organizations were paying attention to Jews of Color ... Rabbi Isaiah Rothstein, a Black Jew ordained at Yeshiva University, asked a few friends to [come] together ... these gatherings [were] meaningful points of connection to be in community with other Black Jews at a time of heightened racial tensions.[23]

One could ask the following question: Why do Black Orthodox Jews need their own space? Why can they just not be included in general spaces for People of Color and in general spaces for Orthodox Jews? The answer is, as with many of these categories, that just because you are part of one identified potentially marginalized group, this does not guarantee that one's entire identity is validated and accommodated. Those who have multiple identity points often need to come together in spaces where their entire being-ness is understood and shared.[24]

This dynamic is expressed by Yonat Shimron, who cites a recent study:

> ... Jews of color are committed to their faith and engage in all the traditional ways white Jews do. They love Jewish ritual, celebrating Jewish holidays and attending synagogue; 75% said working for justice and equality was "very important" for them. At the same time, they also expressed frustration at having to defend and explain their Jewishness and the pain of encountering racism in Jewish contexts.
>
> Participants in the study said they had been repeatedly mistaken for security guards or nannies and presumed to be the non-Jewish partner or guest of a white Jewish person.
>
> 74% percent of respondents said they felt burdened with explaining their identity and 66% said they'd been asked questions about their race or ethnicity that made them feel uncomfortable.[25]

---

[23] https://www.jewishmulticialnetwork.org/our-story.

[24] https://religionnews.com/2021/08/12/study-jews-of-color-love-judaism-but-often-experience-racism-in jewish-settings/.

[25] This challenge of multiple identities and inclusion in various spaces with acknowledgement of all of these identities and how they inform our total being is always a problem. We see this today in our world around discussions of intersectionality and how each person is a complicated Venn diagram of elements, not identified by any single one of those elements to the exclusion of others. Immigrants, those of various descents such as Ashkenazim, Sephardim, or Mizrachim, gender and sexuality diversity, neuro-diversity, cultural backgrounds, and so much else go into the totality of who we are. Too many communities will accept some of these identity markers and exclude others, increasing feelings of exclusion by individuals.

1 A Framework for Inclusion and Exclusion in Jewish Law and Practice

There is an irony regarding Jews of Color. Given the historical rootedness and initial geographical location of the beginnings of the Jewish nation, the point should be made that all were as we would label them today, Jews of Color. Racism, as a phenomenon, is a later development, erroneously traced to roots in the Biblical narrative. For the Jewish people today, it was indeed those who came from Europe, mostly Ashkenazic Jews[26] who utilized this somewhat artificial line of demarcation to express their own superiority. This conflict is still reflected in the State of Israel.

Physical Differences and Disabilities

Regarding how texts are often taken out of context, note this from Leviticus, Chapter 21:

16	The Lord spoke to Moses, saying,
17	Speak to Aaron, saying: Any man among your offspring throughout their generations who has a defect, shall not come near to offer up his God's food.
18	Any man with a defect should not approach: A blind man a lame one, one with a sunken nose or with mismatching limbs;
19	or a man who has a broken leg or a broken arm;
20	or one with long eyebrows, or a cataract, or a commingling in his eye; dry lesions or weeping sores, or one with crushed testicles
21	Any man among Aaron the Kohen's offspring .... There is a defect in him; he shall not draw near to offer up his God's food.[27]

---

[26] This notion of Jews of Color has played out significantly in Israel through the years as the indigenous groupings were Sephardim and Mizrachim from the Spanish and African world respectively, of darker tone and more familiar with the terrain and reality of the region. When the Eastern European Jews, the Ashkenazim, came on various Aliyot, groupings of those coming to Palestine in pre-Israel years, they brought with them their prejudices towards what they considered to be people of color discussed elsewhere in this study and exerted their feelings of superiority over those who had already been located there. This conflict has yet to be resolved. For one study of this phenomenon, beyond the scope of this study, Shabi, Rachel, *We Look Like The Enemy: The Hidden Story of Israel's Jews From Arab Lands,* [England: Walker Books, 2009].

[27] This text from Leviticus is a good example of the inclusion/exclusion line of demarcation to function for the entire community and the needs thereof, and not due to an individual per se, but rather due to the role played in the collective. It must be read in its context regarding the ongoing role of this class of people and not extended or misappropriated to other groups.

While this text refers to a specific group [the Priestly class] who were to perform various ritual roles for the entirety of the Jewish people and had many restrictions placed on them in addition to these, it cannot be ignored that texts such as this are often taken out of context to validate prejudices that will ultimately lead to exclusions or denials of presence of some of our community members with physical differences.

Elsewhere in Torah and Jewish Law, there are exclusions due to precision of language. For example, because a specific spoken formula serves as a contractual agreement, one who is hearing impaired cannot be party to it. Due to the words of Torah indicating that all must be seen and consequently see as well when participating in communal gatherings that are dictated as obligatory, visually impaired persons are exempt from participating in such.[28]

While these examples and others like them limit participation as a result of that literal understanding of words, this has led to misuse and abuse of them to justify exclusion of those with various disabilities and physical differences. This is not within the spirit of the law, as we determine such usage. In fact, accommodations are made for those of the Priestly Class who may not have the intellectual prowess to perform certain tasks and how we help them do so.

Furthermore, Torah clearly indicates that disabilities do not lessen a person's worth or participation in the community. Note this statement from Exodus:

> Moses said to God, 'Please, O Adonai, I have never been good with words, either in times past or now that You have spoken to Your servant; I am slow of speech and slow of tongue.' And the Eternal said to him, 'Who gives humans speech? Who makes them dumb or deaf, seeing or blind? Is it not I, the Eternal?' (4:10–11)

---

[28] Disabilities and "Mumim" is related to the issue in the footnote above. It is clarified that even with these categories, there was an acknowledgement that while physical, spiritual and other types of perfection may be aspirational, they are not realistic and there are accommodations to be made. For example, as Passover was central to the community as a whole and there are so many requirements involved, there was a provision made for a Second Passover /*Pesach Sheni* so that those who could not participate in the first gathering due to impurities would be able to observe and celebrate. If more than a critical mass of the community suffered from mitigating factors that would preclude their participation, it was allowed for all to gather anyway at the originally prescribed time. Here, inclusion overrides any factors that would have indicated exclusion. The Talmud in Masechet Hagiga emphasized the difference between being exempt from participation versus being forbidden. For a fuller discussion of this text and application, the reader is referred to" Inclusion of Women and LGBTQ Persons in Orthodox Judaism," Dr. Saundra Sterling Epstein.

1 A Framework for Inclusion and Exclusion in Jewish Law and Practice

We note others who are not perfect physical specimens, such as David who was to become King though his small stature did not make him a likely candidate. Isaac became visually impaired in his later years, Jacob had a limp, many of our foremothers had difficulties conceiving, and the list goes on. Some prophets were thought to suffer from what we could categorize today as mental illness, or neuro-diversity. The Talmud cites instances of individuals with these challenges. Why are we so open about these differences when others feel so much shame about them? There is a valuable teaching here—that we are all in some way lesser able or disabled, and thus we should include all in our community.

Faith Fogelman in her article, Disability Matters Within Judaism, explains:

> ...disability touches most people ... to varying degrees. Limited disability exposure may contribute to approaches which are misguided and driven by one's own emotional discomfort. Optimal engagements depend on disability awareness to develop a foundation, a toolbox for appropriate interactions to individualize per person and disability. Followers of the Torah are also guided by a concomitant study of the intersections of Judaism and disability. These intersections serve as starting points for developing appropriate and realistic attitudes toward disability ... leading to greater understanding of "that which is hateful to others" in disability matters.
>
> ...Throughout Tanakh, there are references to the intersections of Judaism and disability. [In] Rabbinic and current commentary ... [s]ome ... reinforce Judaism's compassion toward disability, while others provide a historical account of how approaches toward disability have changed. There is also a body of disconcerting literature by sages, ...reflecting discomfort with disability, which claims that people with disabilities, depending on the condition, should be permanently relegated to subordinate statuses. This approach ... received widespread, but not universal, support; and vestiges still remain.[29]

The stigma that disabilities evoke is evident in BaMidbar Rabba 7.1:

> When Israel came out of Egypt, the vast majority of them were afflicted with some blemish. Why? Because they were working in clay and bricks and climbing to the tops of buildings. Those engaged in building became maimed through climbing to the top layers of stone. Either a stone fell and cut off the worker's hand, or a beam or some clay got into his eyes and he was blinded. When they came to the wilderness of Sinai, God said, "Is it consonant with the dignity of the Torah that I should give it to

---

[29] Fogelman, Faith, Disabilities Matter within Judaism, Institute for Jewish Ideas and Ideals, New York, 2010, found at https://www.jewishideas.org/article/disability-matters-within-judaism. This writing is a well-developed treatment of this dilemma from both a religious and historical perspective.

a generation of disfigured persons? If, on the other hand, I wait until others take their place, I shall be delaying the Revelation." Then God bade the angels come down to Israel and heal them.[30]

Furthermore, within the cultural and social dimensions of the religiously pitched Jewish community, there is the element of shame. This is encouraged by an established norm that if one follows a religious life properly, no harm will come to them or their children. Any disability or difference is seen as a punishment for something done wrong; therefore, it needs to be hidden, as do the persons who suffer from it. This is reinforced socially to the point of exclusion, which so many families and individuals feel. As Fogelman states at the end of her writing, "people with disabilities frequently claim that attitudes are the greatest barriers toward integration."[31]

It is community fear, shame, sanction, or lack of consideration that causes this exclusion, not Jewish Law. We are to include all members in our community as affirmed in our texts. Masechet Hagiga in the Babylonian Talmud is such a text[32] in which the distinction is clarified in terms of who is obligated to participate in communal gatherings and who is exempt. However, there is clarification that if those who are exempt wish to participate in the community for a variety of reasons, they are welcome to do so. This is amplified in other aspects of Jewish Law as well.[33]

---

[30] We see an additional element of exclusion in our complicated Venn Diagram. We are all aware of socio-economic and professional types of exclusion. Here we learn that noble work can be physical labor as much as academic or professional pursuits and that we include all whom God loves and embraces.

[31] Fogelman, ibid.

[32] *Babylonian Talmud, Masechet Hagiga.* In this Tractate of the Talmud, the distinction is made regarding being exempt from obligation and participating in various actions due to one's intentional wish to be part of a ritual, community or ceremony. One of the seminal concepts in this discussion is *nachat ruach,* or what we might think of today as emotional and psychological well-being. This is a an important criterium in thinking about inclusion.

[33] A visually impaired woman is not obligated to light Shabbat candles, due to potential dangers. However, Rabbinic authorities explain that she may indeed do so, with the help of someone guiding her hand. Use of interpreters and technology for hearing impaired people, etc. ensures their participation. Various technological advances in the use of wheelchairs and other forms of allowing for movement is yet another oft approved means of including physically limited persons.

At no point is the community to exclude people for any unstipulated reason. This one teaching in the middle of Leviticus 19, called the Holiness Code exemplifies this:

> Do not curse a person who is deaf and do not place a stumbling block in front of a person who is blind. (Leviticus 19:14)

We are to treat all with respect, never act as though they are not there and facilitate their involvement. Today there are various resources that help with these efforts such as the **Jewish Braille Institute** and **Zomet**, as well as others, addressing the needs of, and making, Jewish life, texts, and living accessible to those who are visually or hearing impaired, respectively.[34]

This reformulation of how we address those with various needs or deficits has led to an explosion of organizations, school programs, camps, and agencies who realize that the Jewish community is obligated to include all members to the degree that individuals are able. **Parents for Torah for All Children [PTACH]** began in 1976 to reflect this need, parallel to the increased sensitivity to this issue in the general American educational scene, and continues to be expand this work.[35] The initiatives of this organization have resulted in increasing efforts to ensure that every child learns within the Jewish community to the degree they are able, continuing into adulthood.

This is not a new concept, but rather once again returning to the framework which was always intended. As we learn in Maimonides' Mishneh Torah, HIlchot Talmud Torah 10:

> Every member of the people of Israel is obligated to study Torah—whether one is rich or poor, physically able or with physical disability.

Another important organization that has been working for inclusion of all young members of the Orthodox Jewish community is **Yachad/National Jewish Council**

---

[34] The Jerusalem Center for Research in Medicine and Halacha is found at http://www.j-c-r.org/about.html and is foremost in research that allows for accommodation related to various challenges, ensuring more accessibility for people with various impairments. Jewish Braille Institute found at https://www.jbilibrary.org, Jewish Deaf Resource Center at https://www.jdrc.org, and Zomet at https://www.zomet.org.il/eng/?CategoryID=253&ArticleID=142 for hearing aids that are Shabbat enabled. Other initiatives bring together our technological progress with ensuring accessibility for more people.

[35] https://www.ptach.org.

for Disabilities. It is dedicated to the involvement of all Jews with disabilities in every aspect of Jewish life. Yachad/NJCD offers summer camps; Israel trips; social programming for all ages; social skills development; support services, case management, counseling for individuals, siblings, and families; religious holiday and Sabbath gatherings; educational opportunities and special needs yeshivas; and vocational services.[36]

In these many offerings, the larger Jewish community learns and benefits as well from the talents and abilities of these individuals that would have been excluded in the past, reinforcing the lesson as articulated in Mishnah Sanhedrin 4:5:

> A human being mints many coins from the same mold, and they are all identical. But the Holy One, Blessed be G-d, strikes us all from the mold of the first human and each one of us is unique.

It is incumbent upon us to teach each according to their means. This lesson is amplified by Moses, the paradigmatic Jewish leader, in the Talmud Yerushalmi, based on Exodus, Chapter 32.

> Rabbi Yochanan said: 'Each of the 40 days that Moses was on Mount Sinai, God taught him entire Torah. And each night, Moses forgot what he had learned. Finally, God gave it to him as a gift. If so, why did God not give the Torah to him as a gift on the first day? In order to encourage the teachers of those who learn in a non-traditional manner.'"[37]

Similar to the trajectory of women becoming more educated and able, as our diversely capable individuals are encouraged and enabled to achieve so much, they are now more present in the public community. Thus, all benefit from observing the teaching of Proverbs 22.6, enjoining us to "teach a child according to their ways." We are to recognize the blessing that these members of our community are to all and acknowledge the many lessons we can learn from them.[38]

---

[36] https://www.yachad.org/resourceguide/.

[37] This general teaching appears often in the Talmud (e.g. Tractates of Berachot and Menachot) and in the words of Commentators (e.g. Sforno and Abrabanel).

[38] There are special blessings we invoke when we are in the presence of those with challenges or in unusual circumstances. (Berachot 58b).

Those Who Are Different: Do Not Oppress the Other (Whomever That May Be)

A foundational teaching appears thirty-six times in the Torah text and elsewhere as well. We are to facilitate inclusion of all in the community to the highest degree possible. In cases of socio-economic need, we learn:

> If there be among you a person with needs, you shall not harden your heart, but you shall surely open your hand. (Deuteronomy 15:7)

More expansively, Deuteronomy 24:17 and 27:19, and Jeremiah 22:3, and many other texts of the Jewish Bible teach us "not to oppress the stranger, the orphan and the widow." These three are offered as examples of the weakest, least protected members of society. The Torah repeatedly delineates that this support must be offered with dignity and graciousness.

This sentiment is present in accommodations in sacrifices, community participation, and participation in deeds of *tzedakah* (sharing and caring with one's resources) that facilitate the purposeful involvement of all members of the community, regardless of their own resources. Additionally, there are laws regarding the distribution of vegetation and the fruit of the earth so that there not be people who are suffering from food or home insecurity according to the laws as articulated in the Torah, Talmud, and subsequent codes of practice.[39]

Regarding those we may not like or feel comfortable with, in Pirke Avot 4:3, we learn:

> Do not despise any [person], and do not discriminate against anything, there is no person that has not their hour ...

We see in Masechet Ta'anit in the Talmud, 20 a –b

> Rabbi Elazar son of R. Shimon was coming from Migdal Gedor, from the house of his teacher. He rode along the riverside on his donkey, and was feeling elated because he

---

[39] Jewish Law makes clear that those with resources are not allowed to exclude others in the community who may not be as fortunate in any number of ways. All have the responsibility of distribution which dictates how one gathers the produce from one's field, leaving portions for others to collect (e.g. Book of Ruth). Tzedakah or the required sharing and caring with one's resources includes all members of the community as there is always someone in more need than even the needy. Pride of participation, dignity of giving and sharing and the notion that all have something to contribute is central in so many ways in Jewish Law.

had studied much Torah. He met an exceedingly ugly man, who greeted him, "Peace be upon you, my master!" R. Elazar did not return his salutation but instead said to him, "How ugly this person is! Are all the people of your city as ugly as you?" "I do not know," said the man. "But go to the craftsman who made me, and say to God: How ugly is the vessel which you have made!"

There are many such texts regarding inclusion of all in our collective and the required attribute of humility in remembering that G-d created all of us. We must carefully look at the reasons and criteria when there are instances of exclusion and consider how we can be more lenient in including all. We learn this in the Gemara, where some who were exceedingly strict in their practice learned about the practice of others and became more lenient.

Amplifying this sentiment, our texts clearly "All is Israel is responsible one for the other (Sanhedrin 4:5)." Regrettably, at this time in our historical reality and cultural context, too many reasons are presented for the purpose of exclusion of others and doing so by relegating the other to the "stranger"/the *ger*, precisely the person we are to protect and embrace. This continues to be an issue in the more religiously pitched Jewish community, in which political and cultural conservatism unfortunately often outrun Jewish Law in decision making.

Rabbi Lord Jonathan Sacks teaches this is antithetical to the Jewish notion of both community and the human family of which we are all part:

> The test of faith is whether I can make space for difference. Can I recognize God's image in someone who is not in my image, whose language, faith, ideals are different from mine? If I cannot, then I have made God in my image instead of allowing Him to remake me in His.[40]

Sacks, a most important voice for this generation, articulates clearly what is stated in Jewish text and law and what is not part of its teachings. He often challenges all to consider we are most connected to the Divine when we respect the differences that God ordained should be part of our world.[41]

Groups have been founded to respond to this misinterpretation and misuse of language and its resulting mistreatment and abuse of people. Foremost among them in Israel is **ITIM**, which Rabbi **Seth Farber, PhD**, founded in 2002 to strengthen Israelis' connections to Jewish rituals at the most significant milestones

---

[40] Sacks, Rabbi Jonathan, *The Dignity of Difference*, [Britain: Bloomsberg Publishers, 2002], p. 201.

[41] Sacks, Rabbi Jonathan, *Radical Then, Radical Now*, [Britain, Continuum Publishers, 2001] p. 8.

in their lives, feeling included and valued. Rabbi Farber witnessed how many Israelis felt alienated from Judaism, because government and Rabbinic authorities that administer matters of Jewish life like marriage and conversion were disrespectful, unresponsive, or exclusionary. ITIM took on the mission to increase participation in Jewish life by helping people navigate Israel's religious bureaucracy. In 2005, ITIM established an **Assistance Center** to provide free information, individualized guidance, and problem-solving on every state-administered issue of Jewish life—from birth to burial.[42]

Other initiatives invested in supporting all groupings discussed emphasize that foundational Jewish teachings demand that we are all obligated—*Mechuyavim*—to welcome and accommodate all members of the Jewish collective in public spaces, communities, synagogues, and daily lives. If there are any limits, it is according to their choices, needs, and Halachic standards, not community sanction.

Conclusion and Reclaiming Our Foundational Principles

From one original earth-being that was human, we all have evolved. This was God's design. In the Mishneh of Sanhedrin 4:5, this is stated:

> Human beings were created as a single individual to teach you that anyone who destroys a single life is as though that person has destroyed an entire world, and anyone who preserves a single life is as though an entire world has been preserved. This was also done for the sake of peace among humanity, so that no person could say to another, "My parent is greater than yours."

Simultaneously, we are united by each person's individuality and the fact that we are different from one another probably more than any other factor. The act of creating the human being in the image of God is indication of God's love as G-d bestowed the greatest gift of all to humanity, that of knowledge. We are to use that knowledge properly for the benefit of all, not abuse it to the detriment of others. In the words of Rabbi Jonathan Sacks, "We are all different, but we each carry in our being the trace of the one God."[43]

Something has clearly gone horribly wrong. We know all too well that anachronistic reasoning and co-opting of modern phenomena that are self-serving to those

---

[42] From https://www.itim.org.il/en/.

[43] Sacks, Rabbi Jonathan, Not in God's Name, [United States: Schocken Publishers, 2017] p. 172.

who prefer a class structured history are utilized to justify their ends by the means of misuse and abuse of Biblical and other religion-based texts. It is herein proposed that we embrace those who emphasize a return to foundational principles, informing the interpretation and activation of the Torah given law as intended, including all we can without compromising either the spirit or the letter of the law.

How do we do this? As many teach, the measure of the decency of a society is determined by how it cares for and includes its least powerful members in an equitable manner. This reinforces the notion that while we are indeed different, we all share the same basic beginning and are enjoined to include all as we gather in our various collectives. By honoring God's intentions and love for every human being, and observing the basic requirement to act in a way that embraces all and make accommodations for our various community members, it is hoped that we can heal the divisiveness that has so hurt our community, the exclusions that have been nothing less than devastating to individuals and remember that the sum of the whole is greater than the total of individual parts. In this manner, all who may be vulnerable or different must be included and afforded the protection maintained in those teachings that accord with the foundational roots of the Jewish community. Only then will our community reflect the original paradigm in which all human beings are created in the image of God and worthy of the honor of inclusion.

Bibliography

Burrell, Kevin. 2021. Slavery, the Hebrew Bible and the Development of Racial Theories in the Nineteenth Century, Department of Religious Studies, Burman University, Lacombe, AB 6730, Canada, September. https://doi.org/10.3390/rel12090742

Fogelman, Faith. 2010. Disabilities Matter within Judaism. Institute for Jewish Ideas and Ideals, New York. https://www.jewishideas.org/article/disability-matters-within-judaism

On-line compilation of many Jewish texts. http://mechon-mamre.org

Sacks, Rabbi Jonathan. 2001. *Radical Then, Radical Now*. Britain: Continuum Publishers.

———. 2002. *The Dignity of Difference*. Britain: Bloomsberg Publishers.

———. 2017. *Not in God's Name*. United States: Schocken Publishers.

Scherman, Rabbi Nosson, ed. 2000. *The Stone Edition: The Tanach*. New York: Mesorah Publications, Third Impression.

Schottenstein Edition of the Babylonian Talmud. 1983 ff. New York: Mesorah Publications, Ltd.

Shimron, Yonat, 2021. Study: Jews of Color Love Judaism but Often Experience Racism in Jewish Settings. *Religion News Service*, USA. Found at The Jerusalem Center for Research in Medicine and Halacha, Israel: Jerusalem. http://www.j-c-r.org/about.html

Use of texts from Torah, Talmud, etc: These quotes and references appear in the body of the paper and come from the original Hebrew texts cited.

Zamperini, Ariano, Marialuisa Menegatto, Miriam Mostacchi, Simone Barbagallo, and Ines Testoni, 2020. Loss of Close Relationships and Loss of Religious Belonging as Cumulative Ostracism: From Social Death to Social Resurrection. *Behavioral Science*, June. https://www.ncbi.nlm.nih.gov/pmc/articles/PMC7349362/

Saundra Sterling Epstein received her BA, MS, and EdD from the University of Pennsylvania. Dr. Epstein directs Beyachad, a program bringing Jewish living, and learning together. She has been teaching texts, regarding challenging issues around the world in hopes of reaching and inspiring students. Dr. Epstein has been published widely in a variety of venues regarding various topics including Women in Faith, Inclusion of LGBTQ members in our Communities of Faith, environmental sustainability, prayer, G-d talk, and many more. Dr. Epstein also works nationally and internationally on multi-faith learning, dialogue, and understanding. It should be noted, her book, *Life Journeys: Stepping Back and Moving Forward*, was published in February 2017 and is available through Amazon.com. Dr. Epstein is presently serving as the director of the Welcoming Shuls and Communities project of ESHEL, which is the National LGBT Inclusion Consortium for the Orthodox Jewish Community.

2

Does *Everyone* Get to Ride the "Great Vehicle"?: Exclusive Inclusivism in the Lotus Sūtra

John M. Thompson

Introduction

These days we are increasingly aware of our tendency as *homo sapiens* of selecting only certain people for our consideration, dismissing others as "unworthy," particularly when it comes to religion. Certainly, when this subject comes up, I reflexively think of Biblical passages about the "Son of Man" coming to separate, "the sheep" from "the goats,"[1] or *Qur'anic* statements of Allah rejecting "unbelievers."[2] Yet themes of exclusion and inclusion are not confined to the Abrahamic traditions, we also find them in the *Lotus Sūtra* (Skt. *Saddharma Puṇḍarīka Sūtra*, Ch. *Miaofa lianhua jing*), one of the most popular texts in the Mahāyāna ("Great Vehicle") branch of Buddhism. Famous for its "innumerable meanings,"[3] and its revelation of

---

[1] Matthew 25: 31–46 (NRSV).
[2] Qur'an 3: 85.
[3] Skt. *Anantanirdeśa*, Ch. *Wúliángyì*.

J. M. Thompson (✉)
Department of Philosophy & Religion, Christopher Newport University, Newport News, VA, USA
e-mail: john.thompson@cnu.edu

© The Author(s), under exclusive license to Springer Nature Switzerland AG 2024
M. Shafiq, T. Donlin-Smith (eds.), *Inclusion or Exclusion in the Sacred Texts and Human Contexts*, https://doi.org/10.1007/978-3-031-70180-1_2

the Buddha's wondrous *upāya* ("skillful means," "expedient devices") in preaching the Dharma,[4] the *Lotus* has long been the focus of intense devotion. More importantly, the *Lotus* proclaims the Buddhahood of all beings, espousing a Buddhistic "universal salvation." On the face of it, this makes the *Lotus* an *inclusive* scripture. Yet the *Lotus* also has a strong *exclusivist* dimension. This basic contradiction makes the *Lotus* a fascinating yet frustrating text to work with. What are we to make of such a text that seems so fundamentally at odds with itself?

In this chapter I address some of these issues, highlighting examples of the text's play between inclusivism and exclusivism, and also the problems this poses. My point is *not* to resolve such matters so much as to bring the *Lotus* into these discussions. I contend that by deliberately resisting attempts to impose a definitive message, the *Lotus* draws us into a dynamic that pushes us to revisit our initial assumptions, thereby challenging our desire for easy certainties. Ironically, then, by excluding finality, the *Lotus* actually fosters continual engagement—what could be more inclusive?

Exclusivism and Inclusivism: Some Initial Points

First, though, I must clarify some terms. As I understand it, "exclusivism" refers to the practice or policy of leaving out a person or group from a place or privilege. "Exclusivism" focuses on distinction, keeping things (persons, groups) separate. By contrast, "inclusivism" refers to the practice or policy of embracing or incorporating diverse persons or groups into a larger whole. Unlike "exclusivism," "inclusivism" begins with diversity but aims at togetherness. However, in theological circles, these terms have specialized senses. At its simplest, religious exclusivism maintains the absolute truth of its adherents' faith while denying the spiritual validity of any other. Religious inclusivism, by contrast, maintains the truth of its adherents' faith but sees this salvific truth as present in other religious traditions to a lesser extent. Moreover, both exclusivism and inclusivism contrast with "pluralism," the view that there are multiple legitimate faith traditions, with none more valid than the others.

This tripartite scheme for addressing religious diversity is more complex than I make it out to be, and each position includes various levels and degrees, but it does provide a useful starting point for discussion. Ken Rose, a scholar of Comparative Theology, explains:

---

[4] In this paper I use the term "Dharma" for the more technically proper "Saddharma" ("True Teachings").

Exclusivism may be defined as taking one of the many available bodies of religious teaching as final to the exclusion and even negation of other bodies of religious teaching; *inclusivism* may be defined as a weaker or minimal expression of exclusivism that takes terminology in the home tradition as the "final vocabulary" to interpret all religious phenomena; and *pluralism* (as a theological and philosophical stance rather than just as the reality of religious diversity) may be defined as the view that the existence of multiple self-consistent and internally plausible final religious vocabularies undercuts claims that a particular body of religious teaching is final, normative, or universally binding.[5]

Rose further maintains that exclusivism and inclusivism are stronger and weaker forms of "particularism," the "view that one particular body of religious teaching and practice is final and thus exclusively binding on humanity."[6] As we can see, scholarly discussion of issues surrounding religious diversity and the ultimate status of different religions vis-à-vis each other poses significant, perhaps irresolvable philosophical difficulties.

Rather than dive into such arguments myself, however, I make a few observations. First, these stances of "exclusivism," and "inclusivism," "pluralism" arose out of Christian missionaries' efforts to spread the gospel to the "heathens" encountered during European colonial expansion.[7] As such, these theoretical ideas developed in a context concerned with overcoming obstacles to global Christianization. Even today, exploring interfaith relations is often framed as a *Christian* theology of religions, betraying traces of a mindset that presumes to dictate the terms by which this "problem" should be "solved." Second, it's clear that the terms "exclusivism," "inclusivism," and "pluralism" themselves have various meanings. For example, "inclusivism" typically comes down to accepting (some) "Others" while subordinating them to the dominant (Christian) faith. Nonetheless, in a traditional Chinese perspective "inclusivism" does *not* have the "hidden exclusivist" tendency that some of its critics maintain. We see this clearly in the ideal of "harmony" (和, *he*), a complex ethical and metaphysical notion that avoids both conflict and forced conformity. As such, "harmony" is a process that

---

[5] Ken Rose, "Religious Pluralism and the Upaniṣads," Embodied Philosophy.com, October 8, 2018, accessed May 1, 2023, https://www.embodiedphilosophy.com/religious-pluralism-and-the-upani%E1%B9%A3ads-2/?_gl=1*1n7vqps*_up*MQ..*_ga*MTIzNTU5OTUyNC 4xNjgzOTE4MDQz*_ga_VZ66VKPMTH*MTY4MzkxODA0MS4xLjAuMTY4MzkxOD A0MS4wLjAuMA..#easy-footnote-10-2410.

[6] Ibid.

[7] Dale Tuggy, "Theories of Religious Diversity," in *The Internet Encyclopedia of Religion*, 2015, accessed May 3, 2023, https://iep.utm.edu/reli-div/.

doesn't posit a predetermined order,[8] and as a guide for dealing with diversity, it is decidedly "inclusive" yet non-exclusive.

Exclusivism and Inclusivism in the *Lotus*

My foregoing remarks sketch out the fraught nature of religious exclusion and inclusion. Now I turn to issues of religious exclusion and inclusion in the *Lotus Sūtra*. Of course, since the *Lotus* is such a complex scripture, I only touch on a few examples of the text's contradictory dynamic.

The most famous exclusivist passage in the *Lotus* occurs in Chapter Two, where the Buddha first reveals that up until this point, he has not preached the full Dharma, as it is beyond the capacity of ordinary beings. Instead, he has resorted to lesser teachings that his audiences can grasp before praising the many skillful techniques (*upāya*) that have enabled his followers to gain *some* understanding. However, if he were to teach the True Dharma, many of his followers would be alarmed and disbelieve it due to their pride at their spiritual knowledge. Śāriputra, the Buddha's foremost monastic disciple, though, begs him to teach the FULL Dharma and the Blessed One agrees, stating that he will now teach the Dharma explicitly for all present.[9] Immediately 5000 monks, nuns, and laypeople get up and leave due to their "overweening pride" at (falsely) believing that had awakened to the full Truth. The Buddha remains silent, making no attempt to stop them, but his comment after they leave is telling: "My assembly has no more branches and leaves, it has only firm fruit," adding that it is just as well that "such arrogant ones" have left.[10] This is a key scene in the *sūtra*, as it sets up the Buddha's discussion of the One Vehicle (*ekayāna*) and his assurances that everyone will eventually attain Buddhahood. However, the Buddha seems remarkably condescending toward those who left. Is their mistaken self-pride in their attainments (from following the teachings the Buddha has already given) so great as to bar them from now hearing the True Dharma? Presumably these "arrogant ones" will eventually come around, but for the time being, they are excluded.

---

[8] For a detailed discussion, see Chenyang Li, Sai Hang Kwok, and Dascha Düring, eds., *Harmony in Chinese Thought: A Philosophical Introduction* (Lanham: The Rowan and Littlefield Publishing Group, 2021).

[9] Leon Hurvitz, trans., *Scripture of the Lotus Blossom of the Fine Dharma* (New York: Columbia University Press, 1976), 22–29.

[10] Ibid., 29.

Even more disturbing evidence of exclusivism in the *Lotus* comes in its threats against those who "slander the *sūtra*." One memorable passage occurs in Chapter Three, where after explaining his "skillful means" through the infamous "Parable of the Burning House," the Buddha admonishes Śāriputra to preach its words only to those who are worthy. He then elaborates in painful detail the fate of those who criticize the *sūtra*, promising that they will be reborn in the worst "hells" for eons only to continue to endure horrific suffering:

> From hell emerging,
>   They shall fall into the rank of beasts.
> If they are dogs or jackals,
>   Their forms shall be hairless and emaciated,
> Spotted and scabbed,
>   Things from which men shrink.
> They shall also by men be
>   Detested and despised,
> Ever suffering from hunger and thirst,
>   Their flesh and bones dried out and decayed…
> If they become camels,
>   Or if they are born among asses,
> On their bodies they shall carry heavy loads
>   And suffer the blows of rods and whips,
> Thinking only of water and grass
>   And knowing nothing else.
> For maligning this scripture
>   They shall suffer punishments such as these.[11]

The Buddha continues to emphasize the horrid fates of those who slander the *Lotus*, relating how even should they attain a precious human rebirth, they must bear various deformities and maladies, never having the opportunity to hear the Dharma. Instead, they shall be deaf and dumb, adding, "Camels, asses, pigs, and dogs – these shall be their companions."[12]

Further evidence of exclusivism comes in Chapter Fourteen, when the bodhisattva Mañjuśrī asks how one should preach the *Lotus*. In response, the Buddha imposes various constraints on those to whom devotees may preach. The rather extensive list is somewhat confusing, as it includes "kings and princes of realms," ministers and senior officials, "followers of external paths" (singling out brahmins and Jain monks), people who "provide wicked amusement" (violent contests, dancers, actors, and magicians), *caṇḍālas* ("outcastes"), people who raise livestock

---
[11] Ibid., 77–79.
[12] Ibid., 80.

(pigs, sheep, chickens, dogs), hunters and fishers, and people who "cultivate other evil practices."[13] While *Lotus* devotees tend to present such passages as helping preachers develop their skills by starting with more receptive audiences, the Buddha's admonitions still distinguish between "insiders" and "outsiders." Clearly, the full revelation of the Dharma (including the promise of universal Buddhahood) must be withheld from certain people. Whether these lines reflect Indic social norms of "pollution and purity" or the fragile status of early communities in which the *Lotus* circulated, this passage *is* discriminatory, echoing the tone of U.S. laws during the Jim Crow era. Moreover, from a position of universal compassion, such "outsiders" are in dire need of the *Lotus*' hopeful message, yet these passages declare that devotees of the *Lotus* must exclude them at least for now.

What is most disturbing in these examples is that the Buddha not only discriminates against "outsiders" but promises *punishments* for those objecting to these teachings. Most scholars maintain that such passages are later interpolations responding to negative reception of the *Lotus* (even persecution of those preaching the *Lotus*), reflecting a "minority consciousness" among devotees early in the text's composition. However, with their gruesome details of blasphemers' fates, these passages evince a hostility toward those who are unreceptive of the *Lotus* and even hint of delight in unbelievers' future suffering. In such passages the *Lotus* confirms our worst fears about the ethical implications of exclusivism.

Nonetheless, the *Lotus* also contains passages demonstrating a truly open inclusivism. This inclusive spirit shows in the structure of the *sūtra* itself, beginning in its opening scene with its detailed descriptions of its audience that extends to myriads of beings from other worlds in later chapters. We see this inclusive attitude explicitly in Chapter Twenty-two, where the Buddha entrusts the *Lotus* to his audience and tells them, "You must all accept and keep, read and recite, and broadly proclaim this Dharma, enabling all beings universally to know and hear it."[14]

One memorable example of inclusivism comes at the beginning of Chapter Three where Śāriputra dances with joy at realizing that the Buddha's teachings mean that he will attain full Awakening. The ecstatic monk says, "I have gained something I never had before....Formerly, when I heard such a Dharma as this from the Buddha, I saw the bodhisattvas receive the prophecy that they should become Buddhas; but we had no part in this. I was sore grieved... This day, at long last, I know that I am truly the Buddha's son, born of the Buddha's mouth, born of Dharma-transformation. I have gained a portion of the Buddha's Dharma."[15] The

---

[13] Ibid., 208–209.
[14] Ibid., 291.
[15] Ibid., 49.

Buddha confirms this, giving a prophecy of Śāriputra's future as the Buddha Padmaprabha ("Flower Glow") who will preside over a magnificent realm called Viraja ("Free of Defilements").[16] Predictions of future Buddhahood for other disciples follow in Chapters Six and Eight, where the Buddha predicts the eventual Buddhahood of some 500 disciples currently in the assembly.[17] Such passages demonstrate how in the *Lotus* previously ignorant people rejoice when they understand that the Buddha's wisdom and compassion extends to them. Those who felt *excluded* realize that they were *included* all along.

Other examples of inclusivism in the *Lotus* occur in Chapter Twelve, which opens with the Buddha explaining how long ago a king renounced his throne to seek the True Dharma. Eventually this king met a seer who promised to bestow upon the king the Dharma of the *Lotus sūtra* itself, doing so after the king spends years serving him. The Buddha then reveals that he himself was this king, and that Devadatta, one of the great villains in Buddhist history,[18] was the seer who instructed him in the *Lotus*, calling him a "good friend," and predicting Devadatta's future Buddhahood.[19] In the same chapter, moreover, we witness a *nāga* ("dragon") princess, whom Mañjuśrī praises for her profound insights, become a full Buddha right before the assembly's eyes.[20] In response, the cosmos quakes its approval and everyone bows in honor of her accomplishment. Traditionally, devotees of the *Lotus* point to her as proof that non-humans and females can attain Buddhahood. Her incredible transformation directly counters earlier declarations by the bodhisattva Prajñākūṭa ("Wisdom Accumulation") and Śāriputra that they doubt the princess' abilities; Śāriputra's comments explicitly draw on traditional Indic views that women cannot attain Buddhahood due to their karmic "impurity."[21] In effect, the entire chapter presents the *Lotus*' teachings on the potential of *all* beings to at-

---

[16] Ibid., 53.

[17] The Buddha extends predictions of future Buddhahood to his personal attendant Ānanda and his biological son Rāhula (Chapter Nine), and to his foster mother Mahāprajāptī and his former wife Yaśodharā in Chapter Thirteen.

[18] According to Buddhist lore, Devadatta sought to usurp control of the Sangha and even attempted to kill the Buddha several times. As punishment, he was swallowed up by the earth and condemned to the deepest of hells.

[19] Hurvitz, trans., *Scripture of the Lotus Blossom*, 195–197.

[20] Ibid., 199–201. *Nāgas* are mythical beings associated with water, and often considered guardians of the Dharma. In one early sutra, though, the Buddha rejects a *nāga*'s request for ordination, explaining that only humans can become monks – the implication being that they are incapable of becoming Buddhas.

[21] Ibid., 200–201.

tain Buddhahood as including even those who in earlier Buddhist tradition were excluded from such opportunity.

Another example of the *Lotus'* inclusivism comes in Chapter Twenty-six, a chapter focusing on *dhāraṇīs*[22] to protect devotees from various harms. After several bodhisattvas and devas step forward to offer their own protective "spells," a group of "ogres" (*rākṣasas*) in the audience volunteer to be protectors of the *Lotus* and those who preach its words, vowing to the Buddha: "O World-Honored One! We, too, with our own persons will protect those who accept and keep, read and recite, and put into practice this scripture, thus enabling them to gain tranquility and separate themselves from decline and care, to dry up the multitude of noxious medicines."[23] In response the Buddha welcomes them into the fold, promising the *rākṣasas* that they "shall have happiness incalculable."[24]

It's easy for contemporary readers to dismiss passages involving monsters and magical powers as "ancient superstition" (although most scriptures include their share of supernatural events and beings) and thus overlook their spiritual implications. Among the latter is the idea that even the most "demonic" beings can receive and practice the Dharma. Again, while we may catch echoes of exclusivism here (demonic "guard dogs" *are* rather scary), the fact remains that these hellish beings are swayed by its teachings and vow to protect their fellow devotees. In response, the Buddha happily extends his blessings to them. If such beings can accept the *Lotus* so joyfully, then surely this marvelous text is available to *all* beings.

The examples give a sense of the *Lotus'* back-and-forth play between exclusivism and inclusivism. The text proclaims its messages in deeply contradictory fashion. Still, we should note a deeper issue in even the *Lotus'* more inclusivist passages. To cite just a few examples:

1. In Chapter Twelve, the *nāga* princess who has such amazing insight must first become *male* before attaining Buddhahood, albeit only for a brief moment (thus subtly confirming the sexist bias of early Buddhism).
2. In Chapter Twenty-five, a section detailing the ability of the bodhisattva Guanyin ("Observer of the Cries of the World") to assume myriad forms (a Buddha, various *devas*, a king, an official, a brahmin, a monk, a nun, a boy, a

---

[22] *Dhāraṇīs* are extended mantras or "spells" of power that protect against demonic attack or just "bad luck." Usually in Sanskrit or Pali, these "words of power" play a large role in popular forms of Buddhism.

[23] Hurvitz, trans., *Scripture of the Lotus Blossom* 323.

[24] Ibid., 323.

girl, a *nāga*, etc.), the text makes clear that despite such illusory appearances to aid other "ignorant" beings, s/he always remains Guanyin.
3. In Chapter Twenty-seven, which relates the story of king who attains Buddhahood after being led to the Dharma by his wife and sons, the text is clear that he *must* convert to Buddhism first. The king's initial status as a *tīrthika* (a non-Buddhist) prevents him from receiving the *Lotus'* teachings.

Such passages betray a subtle "exclusivism," in that some (those "in the know," male, and explicitly Buddhist) are superior to those who have yet to hear the *Lotus*, who are just coming to understand it, or, like the 5000 people in Chapter Two, who initially reject its teachings.

Scholarly Ways of Dealing with Ambiguous Inclusivism in the *Lotus*

Of course, scholars have ways of understanding the *Lotus'* contradictory rhetoric. Anyone who has suffered through grad school will likely gravitate toward the notion that rather than being a transcript of a sermon by the Buddha, the *Lotus* was pieced together from various sources over time by many scribes, editors, and commentators. Drawing on techniques from the field of Biblical criticism, scholars have painstakingly identified various layers within the *Lotus* and even reconstructed a history of its composition.[25] Such studies enable us to explain divergent views within the text as reflecting the interests of the various compilers, redactors, and translators of the *Lotus* who shaped and transmitted the *sūtra* over the centuries.

There is much to recommend such approaches to a work as challenging as the *Lotus*. Indeed, such textual critical studies comprise an immense body of detailed scholarship, underscoring the fact that the text we call "the *Lotus Sūtra*" has a complicated history. Furthermore, this complex composition process has resulted in different versions of the *Lotus* in languages as diverse as Chinese, Sanskrit, Japanese, French, English, some of which have may only exist in fragments. Still,

---

[25] For a good summary of this scholarship, see Yoshiro Tamura, "The Process of Formation of the Lotus Sutra," 29–56, in Yoshio Tamura, *Introduction to the Lotus Sutra*, trans. Gene Reeves (Boston: Wisdom Publications, 2014). For detailed English discussions see Donald S. Lopez, Jr., *The Lotus Sutra: A Biography* (Princeton: Princeton University Press, 2016) and Donald S. Lopez, Jr. and Jacqueline I. Stone, *Two Buddhas Seated Side by Side: A Guide to the Lotus Sutra* (Princeton: Princeton University Press, 2019).

this textual approach remains only *one* way to read the *Lotus* (albeit the most academically respectable one), and scholars engaging in such philological methods continue to disagree in their readings.

Even so, there are deeper problems with a textual critical approach than disagreements between experts in ancient languages and manuscripts, particularly for those interested in scriptures as *sacred* texts. Inevitably, analyses aiming at "objectivity" treat a text as an object of critical scrutiny to be poked and prodded, often privileging an "outsider" stance while asserting its superiority over traditional faith-based readings. Is it possible when taking such an objective approach for the *Lotus* as a manifestation of the Dharma to make a claim on *us,* or is it now just a collection of material to be mined for our own academic use? New Testament scholar Luis Menéndez-Antuña describes this situation well:

> Like a scientist, the interpreter – using all types of science proof methods – extracts an original meaning from her object of analysis…In this model, a disinterested, value-neutral critic embodies the ideal interpreter; almost like a surgeon, scalpel in hand, the reader dominates and masters the text to withdraw all usable information.[26]

This image of the interpreter as surgeon (vivisectionist?) reveals disturbing truths about hermeneutic study. While many of us know of instances where someone (perhaps ourselves) has "beaten a text into submission," Menéndez-Antuña reminds us that this "abstractivist" approach tears texts from their formative context and has violent, colonialist overtones.

A larger issue here, though, is whether a sacred text subjected to objective analysis can even be considered "scripture." At the close of a symposium on "Holy Texts," Paul Ricoeur, one of the foremost twentieth-century hermeneutic theorists, raises this very question when he suggests that the "critical editions" of scriptures like the Bible are no longer sacred (except perhaps to the community of scholars).[27] Similarly, that doyen of comparative scriptural studies, Wilfred Cantwell Smith, declares that "Scriptures are not texts!"[28] since by pointing toward some Sacred Reality, scriptures defy a simplistic subject-object relationship. By contrast, submitting a scripture like the *Lotus* to textual critique potentially reduces it to a mere

---

[26] Luis Menéndez-Antuña, "Not a Bridge, but a Tunnel: Reaching out to the limits of what we (want to) know," *Focus: Boston University School of Theology Magazine* (2023): 37.

[27] Paul Ricoeur, "Epilogue: The 'Sacred' Text And the Community,' 271–276, in *The Critical Study Of Sacred Texts*, ed. Wendy Doniger O'Flaherty, Berkeley Religious Studies Series (Berkeley: The Graduate Theological Union, 1979).

[28] Wilfred Cantwell Smith, *What is Scripture? – A Comparative Approach* (Minneapolis: Fortress Press, 1993), 223.

human artifact (albeit one of rare artistry), an object that academic masters of scholarly techniques ultimately own. And while the *Lotus* at times likens itself to a "precious jewel," treating it as a piece of property would seem to preclude it being a means of spiritual enlightenment.

All this talk about the dangers of objectifying scripture reminds us that no sacred text exists alone. *Pace* Luther's motto *sola scriptura* ("by scripture alone"), by definition "scripture" is inherently relational. Smith claims that "scripture" is actually trilateral, in his words, "a relation – an *engagement* – among humans, the transcendent, and a text."[29] In Buddhism, this relationship is known as the "Three Jewels" (Skt. *triratna,* Ch. *sānbǎo,* Jpn. *mitsubishi*): the Buddha (the Teacher), the Dharma (the Teachings), the Sangha (the community). To be Buddhist is to "take refuge" in the "Three Jewels," each of which depends on the others, and it is in this context of interdependence that we need to understand notions of "inclusivism" and "exclusivism" in the *Lotus*.

In fact, the best "evidence" of the *Lotus* as religiously exclusive lies not in the words of the text itself so much as the way it has been taken up by its devotees. Of these, the most famous is Nichiren (1221–82), a powerful personality who lived during the tumultuous Kamakura period. Nichiren began his monastic career in the Tendai school, perhaps the most influential form of Japanese Buddhism, and, due to the *Lotus*' central role in Tendai life, he became engrossed by the text. Eventually he came to see that text as the *only* version of the Dharma that was effective during his "evil age."[30] To that end, he devised a new *mandala* (cosmic diagram) based on the *sūtra*'s title and encouraged devotees to chant the name of the *sūtra* over and over: *Namu myōhō renge kyō* ("Hail the Scripture of the Lotus of the Perfect Truth"). Moreover, he denounced other Buddhist schools (Pure Land, Zen, etc.), advocating for the forceful conversion of their adherents. Nichiren also argued that faith in the *Lotus* was essential to the well-being of Japan and that rulers supporting other sects were courting disaster. Understandably, he and his followers were persecuted, with Nichiren himself narrowly escaping execution and suffering exile twice.

Nichiren's strident proclamation of the *Lotus* as the only Truth makes him more like a fiery Biblical prophet than a stereotypical Buddhist priest, and his militant exclusivism continued among succeeding generations of his followers. Yet before

---

[29] Ibid., 239.

[30] A recurring theme in the *Lotus* is the idea that the Dharma decays, becoming less effective the further we get from the historical Buddha's lifetime. This process culminates in the "Age of the Degenerate Dharma" (Ch. *mòfǎ*; Jpn, *mappō*), during which there will be natural disasters, widespread social unrest, and violent conflict.

condemning Nichiren Buddhists for their intolerance, we should note that their insistence on exclusive devotion to the *Lotus* despite rejection by non-believers has a positive purpose. Doing so enables the *Lotus* "to implant the seed of enlightenment in their minds," establishing a karmic connection that guarantees their future Buddhahood. Thus, Nichiren's proselytizing "was not dogmatic self-assertion, but a compassionate act of bodhisattva practice."[31] The "logic" involved is clear: eventually *all* beings will embrace the True Dharma and attain full Awakening. Moreover, this "hidden inclusivism" underlies exclusivist readings of the *Lotus* at various points in later Japanese history.[32]

To further complicate matters, explicitly inclusivist views of the *Lotus* continue to emerge over time. Among the most prominent are those promoted by members of the so-called "New Religions" (*shinshūkyō*) Risshō Kōsei Kai and Soka Gakkai, two contemporary movements focused on the *Lotus* that have branched off from the Nichiren sect and are now international in scope.[33] Such inclusivist readings of the *Lotus* are by no means limited to Buddhists; several prominent Christian scholars have also delved into the *Lotus'* lines and found much that resonates with aspects of Christian doctrine and practice.[34]

The sheer variety of readings of the *Lotus* indicates that diverse people can intelligently engage with this mysterious text despite its history of intolerant exclusivism and that the *Lotus* still provides insights relevant to our world. More importantly, the fact that even Christian scholars find that the *Lotus'* words illuminate the relationship between different faiths indicates that it speaks to people beyond the Buddhist fold. Once again, the fact that the *Lotus* does *not* exclude people willing to grapple with its ideas means that it is an inclusive text.

---

[31] Lopez and Stone, *Two Buddha's Seated Side by Side*, 86–88.

[32] The most extreme examples are the *Fuju-fuse* ("not giving nor receiving") sect, who refused to have anything to do with members of other religions, even suffering martyrdom at the hands of the authorities. For details see Yoshiro Tamura, *Introduction to the Lotus Sutra*, 133–137.

[33] Both organizations have been sources of controversy but are actively engaged in fostering global understanding and discussion of the *Lotus*. See "Basic Information: Rissho Kosei Kai International," Rissho Kosei Kai, accessed June 20, 2023, https://rk-world.org/basic-information/, and "About the Soka Gakkai: Soka Gakkai (Global)," Soka Gakkai (Global), accessed June 20, 2023, https://www.sokaglobal.org/about-the-soka-gakkai.html.

[34] See, for example, Schubert M. Ogden, "The Lotus Sutra and Interreligious Dialogue," in *A Buddhist Kaleidoscope: Essays on the Lotus Sutra*, ed. Gene Reeves (Tokyo: Kōsei Publishing Co., 2002), 107–114 and Michael A. Fuss, "*Upāya* and *Missio Dei*: Toward a Common Missiology," in *A Buddhist Kaleidoscope: Essays on the Lotus Sutra*, ed. Gene Reeves (Tokyo: Kōsei Publishing Co., 2002), 115–126.

Some Unsatisfactory Conclusions

So, after all of these remarks, what conclusions can we draw? Certainly, the *Lotus* reveals the fraught nature of our concepts of "inclusivism" and "exclusivism," since this text seems to be both. Perhaps, then, there is an alternative? One that comes to mind is a perspective called "Expedient Means Pluralism." As explained by scholar David Burton, "Expedient Means Pluralism" centers on the notion of *upāya* but applies it not only to earlier versions of the Dharma but also to other religions, and even the *Lotus* itself. Taking this approach effectively means that the *Lotus* contains infinite (innumerable?) meanings.[35] Moreover, this approach fits with the Buddha's words in Chapter Three, where he reminds Śāriputra, "Seek as you will in all ten directions: There is no other vehicle, apart from the expedient devices of the Buddhas."[36] Yet as tempting as "Expedient Means Pluralism" is, it begs the question: can a text can truly mean *something* if it seems to be able to mean *anything*? Regardless, examining the *Lotus* in the context of arguments about religious exclusivism and inclusivism suggests that we cannot cleanly separate these notions. "Inclusivism" and "exclusivism" entail each other, with "pluralism" just expanding the situation and, perhaps, including its *own* "exclusivism."

Interestingly, since the *Lotus* resists efforts to pigeon-hole it as either "inclusivist" or "exclusivist," it raises the possibility that *other* sacred texts do too. Those of us who take scriptures seriously as *sacred*—particularly in the context of interfaith exchange—should bear this point in mind. Rabbi Jonathan Sacks observes that in Judaism there is more than one "correct" way to read *Torah*, citing rabbinic teachings about the "seventy faces" of scripture and the tradition that since *Torah* was originally revealed before some 600,000 Israelites, it can be interpreted some 600,000 ways.[37] This sounds like a Jewish analogue to the *Lotus*' "innumerable meanings," though this does not mean that *Torah* and the *Lotus* say "the same thing."

Ironically, at this point, I find myself seeking refuge in another type of exclusivism, one that excludes definitive labels as "exclusive," or "inclusive." Perhaps we are running up against the limits of language (a familiar theme in Buddhism as well as the apophatic currents of various religions) *despite* the many powers of language in the *Lotus*. In discussing the mysteries of the *Lotus,* Donald Lopez and Jacqueline

---

[35] David Burton, "A Buddhist Perspective." In *The Oxford Handbook of Religious Diversity,* ed. Chad Meister (New York: Oxford University Press, 2010): 321–336.

[36] Hurvitz, trans., *Scripture of the Lotus Blossom of the Fine Dharma,* 74.

[37] Rabbi Jonathan Sacks, *Not in God's Name: Confronting Religious Violence* (New York: Schocken Books, 2015), 218.

Stone observe that we readers of religious texts engage in a complex process of "hermeneutical triangulation," groping for an understanding of scripture that is always mediated by our biases and the influences of our cultural-historical context.[38] Invariably we end up excluding and including various points and perspectives.

But there's more. In her scholarly "memoir" *Encountering God: A Spiritual Journey from Bozeman to Banaras,* Diana Eck observes, some of us find ourselves sliding back and forth through "exclusivist," "inclusivist," and "pluralist" attitudes at different points in our faith journeys.[39] Indeed, a few of us even discover that the boundaries of our faith identities prove more porous than we anticipated as we come to include previously "other" sacred texts and practices in our lives. In such cases, we find we are in situations of "multiple religious participation."[40] This may be especially troubling to adherents of the Abrahamic traditions, which have long defined themselves in terms of exclusive faith commitments, but "MRP'ing" is the norm in East Asia, and I suspect that if we are honest, we will admit that it is far more common than we initially have thought.

Before finishing these reflections on exclusivism and inclusivism in the *Lotus*, I feel I must lay my own cards on the table: my sense of the Dharma is that it includes *everyone* and *everything* while not excluding any spiritual path. Instead, it takes us past settled opinions into a radical openness to the Mystery of Reality beyond our wildest imaginings. I see this in the *Lotus'* opening scene where myriads of people from all walks of life (the text does *not* explicitly identify all of them as "Buddhist") gather alongside of all manner of beings to be illuminated by the Buddha. I see it also in the example of Bodhisattva "Never Disparaging" (Sadāparibhūta), who in Chapter Twenty says even to his abusers, "I dare not hold you in contempt! You are all treading the Path, And shall all become Buddhas!"[41] Can we entertain the possibility that the *Lotus'* expansive vision offers? I hope so. *Namu myōhō renge kyō*, my friends.

---

[38] Lopez and Stone, *Two Buddhas Seated Side by Side*, 34.
[39] Eck, *Encountering God*, 170.
[40] John H. Berthrong, "Considering the Lotus Sutra," in *A Buddhist Kaleidoscope: Essays on the Lotus Sutra*, ed. Gene Reeves (Tokyo: Kōsei Publishing Co., 2002), 95–96.
[41] Hurvitz, trans., *Scripture of the Lotus Blossom*, 283.

Bibliography

Berthrong, John H. 2002. Considering the Lotus Sutra. In *A Buddhist Kaleidoscope: Essays on the Lotus Sutra*, ed. Gene Reeves, 95–106. Tokyo: Kōsei Publishing Co.
Burton, David. 2010. A Buddhist Perspective. In *The Oxford Handbook of Religious Diversity*, ed. Chad Meister, 321–336. New York: Oxford University Press.
Eck, Diana L. 1995. *Encountering God: A Spiritual Journey from Bozeman to Banaras*. New York: Penguin Putnam Inc.
Fuss, Michael A. 2002. *Upāya* and *Missio Dei*: Toward a Common Missiology. In *A Buddhist Kaleidoscope: Essays on the Lotus Sutra*, ed. Gene Reeves, 115–126. Tokyo: Kōsei Publishing Co.
Hurvitz, Leon, Trans. 1976. *Scripture of the Lotus Blossom of the Fine Dharma*. New York: Columbia University Press.
Li, Chenyang, Sai Hang Kwok, and Dascha Düring, eds. 2021. *Harmony in Chinese Thought: A Philosophical Introduction*. Lanham: The Rowan and Littlefield Publishing Group.
Lopez, Donald S., Jr. 2016. *The Lotus Sutra: A Biography*. Princeton: Princeton University Press.
Lopez, Donald S., Jr., and Jacqueline I. Stone. 2019. *Two Buddhas Seated Side by Side: A Guide to the Lotus Sutra*. Princeton: Princeton University Press.
Menéndez-Antuña, Luis. 2023. Not a Bridge, But a Tunnel: Reaching Out to the Limits of What We (Want to) Know. *Focus: Boston University School of Theology Magazine*: 34–37.
Ogden, Schubert M. 2002. The Lotus Sutra and Interreligious Dialogue. In *A Buddhist Kaleidoscope: Essays on the Lotus Sutra*, ed. Gene Reeves, 107–114. Tokyo: Kōsei Publishing Co.
Ricoeur, Paul. 1979. Epilogue: The 'Sacred' Text And the Community. In *The Critical Study of Sacred Texts*, Berkeley Religious Studies Series, ed. Wendy Doniger O'Flaherty, 272–276. Berkeley: The Graduate Theological Union.
Rissho Kosei Kai. Basic Information: Rissho Kosei Kai International. Accessed June 20, 2023. https://rk-world.org/basic-information/
Rose, Ken. 2018. Religious Pluralism and the Upaniṣads. *Embodied Philosophy.com*, October 8. Accessed May 1, 2023. https://www.embodiedphilosophy.com/religious-pluralism-and-the-upani%E1%B9%A3ads-2/?_gl=1*1n7vqps*_up*MQ..*_ga*MTIzNTU5OTUyNC4xNjgzOTE4MDQz*_ga_VZ66VKPMTH*MTY4MzkxODA0MS4xLjA.uMTY4MzkxODA0MS4wLjAuMA..#easy-footnote-10-2410.
Sacks, Rabbi Jonathan. 2015. *Not in God's Name: Confronting Religious Violence*. New York: Schocken Books.
Smith, Wilfred Cantwell. 1993. *What is Scripture? – A Comparative Approach*. Minneapolis: Fortress Press.
Soka Gakkai (Global). About the Soka Gakkai: Soka Gakkai (Global). Accessed June 20, 2023. https://www.sokaglobal.org/about-the-soka-gakkai.html
Tamura, Yoshiro. 2014. *Introduction to the Lotus Sutra*. Translated by Gene Reeves. Boston: Wisdom Publications.
Tuggy, Dale. 2015. Theories of Religious Diversity. *The Internet Encyclopedia of Religion*. Accessed May 3, 2023. https://iep.utm.edu/reli-div/.

John M. Thompson is currently Professor of Philosophy and Religion at Christopher Newport University, where he teaches a variety of courses on religious and philosophical traditions. Dr. John Thompson is a specialist in Buddhism and East Asian traditions. Also, he currently serves on the steering committee for the AAR's unit on Comparative Approaches to Religion and Violence. Dr. John Thompson is also a practitioner of martial arts and meditation, as he is deeply committed to mentoring undergraduates who are interested in philosophy and religion. His scholarly interests include comparative religion, myth and ritual, mysticism, scriptures of the world, violence and religion, pop culture, as well as religion and philosophy.

Inclusive Evangelicalism? Toward An Ontology of Inclusion in Evangelical Christian Traditions

Jason Okrzynski

"Evangelical" in Contemporary Usage

It seems that a significant section of American Christianity is suffering from a theological crisis that it does not identify. This claimed is evidenced by the documented statistic that 81% of "evangelical Christians: voted for Donald Trump in the 2016 election; a statistic that declined only marginally in 2020. This phenomenon has been both angered, and even more so, confounded Christians of many stripes; this author included.[1] Turn the television to any political pundit discussing this demographic today, and it will seem that the term "Evangelical" is a clearly identifiable term, with a clearly defined group of Christians, passionately united in a shared confession and belief.

---

[1] See: Whitehead, Andrew L., and Samuel L. Perry. *Taking America back for god: Christian nationalism in the United States.* New York: Oxford University Press, 2022.

J. Okrzynski (✉)
United Protestant Church, Grayslake, IL, USA
e-mail: seniorpastor@upcgl.org

© The Author(s), under exclusive license to Springer Nature Switzerland AG 2024
M. Shafiq, T. Donlin-Smith (eds.), *Inclusion or Exclusion in the Sacred Texts and Human Contexts*, https://doi.org/10.1007/978-3-031-70180-1_3

The truth of who the so-called Evangelicals are, however, could not be further from this simple definition.[2] Anyone defining this term clearly must begin with the sociological reality that the use of the term (whether as "evangelical" or "Evangelical) represents a self-described affiliation, leaving its ultimate meaning amorphously subjective. However, the most minimal interrogation of black voters revealed an equally significant cohort of self-described "evangelical" voters supported Hillary Clinton in 2014 and Joe Biden in 2020. In fact, the support of Democratic candidates among black "evangelicals" is actually the longest, clearest, and strongest cohort voting fidelity dating back at least to the Civil Rights era.

Precarious to this term is the prevalence of a single letter. Creating a semantic distinction by capitalizing the "E" in "Evangelicals" is a surprisingly recent phenomenon. Use of evangelical as a proper title did not become commonplace until just after the Civil War. Throughout Europe and America historically, the terms "protestant" and "evangelical" were used interchangeably until that time. In post-war America, survival demanded these denominations into forced and hasty reunion, with little time to tend to real reconciliation. It was during this time that the use of "Evangelical" became quickly prominent.[3] With the formation of the National Association of Evangelicals in 1941, The Evangelicals managed to create for themselves a centralized bully pulpit, whose institutional history paints a not-so-subtle picture, of judgment, exclusion, and marginalization of all female, black, brown, and LGBTQIA+ voices or membership within the circle of so-called Evangelicals.[4]

However, all these explanations of evangelicals, enlightening as they are still leave one of the most confounding realities of the "evangelicals" and Trumpism utterly unexplained. For their complicated racial and political history, evangelicals' identity, even at its worst, hides behind a thin veil of performative piety. Historically, it was a given that white, American protestant-evangelical Christians insisted on good clean language from their leaders and heroes. Historically evangelical (or protestant) faith has been tied to an assumed cultural ascent to proper moral, ethical, and civil behaviors arising from a long, powerful, and shared tradition of "good Christian behavior" beginning with the Ten Commandments, but commonly highlighting conservative sexual morality, tame talk, obedience to the rule of law and an

---

[2] For a clear definition on this dodgy term and its history see: 1. David William Bebbington, George M. Marsden, and Mark A. Noll, essay, in *Evangelicals: Who They Have Been, Are Now, and Could Be* (Grand Rapids, MI: William B. Eerdmans Publishing Company, 2019).

[3] See Marty, M. E., & Marty, M. E. (1986). Protestantism in the United States: Righteous empire. Scribner's.

[4] See: Sharp, Isaac B. The other evangelicals: A story of liberal, black, progressive, feminist, and Gay Christians - and the movement that pushed them out. Grand Rapids, MI: William. B. Eerdmans Publishing Company, 2023 or Kobes, Du Mez Kristin.

abiding respect for the poor, the infirm, and the "least of these." All this changed abruptly on October 7, 2016. On that date now infamous audio leaked containing an Access Hollywood Recording of Trump claiming he could walk up to a woman and grab them by their private parts, because he was so famous.

Trumps very character has shockingly, and without ceasing thumbed his nose at all these values; and yet his "evangelical" supporters have been as brash as to describe him as a vessel for God. How to explain this? I suggest that by linking the term "evangelical" with one of its most significant intellectual progenitors, Martin Luther, can both shine light on the genesis of this phenomenon; but even more so craft an alternative path beyond the ugliness of the last century, to reform, and perhaps even reclaim "evangelical" as a positive identifier into the future.

Luther's Rage

In the fourteenth- and fifteenth-century Reformation, "evangelical" was used *at least* as prominently by early Reformation figures; and significant for our concern, evangelical was The Reformer, Martin Luther's preferred title. The connection between Luther's thought and the emergence of Evangelical Trumpism is both obvious, and yet due to the amorphous, and intentionally equivocating nature of the Evangelical culture, is itself ambivalent. However, on the surface, a reading of Luther's key theological themes will find obvious correlation in the published Tenets of the NAE.[5] Luther's key stress on the authority of scripture, Justification by faith, the (divinely) revealed nature of the Creeds, as well as his conviction that the "true church" was not the visible church of traditions, denominations, and institutions but of the believer convicted by The Spirit of Biblical truth. What is more, Luther's stress on, justification by *grace alone, faith alone* and *scripture alone* has a history of taking on a disembodied and ahistorical nature. In Luther's methodology, this strong conviction about the authority of Biblical Revelation for knowing about God was paired with an equally strong conviction about the role of empirical, scientific reason for knowing about earthly and worldly matters. We will return to that later. For now, let it simply be said that one aspect of Luther's thought can *seem* to state, in no uncertain terms, that Christian behavior is irrelevant compared to faith as trust in the grace of God. This (mis)reading of Luther, combined with his famously belligerent temperament, goes a long way to explain how simple God-loving Christians can justify offering blind fidelity to Trump. However, keep-

---

[5] Isaac B. Sharp, The (Other) Evangelicals Sharp, Isaac B. (Grand Rapids, MI: William. B. Eerdmans Publishing Company, 2023), p. 38.

ing in mind the racialized political history of "Evangelical" goes even further to connect its genesis to Luther's writings and legacy.

Luther was famous for raging against his opponents. He regarded the revealed God of saving with apocalyptic ultimacy. This ultimacy, however, becomes even more dangerous when he raged against the opponents to true doctrine. For Luther, Christ is truly present in faith; thus, an attack on doctrine was akin to crucifying God himself. Luther could turn with incredible petulance towards anyone who he perceived as such. Luther's rage, as expressed in angry vitriol and verbal polemics against, is almost as famous as his almost singular historical significance. Nowhere is it hotter or more dangerously stated as it was in his rhetoric against those he perceived as the religious opponents of the Christian Church Jews and Muslim; people who have been further distinguished in liberal-modern thought by being labelled as of a distinct race.

Luther's thorough and unrelenting theology of Grace and gift have drawn me into a lifelong academic and pastoral conversation with man. However, the writings I am about to explore are embarrassing, at best. At worst they are dangerous and fill me with both fear and anger. I want to make clear that I have absolutely no interest in excusing them, softening them or anything short of condemning them in this chapter. I outline them here in the hopes that I can draw the connection between Luther's temperament and Trump; and in the next part of the chapter, to deconstruct the esoteric chauvinism in Trump's entitlement precisely by highlighting the best of the Biblically revealed truths and thought of Luther.

Luther's Rage and the Jews

Luther's first writings about Jews came in his 1523 tract *That Jesus was Born a Jew (1523)*.[6] The goal of the writing is to offer an own response to a series of rumors and accusations about Luther that are false. There Luther is clear that he wishes for Jews to convert to Christianity. However, it is also clear that he makes no racial or ontological distinction between Jews and Christian. Rather, it is faith and theology that make for the distinction. However, even within that distinction, Luther ultimately respects the integrity of the Jewish faith, and he does so in a humble and even self-critical vein:

> If the apostles, who also were Jews, had dealt with us Gentiles as we Gentiles deal with the Jews, there would never have been a Christian among the Gentiles. Since they dealt with us Gentiles in such brotherly fashion, we in our turn ought to treat the

---

[6] LW 44:195–230.

Jews in a brotherly manner in order that we might convert some of them. For even we ourselves are not yet all very far along, not to speak of having arrived.[7]

To say that the entirety of the work represents a positive and affirming review of the Old Testament is not saying enough. Luther painstakingly reviews the entire cannon explicating the integral authority of each text and in turn demonstrates the utter and absolute dependence of the New Testament and all Christian faith and theology on The Old Testament. He used language like that to assess the Abrahamic Promise in Genesis 22:18:

> It is a short saying, to be sure, but a rich gospel, subsequently inculcated and used in marvelous fashion by the fathers both in writing and in preaching. Many thousands of sermons have been preached from this passage, and countless souls saved. For it is the living word of God, in which Abraham and his descendants believed, and by which they were redeemed and preserved from sin and death and the power of the devil.[8]

Even more instructive for modern readers is a middle section in which Luther squabbles about the Judaic assessment of the virgin birth. Luther's medieval worldview not only assumes that Jews and Christian are naturally open to intelligent debate about the interpretation of scripture but also that he believes that what is keeping Jews from sharing his Christology is not that Jews are stupid, evil nor are they *ontologically* different from other human beings. Rather, he argues that they have just not been taught correctly. It is implicit to Luther's understanding that Jews and Christians share the exact same theological, ontological, anthropological, and soteriological characteristics. What separates Jews and Christians is faith; defined as an orientation towards God as opposed to a racial, ontological or soteriological category. In the concluding paragraphs, Luther takes it on himself to include some apologetics aimed at evangelizing Jews.

By 1546, Luther's writings and thoughts had taken an ugly turn for the worse. His early stress on Jews as deserving of respect and friendship as well as his positive assessment of their given openness to God and his hopes for conversation shifted. Somewhere, the Jews became an enemy, not personally, but pastorally, as opponents to the gospel. The impetus for writing the work was Luther's understanding that there were Judaist religious traditions. In Luther's mind, this was an abomination, denying God's full glory and possibly leading to eternal damnation.

---

[7] Ibid.
[8] Ibid.

The tour de force of Luther's later, anti-Judaistic sentiments is his 1543 tract *On the Jews and Their Lies*,[9] a text so ugly that it moved Dietrich Bonhoeffer to comment he wished Luther had died before writing it. In it, Luther scribes a tirade against the Jews that go so far as to outline the course of action that will later be taken by the Third Reich in *Chrystal Nacht*. The writing is quite long, and somewhat like the 1527 piece in that most of it is concerned with an exhaustive exegetical commentary on the Old Testament. However, throughout Luther utilizes several key strands from the OT to make sweeping judgments against the Jews.

The first concept that Luther weaponizes against the Jews is the punishment on God upon Israel for her unfaithfulness. Beginning in Exodus and throughout the prophets, David's reign and perhaps most significantly the Babylonian Exile, the Hebrew scriptures present self-understanding as that in anger God has (for a time) withdrawn divine blessing and providence from Israel so that she might repent and return to God. Luther explicates every one of these texts' *ad nauseam*, with each exegesis ending in the same conclusion: the Jews have rejected Christ because they have incurred God's divine wrath and unable to return to him. The both The Roman Catholic Papacy and the very existence of Islam are similarly included on the list of divine stumbling blocks God has imposed on the world as recourse to sinfulness.[10]

The second theme that Luther utilized from the Old Testament is the various statements condemning Israel's worship. In this vein, Luther does refer to the Jews and their "race."[11] However, what can be confounding to the modern mind is that Luther's mockery is precisely that it is circumcision that divides them as a race. Luther does not view them scientifically, ontologically, or anthropologically as racially distinct. Rather, as a fellow human, he finds it incomprehensible that they would not convert to Jesus who he unequivocally understands as to be the Son of God and objectively more superior to the religion of Moses. In fact, race is not understood genetically for Luther but religiously; as a consquence of bearing embodied, physical sign of the covenant God established freely by grace. Luther believes that Jews' rejection of Jesus is an assault against the Divine Grace made known in Jesus.

In this vein, Luther's anger climaxes at the conclusion of the writing. Christians are saved by faith, apart from circumcision. Thus, challenging the faith is a serious evil for Luther. Politically, Luther understood the role of the state's power exists only to limit evil and encourage external righteousness (good behaving) from its

---

[9] LW 47:121–306.
[10] Ibid., 161.
[11] Ibid., 149.

citizens. Therefore, given that Judaizing is an affront to both, Luther makes proscriptive judgments to the church and the princes regarding their treatment asking, "What shall we Christians do with this rejected and condemned people, the Jews?" Luther's deplorable answer is sevenfold, including but not limited to burning Jewish buildings, taking their businesses and scriptures away by force, gathering them into ghettos and submitting them to forced labor.[12]

Luther's Rage and the Turks

In many ways, Luther's view of Islam is similar.[13] If not an outright defender of Islam, Luther was at the very least a tolerant advocate. This is surprising given the fact that in Luther's day fear of Islam was rampant in Germany as the "Turks were at Vienna's doorstep."[14] Nonetheless, Luther fought against the Imperical ban on publication of the Quran in Latin so that Christians could read it. He himself owned a Latin translation which he read in its entirety. When the ban was removed and publication ensued in 1543, it was Luther and his colleague Phillip Melancthon who wrote the preface! Luther shared his original thoughts on the Quran and the Islam in 1529.

Luther's first words on Islam came in his reformation tract, *On War Against the Turks*.[15] There is much in this work that may be helpful in the quest for an inclusive

---

[12] "First, to set fire to their synagogues or schools and to bury and cover with dirt whatever will not burn, so that no man will ever again see a stone or cinder of them… Second, I advise that their houses also be razed and destroyed. For they pursue in them the same aims as in their synagogues. Instead, they might be lodged under a roof or in a barn, like the gypsies…. Third, I advise that all their prayer books and Talmudic writings, in which such idolatry, lies, cursing, and blasphemy are taught, be taken from them… Fourth, I advise that their rabbis be forbidden to teach henceforth on pain of loss of life and limb… Fifth, I advise that safe-conduct on the highways be abolished completely for the Jews. Sixth, I advise that usury be prohibited to them, and that all cash and treasure of silver and gold be taken from them and put aside for safekeeping. Seventh, I recommend putting a flail, an ax, a hoe, a spade, a distaff, or a spindle into the hands of young, strong Jews and Jewesses and letting them earn their bread in the sweat of their brow, as was imposed on the children of Adam (Gen. 3 [:19]) …. one should toss out these lazy rogues by the seat of their pants." Ibid., 268–273.

[13] Take note that Luther refers to Islam and Muslims in shorthand most commonly referring to the "The Turks".

[14] Christine Helmer, Paul Helmer, and Munib A. Younin, "Beyond Luther: Prophetic Interfaith Dialogue for Life," essay, in *The Global Luther: A Theologian for Modern Times* (Minneapolis: Fortress Press, 2009), 56.

[15] LW 46:154–205.

evangelicalism today. The works focusses on the question of warring against Islam globally. Luther's simple answer is that in Christ God calls all people of faith to repent of the sword. From a spiritual standpoint, the Christian has no business whatsoever in going to war. In fact, Luther is clear that beginning with the crusades the church's wars against the Muslims are truly a front to cover their greed and arrogance. Luther insists that if all the rulers in the world were true Christians, there would likely be no wars.

The Turks, however, have no more right to wage war and violence nor to invade and claim the lands of others. Explicit concession is given for the state to go to war, but only to the extent that they are seeking to protect people. Luther highlights the Quran's positive view of Mary and Jesus, but ultimately urges prayerful resistance to Islam in defense of the divinity of Christ, the Christian state, and the estate of Christian marriage (monogamy).[16] In this vein, the state indeed has the right to war in defense of Christian liberty, and the Christian is at liberty to serve therein.

Luther quickly followed in 1530 with *Preface to the Tract on the Religion and Customs of the Turk,*[17] in response to several popular commentaries on the Quran and Islam. Luther opens the tract with harsh criticisms for the insufficiency of these writings which offer "the most base and absurd things that arouse hatred and can move people to ill-will, at the same time they either pass over without rebuttal or cover over the good things it contains." Seeking a more respectful, generous, and accurate account, Luther picks up his pen stating that Christendom could learn a lot from Muslims who he praises at length for their religiosity and fidelity in living holy and clean lives. Compared to what Luther understands as the reality of God in Christ, the Christian need not fear or even resist Islam. For Luther, the God of grace who came as an infant, suffered, died, and rose again for humanity's sin is a faith so good and true that it will resist all challengers. Repentance and revival are God's right work in the encounter with the Turks.

Finally, *Appeal for Prayer Against the Turks* (1541)[18] is a letter written on the request of the princes, addressing the fears of Germans regarding their Islamic neighbors. Luther, however, was occupied with a pastoral concern for Germany, lamenting the bad behavior of the people, their lack of villainy, and even the predatory nature of banks and lenders. He describes the Muslim as the *"schoolmaster"* sent by God to punish, warn, and christen the German people to revived obedience.[19] His primary concern is not attacking Islam but rather to ensure that the

---

[16] Ibid., 176–182.
[17] https://wordandworld.luthersem.edu/content/pdfs/16-2_Islam/16-2_Boyce-Henrich.pdf
[18] LW 43:215–41.
[19] LW 43:224.

flourishing of Germany, her Church, and the pastoral vocation. To these ends his prescription is that German Christians take responsibility for themselves before God through Repentance and the ardent practice of true faith in the God of grace and gift. Luther is critical of the "Turkish, Epicurean philosophy," [20] in which he views Islam as trading justification by faith in Jesus for the promise of carnal delights in eternity in reward for good works in earthly life. He takes the opportunity to stress that the real battles against the Turkish armies is not a battle of "flesh and blood," but instead a spiritual battle. In fact, while the political state has mandated to fight against incursive armies, the only right weapon of the Christian man or woman is prayer before God for saving faith.

Ultimately, Luther's thought demonstrates the theological certainty of a medieval thinker. What is more, his critical innovations, as well as his innovations, drew largely from various competing strands in the scholastic theology of the time. Ultimately, when Luther took up his pen for political purposes he more often than not would could rage against his enemies in belligerent and belittling generalizations, strikingly similar to Donald Trump. It is not a huge leap to see a rhetorical history that has remained nebulously present in evangelical culture since Luther. From a biblical standpoint, such judgment, belligerence, and hatred as easily judged. However, there is more to be gleaned from Luther than an examination of the ugliness of contemporary (evangelical) thought and rhetoric. We turn to the wider content of Luther's biblical theology now.

Martin Luther's Ontology and Anthropology

It is essential before turning to Marin Luther's ontology, to take a broader view to Luther's approach to Theological method. In concern to evangelical thrology, Luther's method wields sifnificant ability to give absolute theological-revelational authority to scripture without eschewing other epistemologies. This method is laid out in his short but enlightening work, *Disputation on Humanity*,[21] a sort of philosophical first things. Interrogating the scholastic methods dominant in his day; Luther strikes an argument for the proper process for generating knowledge; he assigns a particular place and epistemic source to the role of both ontology and anthropology that remain surprisingly coherent today. We will begin there, and then explicate his ontology and finally offer a brief examination of his wider theological themes with his ontology in mind.

---

[20] Ibid., 235.
[21] LW 34: 133–134.

Luther begins his argument by commending human reason with high praise. In fact, he opens with an ontic assessment that reason is the God-given gift that defines and unites *all* human beings as a (created) species. Further reason is the highest and best of human endowments and deserves credit for the best of human achievement including "science, art, medicine, politics, and ethics." However, he states (perhaps better even than modern observers today) that there are boundaries to epistemological realm of Reason. Human Reason is a powerful tool for generating knowledge because it relies on gathering information through sense data about the outside world (what we today commonly refer to as empirical nature). Reason comes to reliably know thinkgs, precisely because it uses the human senses to gather real data about the material world and reality, in material history, and study that reality as it is. This means that reason is able to come to know only so far as it can gather sense data on the attributes, history, capabilities, and limits on a given object, people, or thing.

By extension this also means that human reason is always and ultimately limited in what it can accurealty claim to examine. Namely, reason cannot plumb the mind and nature of God beyond what God reveals about God's self. What is more, reason cannot know anything about the original cause of existence, that is why we, or anything, exist. Neither can reason authoritatively generate knowledge about the ultimate and highest purpose fo any given human life or about the ultimate purpose for all that exists; including the purpose and callings of humanity. For Luther, existential and theological question belong rightly to God and are thus are belong to the realm of faith, not reason. Thus, generating knowledge about God, human destiny, and the meaning of life must rely solely on revelation, grace and faith for proper reception.

It is at this point that we can begin to examine Luther's ontology. The *Word Alone* is for Luther the source that reveals an effective ontology of the cosmos and correlating anthropology. The primary locus for these questions begins in the book of Genesis, which attributes to God the role of creator. However, Luther goes further than this in his exegetical work. It was very important to Luther that the primary attribute of God was that God is gracious. Only by viewing God as primarily gracious can the Christian rightly understand the Creation and my role in it. Right Christian belief, as he states in the Small Catechism,[22] consists in trusting that:

---

[22] Theodore G. Tappert, *The Book of Concord: The Confessions of the Evangelical Lutheran Church* (Philadelphia: Fortress Press, 1959).

> ...God has created me together with all that exists. God has given me and still preserves my body and soul: eyes, ears, and all limbs and senses; reason and all mental faculties. In addition, God daily and abundantly provides shoes and clothing, food and drink, house and farm, spouse and children, fields, livestock, and all property- along with all the necessities and nourishment for this body and life. God protects me against all danger and shields and preserves me from all evil. And all this is done out of pure, fatherly, and divine goodness and mercy, without any merit or worthiness of mine at all![23]

This little paragraph is the theological ontology that informs all of Luther's thought. Namely that the cosmos is a gift of God the Creator, who gives through creation out of God's graciousness. In other words, even God's love for humanity depends on the prior existence of grace because it is given freely, without any merit of our own. This is the predominant theme and concern in Luther's theology in his earliest lectures and remains consistent in Luther's thought all the way through to the lectures on Genesis.

Receiving this gift from God in faith, trust, and confidence are the one true and highest work of faith. Here the key aspect of faith that makes it so effective and transformative is nothing short of the theological ontology Luther is proclaiming. Faith calls the believer to see the entire cosmos, including oneself, through ontological lens of gift. God is first and foremost the gracious and joyful giver of free gifts, of which I come to include myself.[24]

The full and practical explication and extension of this ontology of gift reaches its height in Luther's masterpiece, The Freedom of Christian.[25] Luther opens the treatise with a famous couplet that is built on the reflexive understanding of placing one trust in this ontology of Gift:

> A Christian is a perfectly free lord of all, subject to none.
> A Christian is a perfectly dutiful servant of all, subject to all.

In this couplet, Luther is taking his theological anthropology and distilling it further into and effective description of his theological anthropology. What this means is that in the death, suffering, and resurrection, all of God's judgment is really and truly put to death by God in the (incarnate) body of Jesus. Faith as such is not the work that forgives us, but the work that opens the Christian to believing, trusting, and understanding this gift. Thus, anthropologically speaking, the Christian is the

---

[23] Ibid., 354–355.
[24] Both the Large and Small Catechism express this view.
[25] LW 33:327–376

liberated lord of all because, in the words of Paul, "there no longer any judgment for all who are in Jesus Christ." Luther singularly takes seriously the bold claim of the Christian scriptures that in Christ all judgment, and even the devil, are put to death once and for all. Thus, the man or women freed by faith in the merit of Christ has no lord to answer to except Christ, who has already freed them.

This bold statement is incredibly powerful in and of itself. However, when received in faith, which Luther described as a "divine work in us" and a "living, busy, active, mighty thing",[26] Christ becomes more than an idea. As an effective hermeneutics, when the implications of this theology are received, believed, and trusted in faith, they are then also applied as the Christians imagined ontology and anthropology. Thus, in faith, the person knows that they are freed from condemnation by the gracious and loving gift of God. However, this soteriological doctrine always follows from the primal doctrine of creation.[27]

Inwardly renewed by the immanent application of the grace and love of God, the end of this can best be described as the perichoretic performance of divine love.[28] Adding his Christology and Pneumatology (both gift) extend this into an anthropology: namely that humans are the intended subjects of God's gift of grace and love. Ultimately then, faith makes the Christian man or women to "put on Christ"; which means to incarnate and embody the divine perichoretic economy of gift; by devoting us in all we do to the service and care of our neighbor. The Christiam reflexively applies the theological ontology and anthropology of gift, received in faith, actively to their neighbor. Luther goes so far in this description as to say that the Christian respond to the gift of faith, declaring:

> I will therefore give myself as a Christ to my neighbor, just as Christ offered himself to me; I will do nothing in this life except what I see is necessary, profitable, and salutary to my neighbor, since through faith I have an abundance of all good things in Christ…Just as our neighbor is in need and lacks that in which we abound, so we were in need before God and lacked his mercy. Hence, as our heavenly Father has in Christ freely come to our aid, we also ought freely to help our neighbor through our body and its works, and each one should become as it were a Christ to the other that we may be Christs to one another and Christ may be the same in all, that is, that we may be truly Christians.[29]

---

[26] LW 35:370.

[27] For more on Luther's view of the Holy Trinity see: Helmer, Christine. *The Trinity and Martin Luther*. Bellingham, WA: Lexham Press, 2017.

[28] These are my words, not Luther's. However, I feel they are the appropriate words as my descrioption will see. For more on the Luther and the doctring of the Holy Trinity see: 1. Christine Helmer, *The Trinity and Martin Luther* (Bellingham, WA: Lexham Press, 2017).

[29] LW 31:367

Luther offers a systematic evangelical theology through a singular generative focus on Grace and gift and grace. That vision is explicated here[30] as the universal human vocation to incarnate the grace of God through service and charity to one's fellow creatures. Taken to its logical ends, these theologies pave the way for practice and formation of radically inclusive, tolerant, and humble faith, extended even into our political policies and rhetoric!. This picture of evangelical theology is the picture *par excellance* of "inclusive evangelicalism" and should be the universal goal for the body of Christ's disciples. That it dovetails with the global and civil needs or the modern, globalized pluralistic world it certainly a benefit. That said, this should not come as a surprise. As early as the first century, the apologies of Justin Martyr, aimed at gaining sympathy and political trust from the Roman Empire, asserted just this point.

Conclusion

Luther's view on Jews and Christian makes it clear that he is no modern pluralist. Given Luther pen however, it is compelling and relevant to our purposes that on the whole Luther's writings advocate for the Christian faith to be almost exclusively concerned with a reflexive theology of grace and effective ontology of Gift. Our modern ontologies pose a particular challenge precisely because of modern shifts in anthropology and ontology that change our attitude about race. Whereas Luther opposed the competing faiths, modern social imaginaries construct anthropologies via subjective individualities. Thus the primary connotation of salvation, faith, and perhaps most important sins is associated with a personal history; as opposed to a premodern Luther whose default was to imagine the species as an (ontological) whole.

What even further complicates this model is the modern repression of sacred, revealed, or received sources in favor of the empirical. Combined with the subjective individual, this on its own creates challenges to spiritual and anthropological formatively. Of particular concern, however, is the emergent construction of racialized ontologies in the modern era.[31] In the age of whiteness, evangelical theology is always in danger of (unconsciously) excluding people of color from the reign of God as being somehow less than human. This is beyond the scope of Luther even

---

[30] Ibid., 368.
[31] See Jennings, Willie James. *The christian imagination: Theology and the origins of Race*. New Haven, CT: Yale University Press, 2011; 1. J. Kameron Carter, *Race: A Theological Account* (Oxford: Oxford University Press, 2008).

in his worst writings. In closing I offer some suggestions for preserving the integrity of evangelical Christianity through anti-racist and inclusive.

First, the scriptural witness cannot be abstracted from wider philosophical questions without danger or distortion. Luther's theology of gift demonstrates a biblically serious approach to lived faith that offers a coherent ontology, cosmology, and soteriology of gift. I hope it is also obvious how imperative it is for evangelical faith that these doctrines be held together. When they are not, distortions and fractures occur, the faith thins becoming irrelevant or worse vulnerable to misuse and abuse.[32]

Secondly, it is essential that evangelicals, not just pastors, engage actively in promoting anti-racist form of practicing their faith and work to intentionally defeat all forms of white supremacist and racialized ontologies. It is insufficient to disavow racism in word alone; deed must follow.[33] Luther's vision of faith urges us to receive life and salvation as a gift. When humanity is falsely divided in races based on color, this falls short of honoring the glory of God's gift.

Finally, I wish to highlight the need for evangelical Christians to claim their political theology. It is not sufficient to claim that one is not interested in politics or to simply claim party allegiance. There is an endless array of options for contemporary evangelical Christians to explore other models for developing a relevant contemporary theological view of the state, democracy, and the Christian life.

Institutionally historically, and sociologically: there is no reason to believe that evangelicals are either more responsible nor more vulnerable to ontological racism. However, if I am correct that Trump demonstrates among white evangelicals a serious crisis regarding race and evangelicalism, there is little doubt that those of who love the evangelical faith must do whatever we can to correct this diabolical trick. There is no doubt that ontological racism is a significant and overwhelming challenge and one it seems that has corrupted the evangelical ontology of gift. Perhaps one clear way that Luther can be of help in this project is in urging all of us to take responsibility for ourselves in worship, prayer, and repentance before the living God.

---

[32] For a few examples see: 1. Mark Charles and Soong-Chan Rah, *Unsettling Truths: The Ongoing, Dehumanizing Legacy of the Doctrine of Discovery* (Downers Grove, IL: IVP, an imprint of InterVarsity Press, 2019); 1. Mark A. Noll, *The Civil War as a Theological Crisis* (Chapel Hill, NC: University of North Carolina Press, 2015); 1. Andrew L. Whitehead and Samuel L. Perry, *Taking America Back for God: Christian Nationalism in the United States* (New York: Oxford University Press, 2022).

[33] 1. Jemar Tisby, *How to Fight Racism: Courageous Christianity and the Journey toward Racial Justice* (Grand Rapids, MI: Zondervan, 2023).

Bibliography

Bebbington, David William, George M. Marsden, and Mark A. Noll. 2019. Essay. In *Evangelicals: Who They Have Been, Are Now, and Could Be*, 282. Grand Rapids, MI: William B. Eerdmans Publishing Company.

Carter, J. Kameron. 2008. *Race: A Theological Account*. Oxford: Oxford University Press.

Charles, Mark, and Soong-Chan Rah. 2019. *Unsettling truths: The Ongoing, Dehumanizing Legacy of the Doctrine of Discovery*. Downers Grove, IL: IVP, An Imprint of InterVarsity Press.

Gillespie, Michael Allen. 2010. Essay. In *The Theological Origins of Modernity*, 177. Richmond, BC: ReadHowYouWant.com Ltd.

Helmer, Christine, Paul Helmer, and Munib A. Younin. 2009. Beyond Luther: Prophetic Interfaith Dialogue for Life. Essay. In *The Global Luther: A Theologian for Modern Times*, 56. Minneapolis: Fortress Press.

Helmer, Christine. 2017. *The Trinity and Martin Luther*. Bellingham, WA: Lexham Press.

Jennings, Willie James. 2011. *The Christian Imagination: Theology and the Origins of Race*. New Haven, CT: Yale University Press.

Jones, Robert P. 2021. *White too Long: The Legacy of White Supremacy in American Christianity*. New York, NY: Simon & Schuster Paperbacks.

Kendi, Ibram X. 2023. *How to be an Antiracist*. New York: One World.

Kidd, Colin. 2006. *The Forging of Races Race and Scripture in the Protestant Atlantic World, 1600–2000*. Cambridge: Cambridge University Press.

Luther, Martin. 1955–1972. *Luther's Works*. Edited by Jaroslav Pelikan, Helmut T. Lehmann, and Christopher Boyd Brown. 75 vols. Philadelphia: Fortress Press; St. Louis: Concordia Publishing House.

Noll, Mark A. 2015. *The Civil War as a Theological Crisis*. Chapel Hill, NC: University of North Carolina Press.

Sharp, Isaac B. 2023. *The Other Evangelicals: A Story of Liberal, Black, Progressive, Feminist, and Gay Christians - and the Movement that Pushed Them Out*. Grand Rapids, MI: William. B. Eerdmans Publishing Company.

Stark, Rodney. 2023. *Rise of Christianity: A Sociologist Reconsiders History*. S.l.: Princeton Univ Press.

Tappert, Theodore G. 1959. *The Book of Concord: The Confessions of the Evangelical Lutheran Church*. Philadelphia: Fortress Press.

Taylor, Charles. 2018. Essay. In *A Secular Age*, 146. Cambridge (Mass.): The Belknap Press of Harvard University Press.

Tisby, Jemar. 2020. *Color of Compromise: The Truth about the American Church's Complicity in Racism*. Zondervan.

———. 2023. *How to Fight Racism: Courageous Christianity and the Journey Toward Racial Justice*. Grand Rapids, MI: Zondervan.

Whitehead, Andrew L., and Samuel L. Perry. 2022. *Taking America Back for God: Christian Nationalism in the United States*. New York: Oxford University Press.

Jason Okrzynski completed his PhD in Practical Theology from Garrett Evangelical Theological Seminary in Evanston, IL, with a focus on Christian Education and Congregational studies. Reverend Okrzynski's work is further informed by the wisdom gained through twenty years of applying theory to practice in the real world via his service in congregations. During his two decades of parish leadership, Reverend Okrzynski developed transformative programming and pedagogies and merged them with his parishioners through teaching, preaching, and pastoral care.

Revisiting Madinah Pact: Towards Rebuilding an Ideal Inclusive Society

4

Muneer Kuttiyani Muhammad and Muhammad Mumtaz Ali

Introduction

The purpose of this chapter is to examine the sacred texts, namely the Qur'anic version of peaceful co-existence and its practical manifestation of the Prophet Muhammad (PBUH) in the context of the seventh-century Madinah city. This chapter evaluates the social conditions of Prophetic Madinah, particularly the contents of Madinah Pact pertaining to inclusiveness[1] and its connection with the universal values of the Qur'an and its principles. This study analyses how the basic human rights of people of different faiths in Madinah were protected. In this chapter, the researchers attempt to investigate on Madinah Pact and its connection to the Qur'anic verses on peaceful co-existence in a way to answering the following

---

[1] Ibn Ishaq. *The Life of Muhammad, A Translation of Ishaq seerat al-Rasul Allah,* translated into English by A Guillaume, (Karachi: Oxford University Press. 1967), 341.

M. K. Muhammad (✉)
Centre for Research & Academic Excellence, Al Jamia al Islamiya, Malappuram, India

M. M. Ali
Department of Usul al-Din and Comparative Religion, Kulliyyah of Islamic Revealed Knowledge and Human Sciences, Kuala Lumpur, Malaysia
e-mail: mumtazali@iium.edu.my

© The Author(s), under exclusive license to Springer Nature Switzerland AG 2024
M. Shafiq, T. Donlin-Smith (eds.), *Inclusion or Exclusion in the Sacred Texts and Human Contexts,* https://doi.org/10.1007/978-3-031-70180-1_4

questions: What is meant by Madinah Pact? What are the major Qur'anic principles which inspired the Prophet Muhammad (PBUH) to initiate such a Peace Treaty with the people of Madinah? What kind of society Madinah was? What were the real motives behind this pact? The following analysis will answer these questions.

Madinah Pact: A Brief Introduction

At the very outset, a brief description about the Madinah Pact seems imperative. The historians have unanimously confirmed the existence of such a pact which has been mentioned in numerous Hadith and historical texts.[2] For denoting this treaty, the Arabic terms such as *kitab*, *watheeqah*, *ahd*, and *sahifah*, have been commonly used.[3] The early historians like Ibn Ishaq used the term *al-Kitab*.[4] Various terms such as constitution, charter, covenant, treaty, contract, and peace negotiation, which all mean the same, are generally used to denote this treaty. Historians have verified that the Madinah Pact was written in the early days of the Prophet's arrival in Madinah.[5] His frequent search to find out a suitable place for Islam[6] was a part of the fulfilment of his mission[7] wherein the Messenger (PBUH) and his followers can live peacefully and enjoy the freedom of practicing their way of life. Hence, the Prophet (PBUH) initiated an attempt to build good relationship with all people by way of developing a treaty of peace.[8]

A careful examination of the various articles of the treaty would reveal that it was not merely a treaty of alliance, but it could be considered as a written constitution laying down the foundation of peaceful co-existence for a civil society.[9] The treaty was written and designed with 47 clauses which guarantee the rights of each tribe involved in the treaty. The people of Madinah, not only Muslims but also the people of other faiths had enjoyed freedom and peace through this

---

[2] Ibid.

[3] Ibid.

[4] Muhammad Ibn Ishaq. *al-Seerah al-Nabawiyyah*, edited, Ahmad Fareed al-Mazeedee, (Bayrut: Dar al-Kutub al-Ilmiyyah. 2004) vol.1, 198.

[5] Ibid.

[6] He had searched such a place in *Tayif* and *Abyssinia* before he and his companions venture their journey to Madinah.

[7] Muhammed Nazeer Kaka Khel, *Foundation of the Islamic state at Madina and its Constitution*. (Islamabad: Muhammad Hamidullah Library). http://iri.iiu.edu.pk/.

[8] The Peace pact is reported to have been formed and signed by the Prophet with different tribes in Madinah in the first of year of Hijrah.

[9] Nazeer Kaka..., 81.

4 Revisiting Madinah Pact: Towards Rebuilding an Ideal Inclusive Society

pact.[10] According to this pact, everyone was treated equally.[11] The identity of each tribe was fully recognised and well maintained.[12] The public rights and duties of every tribe who signed the treaty were the same.[13] For this reason, the Prophet (PBUH) became the most acceptable leader for the entire people of Madinah.[14]

A few but very important social principles such as human fraternity, inclusiveness, social integration, and peaceful co-existence were implicitly included in the pact. The total spirit of the pact was directed to unite the multi-religious, multi-tribal, and multi-ethnic demographic composition in Madinah.[15] The idea of citizenship based on human fraternity was accepted in the said society for equal status and representation.

The Qur'anic Foundations of the Madinah Pact

Before we examine the Madinah Pact, it would be worthy to mention some of the Qur'anic verses which are supposed to have served as the theoretical foundation of such a peace contract. Some noble values such as human brotherhood, peaceful co-existence, inclusiveness, social integrity which are generally acceptable universally for all people irrespective of their religion, caste, race, and language can be considered as the backbone of the actions of the Prophet Muhammad (PBUH) in Madinah. The examination of the Madinah Pact reveals that the Prophet's primary concern was upholding the human fraternity upon which the treaty was primarily established. The principle of human fraternity is considered by all religions, faiths, and ideologies as a universally accepted principle. The Qur'an exhorts clearly that all human beings have been created from a single pair of father and mother. This is

---

[10] Akram Diya' al-Umari, *Madina Society at the Time of the Prophet (pbuh): Its Characteristics and Organization*, Trans. from Arabic by Huda Khattab, (Herndon: The International Institute of Islamic Thought, 1991), 108.

[11] For example, the sixteenth article is written as follows; "to the Jews who follow us belong help and equality. He shall not be wronged nor shall his enemies be aided." Diya al-Umari, 108.

[12] Muhammad Hamidullah. *Majmu' al-Wathaiq al-Siyasiyyah li al-ahdi al-Nabawiyya al-Khilafat al-Rashidah*. (Beirut: Dar al-Nafayis, 1985), 554.

[13] Haza Hanurahaza Md Jani and et al. "A Review on the Madinah Charter in Response to the Heterogeneous Society in Malaysia in *Procedia Environmental Sciences* vol. 28, (2015): 92–99,

[14] W. Montgomery Watt. *Muhammad Prophet (PBUH) and Statesman*, (London: Oxford University Press, 1978), 89.

[15] Hanurahaza..., 95.

the foundation of every society upon which a society can thrive. Allah says in the Qur'an:
> Mankind was but one nation, but differed later. Had it not been for a word that went forth before from thy Lord, their differences would have been settled between them.[16]

> O men! Behold, We have created you all out of a male and a female, and have made you into nations and tribes, so that you might come to know one another.[17]

Islam upholds all human beings are from a single man Adam who is also the first Prophet (PBUH). The Qur'an reiterates this truth from time to time. Social relationship and co-operation were considered as the second principle for peaceful co-existence. We can see references to this principle in the Qur'an with several subthemes like inclusiveness, diversity, freedom of faith, social order, etc. See the following verses:
> Allah forbids you not, with regard to those who fight you not for (your) Faith nor drive you out of your homes, from dealing kindly and justly with them: for Allah loveth those who are just.[18]

> But rather help one another in furthering virtue and Allah Almighty consciousness, and do not help one another in furthering evil and enmity.[19]

The Qur'an exhorted trustworthiness is one of the components of teachings of Islam. Allah says;
> O you who have attained to faith! Be true to your covenants![20]

In short, the above verses collectively exhort for efforts for building a peaceful society in the world irrespective of differences in terms of religion, race, and colour. Formation of society based on the principle of human brotherhood was a major concern in the Madinah Pact. Madinah Pact was and still is considered as a means for realising one or more objectives of the Islamic Law. "Brotherhood, whose corollary is cooperation, plays an important role in the social milieu of human life and that is why great social thinkers, like Bertrand Russel, have attached so much importance to this factor for promoting the cause of humanity and its

---

[16] The Qur'an, 10:19.
[17] The Qur'an, 49:13.
[18] The Qur'an, 60: 8.
[19] The Qur'an, 5: 2
[20] The Qur'an, 6: 1

welfare."²¹ The analysis of Madinah Pact and its relation to the above Qur'anic verses will readily provide the answer that these universal principles, which were taught by God the Exalted, were the driving force which inspired the Prophet Muhammad (PBUH) towards the formation and actualization of the Madinah Pact.

The Socio-religious Structure of Madinah: An Overview

The first question this chapter attempts to answer is, "What kind of society Madinah was?" It will provide the socio-religious background to explain the nature of the society of Madinah. Majority of scholarly discussions on Madinah society revolve around the axis of its political dimension, focussing on "'Madinah' society 'as a nation state' or 'city state'".²² The image of today's nation-state usually possesses a tremendous population ranging from millions to billions with a vast geographical area and abundance of materials and natural resources. However, the Madinah state was completely different from that conception in many ways. Madinah was not that much as bigger than our modern nation-states in terms of its population, geographical area, and material resources. In Madinah, there were 22 tribes with different faiths who were involved in the peace pact.²³

Madinah: An Inclusive Plural Society Based on Human Brotherhood

Upon the arrival of the Prophet (PBUH) in Madinah, he passed an order to estimate the census of Madinah population.²⁴ Akram Diya' al-Umari demonstrated a systematic demographic composition²⁵ of the population of Madinah. According to him, the total number of inhabitants in Madinah at that time was estimated to be about

---

[21] Bertrand Russel, *Human Society in Ethics and Politics,* (New York: 1965), 153.

[22] Montgomery Watt describes the early Medinan society as similar to a federation of nomadic clans or tribes.

[23] Hanurahaza…, 97.

[24] Diya' al-Umari, 45.

[25] The number of Jews was estimated from the warriors of the three principle Jewish tribes, referring to the *sÊrah* of Ibn Hisham. Among them, 700 were from the tribe of *Banu Qaynuqa'*. Whereas the warriors of *Banu Nadir* were also about 700, Banu Quraydah had 700–900 warriors. The warriors alone constituted more than 2000 Jews.

10,000[26] citizens.[27] The Jews had a predominant influence upon that society. *Banu Qaynuqa', Banu al-Nadhir,* and *Banu Quraydha* were the major Jewish clans in Madinah.[28] The number of Jewish citizens in Madinah was roughly assumed to be in several thousand by some scholars.[29] The Jews were estimated around 4000, i.e. 40% of total population. Out of these 4000 Jews, only a few hundreds of men had embraced Islam. After 8 years of the Prophet's (PBUH) stay in Madinah, all the tribes were able to bring 4000 believers to march to Makkah for its liberation.[30] From the above historical account, there is a good reason to believe that a great number of people from both tribes had remained as non-Muslims for years even after the Prophet's arrival in Madinah.

Although there have been differences of opinion on the religious identity of some tribes,[31] some sources have identified those tribes as Jewish.[32] The Christian community from the *Aws* tribe, though small in number, was also present in Madinah. It is believed that there were only fifty Christians.[33] Some companions from the Christian background were given the permission to visit the coffins of their mothers, who were Christians.[34] The Roman Christians who lived in the neighbouring provinces were also given freedom of faith and religious practices.[35] Besides them, a small number of idol worshippers were also present. The slaves, mostly from Abyssinia, also lived there as a small minority.

---

[26] 45% of the total population in the city were followers of different faiths of the Arabs, while 40% were Jews and 15% of the population were Muslims.

[27] Zia H Shah, The Constitution of Medina: A Symbol of Pluralism in Islam, *The Muslim Times,* https://themuslimtimes.info/2012/11/09/the-constitution-of-medina-a-symbol-of-pluralism-in-islam/ (accessed on 6th October, 2017).

[28] Abdullah Abd al-Mun'im al-Aseeli, Al-Tha'addudiyah wa al-Tha'ayush al-Thaqafi fi Dhaw'i al-Shariah al-Islamiyah,' in *Al-Tha'addudiyah wa Haqq al-Ikhtilaf min manzur Islami wa dawr al-Jami'at fi Tanmiyat Dhalika,* (Palestine: Jami'atay al-Khalil wa al-Quds al-Maftuhat, 2012), 148.

[29] Muhammad Hamidullah, *History of Hadith,* (n.p.), 82.

[30] Diya' al-Umari, 45.

[31] Banu Akrimah, Banu Muhammar, Banu Za'ura were the most prominent. Diya' al-Umari, 44.

[32] Diya' al-Umari, 44.

[33] Hamidullah, *History...,* 83.

[34] Abdullah ibn Bayyah, "Sahifat al-Madinah: al-Da'wat wa al-Balagh al-Muwatanah", *al-Tafahum,* vol. 50, 2015, 11–24.

[35] Muhammad Abduhu, Muhammad Rasheed Rida, *Tafsir al-Manar, Surah. 9 Verse 29,* (Beirut: Dar Ihya'u al-Turath al-Arabi, 2002), 255.

Gradually a considerable portion of Muslim presence prevailed there.[36] Accordingly, a list of 1500 Muslim citizens was recorded in the census, in which the emigrants (*muhajir*) and the host (*Ansar*) altogether were included.[37] It is worthy to note here that the hypocrites were also included among the Muslims, although their presence was unnoticeably few in the early years; at least, a third of the population of Madinah consisted of hypocrites.[38]

The Prophetic approach towards the hypocrites is a clear indication of tolerance. In the discourse of the multi-religious society of Madinah, the presence of the hypocrites enjoying all the rights and privileges as Madinah citizens is noteworthy. As a matter of fact, here the researchers choose to consider them as a different community which had distinctive identity like the Jews and the Pagan Arabs in Madinah. The hypocrites in Madinah society were mainly from the *Khazraj* tribe. Abd Allah ibn Ubayy ibn Salul, a chief from the tribe in question, was the leader of the hypocrites. The harm they unleashed within the Muslim society was more destructive than those from external enemies. While the external enemies attacked the Muslims from the outside, which were often predictable and anticipated, the hypocrites attacked Muslims inwardly, which had left behind much harmful results. Once, the hypocrites were revealed to the Prophet (PBUH) by Allah Almighty and some of the companions who strongly demanded to kill them all.[39] In spite of their hypocritical attitude, the Prophet (PBUH) did not do anything to them. Rather, he considered them as part of Muslim society and treated them equally.[40] Abul A'la Mawdudi writes about the hypocrites in Madinah in his monumental exegesis that the "Prophet treated Ubayy, the leader of hypocrites kindly, as he had a large group of the hypocrites behind him."[41]

According to modern nationalistic and patriotic perspective, the hypocrites are nothing less than traitors, who deserve the capital punishment. Quite contrary to this, hypocrites were granted equal status, and no legal case was registered against them nor was any war launched.[42] But rather, they were considered as a part of the

---

[36] Al-Aseeli, 148.

[37] Hamidullah, *History*...., 83.

[38] Sayyid Abul Ala Mawdudi, Tafhim al-Qur'an, Surah Al-Munafiqoon (The Hypocrites), http://englishtafsir.com/Quran/63/index.html (accessed on 8th October, 2017).

[39] Muhammad Ammarah, *Al-Islam al-Ta'addudiyah al-Ikhtilaf wa al-Tanavvu' fi Itar al-Wahdah*. (Cairo: Maktab al-Shurooq al-Duwaliyah, 2008), 12.

[40] Ibid., 14.

[41] Sayyid Abul Ala Mawdudi, Tafhim al-Qur'an, Surah Al Munafiqun (The Hypocrites), http://englishtafsir.com/Quran/63/index.html (accessed on 8th October, 2017).

[42] ÑAmmÉrah..., 12.

Muslim society, despite their covert enmity towards Islam and Muslims. The Prophetic approach to the hypocrites clearly shows the tolerant and inclusive nature of the Madinah society which is not often found in modern societies today. This was a manifestation of inclusiveness.

People of different faiths and ethnic groups were an integral part of Madinah society.[43] Their professions varied from merchants, businessmen, farmers, and manufactures.[44] In short, Madinah society was a plural and inclusive society.[45] It is noteworthy that in Madinah society there was no distinction like minority or majority.[46] In the plural and inclusive society of Madinah, Jews, pagans, Christians, Ethiopians, and hypocrites were living together besides Muslims. Hence, from the Qur'anic perspective, a pluralistic, inclusive, peaceful society is encouraged at theoretical, as well as practical levels. The Prophet Muhammad (PBUH) manifested such a society in his life time leaving no space for confusion. The evidences put forth here are expected to be sufficient to prove that the peaceful co-existence was evidently prevalent in the state of Madinah.

Social Integration and Unification of Society

The Prophet (PBUH) was able to materialise some of the specific social values through the implementation of the Madinah Pact. Through the pact, he guaranteed peaceful coexistence and social stability. In order to maintain social stability, the unity of society was considered vital. The Islamic society though, not tribal in nature, the Prophet (PBUH) accepted tribes in order to maintain the security, unity, and distinctive identities of various tribes. For this, from the very first day, the Prophet (PBUH) implemented genuinely all the necessary measures. Unity and welfare of the society was his priority as it is greatly emphasised in the Qur'an. Madinah society was organised on the basis of shared goals[47] in order to maintain unity, peaceful co-existence, security, and protection of each tribe reciprocally from external attacks. The unity of people was greatly emphasised. It is significant

---

[43] Bilal ibn Rabah, one of the great companions and prominent figure in Islamic history was an Ethiopian Negro, Salman al-Farisi another companion is hailing from Persia.
[44] Al-Asili, 148.
[45] Ibid.
[46] Ibn Bayyah..., 11–24.
[47] Faatin Haque, *Islam and the West: Bridging the Misconceptions,* (Dhaka: Institute of Hazrat Mohammad, 2007), 15.

4 Revisiting Madinah Pact: Towards Rebuilding an Ideal Inclusive Society

to note that the Madinah society was termed as *ummatan wahida* (one community)[48] by the Prophet (PBUH).[49] The first sentence of the pact is as follows.

> In the name of the Most Merciful and the Compassionate.[50] This is a document from Muhammad (peace be upon him), the Messenger of Allah, to the believers, Muslims of Quraysh and Yathrib, and all those who followed, joined and laboured with them. They constitute one *Ummah* distinct and apart from the rest of the people.[51]

The word Ummah is generally used to denote the global Muslim community of believers. The idea of Ummah is derived from a *jama'at* which reflects unity within the group.[52] However, the Prophet (PBUH) used the term *ummah* for a society which constituted not only Muslims but also people of other faiths.[53] The *ummah* refers to something which consolidates or unites all groups within one.[54] Many scholars have observed that the unity of people of Madinah was a special one which was based upon the locality or territory not on the basis of traditional kinship. Due to this pluralistic and inclusive nature of Madinah society, it is genuinely considered as the first ideal society which was governed by the first written constitution of the world. The inclusion of people of all faiths and ethnicities within a Muslim society constituted the idea of a civil society as a part and parcel of the *Shariah*. By using the word "one community,"[55] the Prophet (PBUH) practiced in Madinah the idea of unity of all people for peaceful co-existence and prosperity. It was a society

---

[48] The document commenced thus: In the name of God, the Merciful, the Compassionate! This is a writing of Muhammad the Prophet (pbuh) between the believers and Muslims of Quraysh and Yathrib (Madinah) and those who follow them and are attached to them and who crusade along with them. They are a single community distinct from other people. Ammarah, 12.

[49] Mahmud al-Sharqawi, *al-Madinat al-Munawwarah*, (Cairo: Dar al-Shu'b, n.d), 59.

[50] Shukri Nasir Abd al-Hasan, Al-Ta'ayush al-Silmi fi daw'i mabaadi'i sahifat al-madinah, in *Wathiqat al-Madinah Dirasat fi al-Ta'seel al-Dasturi fi al-Islam*, edited by Abd al-Amir Zahid, (Beirut: Centre for Civilization for the Development of Islamic Thought, 2014), 22.

[51] Muhammad Nazeer Khaka. *Foundation of the Islamic State at Medina and its Constitution*, (Islamabad: Islamic Studies, 1982), 76.

[52] Carolyn Fluehr-Lobbon, *Islamic Society in Practice*, (Florida: University Press of Florida, 1994). 51.

[53] Muddhathir Abdu al-Rahman, "The Metaphysical and Ethical Foundations of Religious Pluralism in Islam," in *The Question of Minorities in Islam: Theoretical Perspectives and Case Studies*, Ed. Mohamed El-Tahir El-Mesawi, (Kuala Lumpur: The Other Press, 2015), 6.

[54] Shukri Nasir...., 58.

[55] Muddhathir 'Ibid., 6.

which is unified primarily on the basis of love and brotherhood between *Ansar* and *Muhajiroon*, on the one hand, and Muslims and people of all other religious and ethnic backgrounds, on the other. Therefore, it is argued that one of the objectives of the Madinah Pact was the unification of Muslims or social integration with people of other faiths. The Prophet (PBUH) was a lover of order and unity.[56] The concept of one community was generated by the Madinah Pact, which offers equal rights for all communities within the larger community of Madinah as observed by a writer: the "term plurality or heterogeneous society is being recognised as one community and one *Ummah*."[57]

The preservation of the social order was included in the Madinah Pact. As Abdullah Ibn Bayyah categorically expressed, the Madinah Pact was a treaty which was aimed at nothing other than *maslaha* (wellbeing) of people.[58] Ibn Ashur considers it as one of the all-purpose principles (*maqsad Amm*). He writes: "both its general rules and specific proofs indicate that the all-purpose principle of Islamic legislation is to preserve the social order of the community and ensure its healthy progress by promoting the well-being and righteousness of that which prevails in it, namely the human species."[59] Social integration, therefore, was promoted through the Madinah Pact. Contemporary scholars, for this purpose, have emphasised on the urgency of establishing civilisational dialogues with other communities.[60] He could manage to unite a disintegrated society, whose members used to wage war even for trivial reasons. He was successful in diverting the potentials, valour, and influence of conflicting tribes towards achieving the common goals that would serve the whole community.[61] In order to maintain the social order of the community and its stability, the unity of people, even in diversity was considered essential. The concept of one *ummah* ensures that everyone holds the same responsibility to protect Madinah and the suburban areas.[62] None of the contents in the Pact instigates enmity or hatred between people, but all of its clauses are great impulse for all peoples for establishing justice and guaranteeing the wellbeing to people.

---

[56] Ibid.

[57] Hanurahaza, 95.

[58] Ibn Bayyah..., 17.

[59] Muhammad Al-Tahir Ibn Ashur, *Ibn Ashur: Treatise on Maqasid al-Shariah*, (Herndon: International Institute of Islamic Thought, 2013), 91.

[60] Dina Taha, Muslim Minorities in the West: Between *Fiqh* of Minorities and Integration in *Electronic Journal of Islamic and Middle Eastern Law*, vol. 1, (2013): 4, 1–36.

[61] Hanurahaza, 97.

[62] Ibid.

The Preservation of Freedom for Faith

Another important noteworthy aspect in the Madinah Pact is the provision of freedom of faith, which guarantees the freedom of conscience for the members involved in this contract to choose any religion and in turn builds mutual tolerance as well.[63] The 25th clause in the Pact is the clear proof of freedom of faith which states; "The Jews of Banu Auf are an *ummah* with the believers. The Jews shall have their own religion and the Muslims their own."[64] This statement shows how the freedom of faith of other people as citizen was preserved in the Pact like a constitutional right.[65] The Prophet (PBUH) is the one who was deprived of the basic right of freedom of faith while he was at Makkah. Therefore, the moment he arrived in Madinah, the first thing he wanted to establish was freedom for everyone to choose his/her religion. No one in Madinah was forced to believe in Islam. The Jews were given freedom of faith and religious practice. They were allowed to practice on the basis of their religious law, and they could freely perform their rituals and religious activities.[66] Moreover, they were guaranteed the protection and support in case of an external attack happened.[67] Although the tribes in Madinah were integrated under the leadership of the Prophet (PBUH), they were granted the sovereignty to decide for their own affairs within the tribes.[68]

Several Qur'anic verses, for example 2:156, categorically grants freedom of faith to everyone and denounce coercion in matters of faith. God says "Let there be no compulsion in religion, for the truth stands out clearly from falsehood."[69] The above action of the Prophet (PBUH) is driven from this Qur'anic injunction. The very reason of the revelation of this verse is a practical example of the provision of

---

[63] Ibid., 21.

[64] The articles 27–47 in the pact contains the agreement between Muslims and Jews, which was written and signed in the house of Bint al-Haris.

[65] It may be argued that the freedom of other religions was specifically stipulated in the pact. Judaism was the only organised systematic religion in Madinah at that time. Although the freedom was given to the Arab pagans as well, that religion was heterogeneous in character and did not have a system of religious law. It was due to this reason that their name was not specifically mentioned in the pact.

[66] Abduhu, *Tafsir al-Manar*, 255.

[67] Ibn Ishaq, *al-Seerah al-Nabawiyyah*, 287.

[68] Muhammad Hamidullah, *The First Written Constitution in the World*, (Lahore: Sh. Muhammad Ashraf, 1981). 11.

[69] The Quran 2: 256.

freedom of faiths even in the case of two sons of his companion.[70] There is no historical record which shows that either the Prophet (PBUH) or his companions had coerced others to accept Islam or put any restrictions on their faith and religious practices. On account of this reason, the Prophet (PBUH) assured freedom of faith and practice to others as well. If preservation of religion is confined to the religion of Islam alone, as some scholars have argued, why did the Prophet (PBUH) grant freedom of faith to people of other faiths in Madinah? We can safely argue that this Prophetic deed at Madinah is a clear indication that the preservation of faith is not reserved for Muslims alone. Rather, all members in society also have the same right for their religion to be protected. It may be argued that by the protection of religion, Islam must be primarily prioritised for preservation. At the same time, it extends to other religions as well.

The inclusion of the article preservation of faith, not only for Muslims but also for the people of other faiths, is the practical implication of the universal principle of the Qur'an which is, "You have your way (religion), and I have my Way (religion).[71] The statement in the Madinah Pact is evidently written that, "The Jews have their religion and the Muslims have their religion." The word "Jews" specifically mentioned in the treaty does not mean that this right is given to Jews alone. Since the Jews were the prominent majority in Madinah other than the Arabs, their name is specifically mentioned.

The Muslim society in Madinah in which Muslims had the upper hand, they never tried to impose their faith upon others. The Prophet (PBUH) aimed at constructing a multi-religious pluralistic and inclusive society in a manner that allowed religious freedom for all in the society. Here the freedom of religion is not only granted in a social context but it was preserved by the enactment of law as well. In short, the analysis of the Madinah Pact clearly demonstrates a complete picture of a true multi-religious, multi-ethnic, multi-culture community which upholds the higher values such as freedom of faith, human equality and brotherhood, and peaceful coexistence. In this regard, it may be argued that the human history has never before witnessed such a plural multi-religious society like Madinah.

---

[70] The historical account of this incident as it is narrated in various commentaries is given in the fourth chapter.
[71] The Quran 109: 6.

Conclusion

From the above analysis, we can conclude that the Madinah Pact which the Prophet (PBUH) signed with the members of tribes in Madinah was, in fact, an effective means for realising the overall universal principles and social values such as peaceful co-existence, inclusiveness, freedom of faith, and social integrity. The Pact by its own right was not an objective, but it was a means to materialise the real objectives of the Islamic law. The contents written in the Pact undeniably reveals that it was used to protect the five essential higher intents of the Islamic Law such as the preservation of life, faith, wealth, offspring, and honour of all people irrespective of their socio-religious-ethnical differences. Besides these five essential objectives of Islamic Law at individual level, the most important social values such as freedom of faith, human brotherhood, fraternity, peaceful coexistence, and social integration were successfully practiced in Madinah at a collective level. Various actions and programmes for involving all members of various communities were made possible based on the above-mentioned objectives. The higher intents and objectives of Islamic law are recurrently mentioned implicitly in the Qur'an. The actions of the Prophet (PBUH) at Madinah manifest the practical implications of the Prophet Muhammad (PBUH), in a specific human context, which is the Madinah society in the seventh century.

The Prophetic actions in Madinah serve as an exemplary model to preserve the social integration and order of multi-religious societies of the present world. It is also imperative to counter the problems of intolerance and social disintegration in our contemporary societies. Although these societies claim to be plural and inclusive, racial and religious discrimination still exist. Demonstrating the Madinah model as an ideal plural society does not mean that the same model itself is required to be emulated as it is in all times. As time changes, the means to attain the objectives of social integration may also change.

The major social principles of the Qur'an such as human fraternity, inclusiveness, social integration, and peaceful co-existence were implicitly included in the Pact of Madinah. The total spirit of the Pact was directed to unite the multi-religious, multi-tribal, and multi-ethnic communities in Madinah. The idea of citizenship based on human fraternity was accepted in the said society for equal status and representation. In short, the Madinah state and its socio-religious structures certainly offer a model of an ideal as well as inclusive and holistic state of plural society. In order to realise the above objectives in our contemporary plural societies, the political and religious leaders, policy makers, and community representatives from different socio-religious background may develop various measures and policies that are deemed suitable for modern plural societies based on the model of the Prophet Muhammad (PBUH). The ideal Islamic society does not repudiate the existence and peaceful living of people of other faiths but guarantees all of their human rights, dignity, honour at individual and collective levels. The Prophet Muhammad (PBUH) has demonstrated a practical manifestation of what the sacred texts, namely the Qur'an uphold and their universal social principles and noble values such as peaceful co-existence, inclusiveness, and social integration through the Madinah Pact.

Bibliography

Abduhu, Muhammad., Rasheed Rida, Muhammad. 2002. *Tafsir al-Manar, Surah. 9 Verse 29,* Beirut: Dar Ihya'u al-Turath al-Arabi.
Ali Bulaj. April 2006. Wathiqat al-Madinah al-Munawwarah wathiqat al-Salam fi mujtami' muta'addid al-thaqafat wa al-Adyan. *Hirah Magazine* 3: 12–16.
Al-Sharqawi, Mahmud. n.d. *al-Madinat al-Munawwarah.* Cairo: Dar al-Shu'b.
Ammarah, Muhammad. 2008. *Al-Islam al-Ta'addudiyah al-Ikhtilaf wa al-Tanavvu' fi Itar al-Wahdah.* Cairo: Maktab al-Shuruq al-Duwaliyah.
Diya' al-Umari, Akram. 1991. *Madina Society at the Time of the Prophet (pbuh): Its Characteristics and Organization,* Translated from Arabic by Huda Khattab. Herndon: The International Institute of Islamic Thought.
Fluehr-Lobbon, Carolyn. 1994. *Islamic Society in Practice.* Florida: University Press of Florida.
Haque, Faatin. 2007. *Islam and the West: Bridging the Misconceptions.* Dhaka: Institute of Hazrat Mohammad.
Haza Hanurahaza Md Jani, et al. 2015. A Review on the Madinah Charter in Response to the Heterogeneous Society in Malaysia. *Procedia Environmental Sciences* 28 (2015): 92–99.
Ibn Bayyah, Abdullah. 2015. Sahifat al-Madinah: *al-Da'wat wa al-Balagh al-Muwatanah. al-Tafahum,* 11–24.
Ibn Ishaq. 1967. *The Life of Muhammad, A Translation of Ishaq Seerat al-Rasul Allah.* Translated into English by A Guillaume. Karachi: Oxford University Press.
Kaka Khel, Muhammed Nazeer. n.d. *Foundation of the Islamic State at Madina and its Constitution.* Islamabad: Muhammad Hamidullah Library. http://iri.iiu.edu.pk/.
Muddhathir Abdu al-Rahman. 2015. The Metaphysical and Ethical Foundations of Religious Pluralism in Islam. In *The Question of Minorities in Islam: Theoretical Perspectives and Case Studies,* ed. Mohamed El-Tahir El-Mesawi. Kuala Lumpur: The Other Press.
Muhammad Hamidullah. 1985. *Majmu' al-Watha'iq al-Siyasiyyah li al-Ahdi al-Nnabawiyya al-Khilafat al-Rashidah.* Beirut: Dar al-Nnafayis.
Russel, Bertrand. 1965. *Human Society in Ethics and Politics.* George Allen & Unwin Ltd. London.
Sayyid Abul Ala Mawdudi, Tafhim al-Qur'an, Surah Al-Munafiqoon (The Hypocrites). Accessed October 8, 2017. http://englishtafsir.com/Qur'an/63/index.html

Taha, Dina. 2013. Muslim Minorities in the West: Between Fiqh of Minorities and Integration. *Electronic Journal of Islamic and Middle Eastern Law* 1: 4.
Watt, Montgomery. 1978. *Muhammad Prophet (pbuh) and Statesman*. London: Oxford University Press.
Zia H Shah. The Constitution of Medina: A Symbol of Pluralism in Islam, *The Muslim Times*. Accessed October 6, 2017. https://themuslimtimes.info/2012/11/09/the-constitution-of-medina-a-symbol-of-pluralism-in-islam/.

Muneer Kuttiyani Muhammad was born in Aluva, Kerala, India, in 1980. He graduated with a BA in Economics from Mahatma Gandhi University, Kottayam, in 2001 and secured a Master's degree in Da'wa and Comparative Religion from Al Jamia Al Islamiya, Kerala, in 2007. He secured his second Master's degree in Islamic Thought & Comparative Religion from the International Islamic University Malaysia (IIUM) in 2014, where He also completed his PhD in 2020. He has authored a book entitled Religious Co-Existence in Malappuram, published by IIUM Press in 2017. He has also published a number of articles on the universal values of religion and contemporary issues in various academic journals and has presented research papers at various international academic conferences. From 2018 onwards, he has served as the Director of Al Jamia Centre for Research & Academic Excellence and as an assistant professor at Al Jamia Al Islamiya, Santhapuram.

Muhammad Mumtaz Ali started his career as an assistant professor at the International Islamic University Malaysia in 1987. Since then, he has been serving in the same University. Currently he is a professor in the Department of Usul al-Din and Comparative Religion at AbdulHamid AbuSulayman Kulliyyah of Islamic Revealed Knowledge and Human Sciences. He has produced several text books from an Islamic perspective. His books in the area of Islamization of Knowledge are considered bestsellers on campus. In 2014 and 2016 he was awarded the National Book Awards for his works Issues in Islamization of Human Knowledge: Civilization Building Discourse of Contemporary Muslim Thinkers and Islamization of Modern Science and its Philosophy: A Contemporary Civilizational Discourse, respectively. Ali is currently serving as the Chairman of the Committee for Postgraduate Studies in the Department of Usul al-Din and Comparative Religion.

Confucian Exclusivism: A Challenge to Confucian Exemplarist Morality

Mathew A. Foust

Recently, some scholars have advanced the theory of Confucian exemplarist morality (e.g., Olberding 2012; Y. Lai and K. Lai 2022). In the most extensive account of Confucian exemplarist moral theory, Olberding (2012) holds that the *Analects* offers "narrative accounts of exemplary people and lives, as well as the general and abstract concepts and prescriptions that issue from their examples" (p. 13). In short, the *Analects* "is a document that details how Confucius and its authors attempt to explain, to themselves and others, why they admire the people they do" (Olberding 2012, p. 21). Although this interpretation of the *Analects* has received some criticism (e.g., Kim 2012; Li 2020), it is certainly plausible that the *Analects* portrays some morally good people and "is clear in its interest in describing these people, and committed to encouraging others to emulate these people" (Olberding 2012, p. 99).

Original publication: Foust, M. A. (2024). Confucian exclusivism: A challenge to Confucian exemplarist morality. *Asian Philosophy*, 1–12. https://doi.org/10.1080/09552367.2024.2359208

M. A. Foust (✉)
Department of Philosophy and Religion, Appalachian State University, Boone, NC, USA
e-mail: foustma@appstate.edu

© The Author(s), under exclusive license to Springer Nature Switzerland AG 2024
M. Shafiq, T. Donlin-Smith (eds.), *Inclusion or Exclusion in the Sacred Texts and Human Contexts*, https://doi.org/10.1007/978-3-031-70180-1_5

Chief among those whose lives are cast as exemplary in the *Analects* is Confucius. Olberding describes Confucius as unambiguously the major moral hero of the *Analects*, at once a master who discerns the difference between right and wrong and a consummate learner, committed to emulating his own exemplars (e.g., the legendary sage kings). Morally exemplary features of Confucius are depicted on several occasions in the *Analects*, including Confucius's abiding by the moral norms and traditional practices of his day, his abstention from immoral or morally dubious activities and behaviors, his high aspirations and high standards, his deeply refined aesthetic sense, his modesty about his own capacities and generosity in celebrating those of others, his circumspection in judgment, and his devotion to his disciples (Olberding 2012, p. 107). Highlighting aspects of Confucius's gesture, personal style, and communication, Olberding (2012) avers that the *Analects* assigns significance to the styling of conduct "because demeanor and manner appear to display how our actions come about, the motivational, intentional, and emotional forces at work in prompting our actions" (p. 117). Thus, it is not just the case that Confucius performs laudatory actions, but he performs them in the right way, from praiseworthy origins.

The question of precisely what attitudes Confucius embodies is critical to Confucian exemplarist moral theory. Tan (2005) has discussed the importance of emulation of "paradigmatic characters" in the Confucian tradition, detailing the importance of imagination and understanding involved in the process. Discerning what beliefs and attitudes animate another person's actions is critical to judging their virtue and worthiness for emulation. Confucius himself suggests the heuristic value of observing the examples set by others in *Analects* 2.10 (Slingerland 2003, p. 11). He advises in *Analects* 4.17, "When you see someone who is worthy, concentrate upon becoming their equal; when you see someone who is unworthy, use this as an opportunity to look within yourself" (Slingerland 2003, p. 35).

In order to determine whether Confucius is indeed a moral exemplar to be admired and emulated by those who encounter him in the *Analects*, it is necessary to acknowledge and critically confront strands of his thought and action that problematize this description. In this chapter, I would like to focus on what I call the exclusivist strands of Confucius's thought and action. Although the term "Confucian exclusivism" has not yet been developed in the scholarly literature, scholars have invoked similar terms in addressing some of its forms. In a recent attempt at "tracing the Confucian Other," Zhang (2023, p. 16) discusses Chinese ethnic exclusionism and cultural exclusionism in relation to the Confucian tradition, which has significantly shaped Chinese culture. Similarly, Berenpas (2016, p. 161) refers to Confucian particularism in describing Confucius's grounding of moral duties such as hospitality in the nearness of relations between oneself and the other. To wit, some scholars hold that Confucianism privileges blood relations, with one (Liu

2003) assigning the tradition the label of "consanguinitism." There is no question that early Confucian texts emphasize *xiao* (filiality; filial piety) as a moral and cultural value. The foregrounding of obligations to family over and against those to society at large is not equivalent to—but is compatible with—a number of modes of exclusivism. In this chapter, two distinct types of Confucian exclusivism will be discussed, Confucian culturalism and Confucian speciesism. Of course, no such terms were at play during Confucius's time, so the very suggestion of the presence of such -isms in the *Analects* may appear to be anachronistic. However, I think it is not unreasonable to look at a historical text through a modern lens as a way of gauging its contemporary relevance or to respond to other scholars who have engaged with the text with a new vocabulary. Accordingly, drawing on passages from the *Analects*, I will explore the extent to which these forms of Confucian exclusivism animate the most influential of texts from the Confucian tradition.

Confucian Culturalism in the *Analects*?

The case for culturalism in the *Analects* turns on a recurrent distinction therein between the *Huá* (Chinese) and *Yí* (non-Chinese; peoples outside of China proper), the latter commonly cast as barbarians—a term deployed similarly to *yí* being *mán* (rough; reckless). The distinction between the Chinese and non-Chinese in the *Analects* is tied not only to a distinction between *us* and *them* but often to a distinction between *here* and *there*. Even when the distinction between *here* and *there* is not drawn with precision, the *Analects* appears to invoke imagined social-political communities, an idea consistent with the notion of a nation as an imagined social-political community developed by Anderson (1983). Nonetheless, I have chosen "culturalism" over and against other terms such as "nationalism" or "racism," following the suggestion of Nylan (2012, p. 600n48) that the term "culturalism" underscores that "the key difference between Chinese and foreigners was seen to be cultural (not ethnic or biological, let alone racist)."

The term "barbarian" derives from the ancient Greek, *barbaroi*, an onomatopoeia for how the speech of non-Greek-speaking people sounded to the Greek. Huang (2013) provides a trenchant comparative study of perceptions of the barbarian in early Greek and Chinese contexts. The translation of the Chinese *yi* and *man* to the English "barbarian" via the Greek *barbaroi* is easily accounted for. The populations in question are associated with areas outside the borders of the place given a central position, as they are physically located outside the periphery, so too are they culturally, intellectually, and morally. China—*Zhongguo* (Middle Kingdom)—is contrasted with barbarian peoples in all directions: *yi* (East), *man* (South), *rong* (West), and *di* (North). Confucianism "envisaged an ideal social, political and moral order based on humaneness and the observance of proper rites" (Huang 2013); because those outside the center did not follow these ideals, they were considered inferior. Direct evidence of this position may be found at *Analects* 3.5, quoted here in full: "The Master said, 'The Yi and Di barbarians, even with their rulers, are still inferior to the Chinese states without their rulers'" (Slingerland 2003, p. 18). The lack of context in which this remark is situated prevents much in the way of a nuanced reading. However, Confucius's emphasis on the superiority of the Chinese states—even without their rulers—appears to betoken a Chinese culturalism over and against a more inclusive or pluralist orientation toward the outsider. Anticipating the link that I will make between culturalism and speciesism, Ames and Rosemont, Jr. (1998, p. 234n46) point out that "the Chinese language might reflect a certain contempt for such bordering tribes," with the Di tribes classified under the dog (*quan* 犬) radical, the Man tribes classified under the beast/insect (*hui* 虫) radical, and the Mo tribes classified under the reptile/beast (*chi* 豸) radical.

A similar sentiment is conveyed in *Analects* 13.19. In this case, however, we are provided some context. The passage immediately indicates that Fan Chi, a disciple of Confucius, asked about *ren* (humaneness; Goodness). Confucius issues the following reply: "When occupying your place, remain reverent; when performing public duties, be respectful; and when dealing with others, be dutiful. These are virtues that cannot be abandoned, even if you go to dwell among the Yi or Di barbarians" (Slingerland 2003, p. 148). Confucius's remark that these are virtues that cannot be abandoned, even if you go to dwell among the Yi or Di barbarians, may be read in a number of ways. On one reading that would amount to an extreme expression of culturalism, Confucius means that if Fan Chi, a Chinese, has cultivated the virtues of reverence, respectfulness, and dutifulness, it is *impossible* for him to abandon these virtues. Even if he goes to dwell among the Yi or Di barbarians, Fan Chi's character is impervious to their negative influence. More likely, Confucius means that if Fan Chi goes to a place in which the virtues are lacking, such as among the Yi or Di, he ought not to conform to a morally inferior norm. Rather than a comment, then, on Fan Chi's moral fortitude *qua* Chinese, I believe that Confucius's response should be construed as instruction, a word of warning to Fan Chi to work to preserve virtues once they have been cultivated.

It is instructive that *Analects* 13.19 is not the only passage that begins with Fan Chi asking about *ren*. *Analects* 12.22 begins identically, with Confucius tersely replying, "Care for others." Fan Chi then asks about *zhi* (wisdom), to which Confucius equally tersely replies, "Know others." We are told that Fan Chi "still did not understand," so Confucius elaborates, "Raise up the straight and apply them to the crooked, and the crooked will be made straight" (Slingerland 2003, p. 136). Supposing that straightness in this context represents moral rectitude and

5 Confucian Exclusivism: A Challenge to Confucian Exemplarist Morality 79

crookedness represents moral impropriety, Confucius's comment can be applied to the scenario described in *Analects* 13.19. Were Fan Chi to enter the territory of the Yi or Di, as a dutiful Confucian—perhaps indeed as a dutiful Chinese—his task would be to "straighten" the "crooked," joined, perhaps, by compatriots who he has morally empowered, or "raised up."

This reading of *Analects* 12.22 is corroborated by still another passage, *Analects* 6.22. Although the sequence of questions is in the reverse, here too Fan Chi asks Confucius about *ren* and *zhi*. Working to "ensure social harmony among the common people" is described as part of wisdom, while the hardship of self-cultivation is described as part of *ren*. Many commentators believe that Fan Chi is asking for advice in preparation for taking office and understand Confucius's answers as tailored to the duties of an official. One is to cultivate virtue first, and then spread that virtue to effect *min zhi yi*—literally, "rightness [among] the common people" (Slingerland 2003, p. 60). Imagining the situation portrayed in *Analects* 13.19, encountering the barbaric other, it would be the duty of an official to inculcate virtue. How this is to be done is left unstated in these passages, however several other passages recommend the power of influence by example. These include *Analects* 12.19, in which Ji Kanzi, one of the heads of the Ji clan of Lu, asks Confucius, "If I were to execute those who lacked the *dao* in order to advance those who possessed the *dao*, how would that be?" In response, Confucius asks what need there is for execution, asserting, "If you desire goodness, then the common people will be good," likening the leadership of the *junzi* (exemplary person, gentleman) to the movement of wind and the *xiaoren* (petty person; common person) to the corresponding movement of grass (Slingerland 2003, p. 134).

The influence of the *junzi* has the potential to be expansive and enduring. This notion is underscored with reference to the way things could be if not for the legacies of such persons. Consider Confucius's comments on Guan Zhong, who lived about two centuries before him. Although Confucius criticizes Guan Zhong's understanding of ritual in *Analects* 3.22, Confucius idealizes his accomplishments in *Analects* 14.17: "When Guan Zhong served as Duke Huan's Prime Minister, he allowed him to become hegemon over the other feudal lords, uniting and ordering the entire world. To this day, the people continue to enjoy the benefits of his achievements—if it were not for Guan Zhong, we would all be wearing our hair loose and fastening our garments on the left" (Slingerland 2003, p. 161). In other words, if not for the accomplishments of Guan Zhong, all Chinese would be engaging in "barbarian" customs of appearance and dress.

Confucius himself, as is related in *Analects* 9.14, considered dwelling among barbarians—namely, the Nine Yi barbarian tribes, who lived along the Eastern coast of present-day China, possibly including the Korean peninsula (Slingerland

2003, p. 91). This vignette is often connected with passages in the *Analects* in which Confucius expresses frustration with the moral state-of-affairs of his time and place (e.g., *Analects* 5.7, in which Confucius asserts that "If the *dao* [moral way] is not put into practice, I will set off upon the sea in a small raft"). Upon being asked by an unnamed interlocutor, "How could you bear their uncouthness?" Confucius replies, "If a *junzi* were to dwell among them, what uncouthness would there be?" Confucius may be implying that he is himself a *junzi,* or at least that he is closer to the *junzi* ideal those with whom he would be living. Accordingly, he could, in the phrase of Poo (2005, p. 122) "transform the rustic to the sophisticated," forming a community operating under more rational principles than the alternatives.

The notion that the so-called barbarians could be made to be civilized by an individual who immigrates to their territory smacks of not just culturalism, but possibly colonialism as well. However, it is not clear that we need arrive at such a jarring conclusion. It is possible to read passages such as these in a way that is suggestive of a form of inclusivism, rather than exclusivism. In *Analects* 17.2, Confucius is cited as claiming, "By nature people are similar; they diverge as the result of practice" (Slingerland 2003, p. 200). Accordingly, no person lacks the potential to cultivate virtue. As Slingerland comments, this passage suggests that "all people, even non-Chinese barbarians, are born with more or less similar basic stuff, and it is the quality of the tradition into which they are socialized…that really makes the difference" (Slingerland 2003, p. 200). This reading of *Analects* 17.2 complicates the interpretation that I have been developing of culturalism in the *Analects*, insofar as the border between "us" and "them" is not indexed to geography or group affiliation but to moral character.

Confucius's bleak outlook on his disciple, Zai Wo, may cohere with this reading. In *Analects* 5.10, in response to Zai Wo's sleeping during the daytime, Confucius laments, "Rotten wood cannot be carved, and a wall of dung cannot be plastered. As for Zai Wo, what would be the use of reprimanding him?" (Slingerland 2003, p. 43). If Zai Wo is too far mired in laziness to possibly be improved by Confucius's teaching, it is not because he is from outside Chinese borders (as he is not), but because of his lack of exertion. It is notable that Zai Wo is never referred to as *yí* or *mán*, nor is any other Chinese person in the *Analects* of morally inferior or reprehensible status. These are terms that pejoratively mark those outside Chinese borders as morally inferior. At the same time, as is illustrated in the case of Zai Wo, those within Chinese borders are not viewed as immune from embodying similar moral inferiority.

Confucian Speciesism in the *Analects*?

I would like to turn now to the question of whether another form of exclusivism appears in the *Analects*, namely speciesism—the human-held belief that non-human species are inferior to humans. This discussion closely relates to that of culturalism, particularly concerning the figure of the barbarian. Although my focus here is on Confucius—not Mencius—I would like to mention another scholar's comments about Mencius, which bring to the fore the conceptual link between these forms of exclusivism. As Pines (2015) observes, Mencius argued against two leading thinkers of his age, Yangzi and Mozi, in these terms: "Mr. Yang advocates selfishness, which means having no rulers. Mr. Mo advocates universal love, which means having no father. Having neither ruler nor father means becoming birds and beasts." Thus, "bestiality seems to be a social condition, which can emerge even among the Chinese should the doctrines of Mencius' opponents prevail" (Pines 2015, p. 65). Although Mencius is four generations removed from Confucius, he acts here as a defender of Confucian ideals against competing teachings such as Yangism and Mohism. The reduction of non-Confucian teachings to doctrines fit for non-human animals implies an axiological hierarchy between humans and non-human animals that Mencius likely views as consonant with the teachings of Confucius.

Certainly, a number of passages of the *Analects* recommend a privileging of human interests over those of non-human animals. "Speciesism" is certainly not a term that would have been familiar to Confucius, and my invoking it in this context may be viewed as a prime example of anachronistic interpretation. At the same time, reevaluating Confucian thought in light of our own times necessarily involves using current vocabulary, so I think it is reasonable to entertain the idea. The question is whether the privileging of human interests in the *Analects* amounts simply to a hierarchy, wherein humans still have regard for animals and believe they deserve our care—or whether there is a prioritization of human preferences over and against those of non-human animals characterized by indifference to their well-being. Probing several passages from the *Analects* will aid in making a determination.

Consider *Analects* 10.17, in which it is reported, "One day the stables burned. When the Master returned from court, he asked, 'Was anyone hurt?' He did not ask about the horses" (Slingerland 2003, p. 106). It is not clear *which* stables burned, though this detail may not be that important. On the other hand, that horses were a valuable asset is likely salient to this episode being recorded in the *Analects*. I agree with Fan (2010, p. 84) that because they were materially valuable "[t]here had to be some people then concentrating on such material value, ignoring human value." The function of this passage appears to be to highlight Confucius's prioritizing the well-being of human persons who may have perished in the fire over the loss of non-human animals, no matter their value. In his treatment of this passage, Fan distinguishes among devotional love to parents (*qin ai*), benevolent love to humans (*ren ai*), and sympathetic love (*xi ai*) to non-human animals. A charitable reading of the passage suggests that horses warrant lesser degree of concern that humans do, while still bearing "sympathetic value" (Fan 2010, p. 84). It is certainly plausible that this is the appropriate reading of the passage. However, such a prioritization would be signaled by Confucius asking *first* whether anyone was hurt, and asking *second* about the horses. Confucius's having not asked *at all* about the horses at least raises the question of whether Confucius is indifferent to their well-being.

A similar question arises in *Analects* 3.17. Here, we learn that a disciple, Zigong, "wanted to do away with the practice of sacrificing a lamb to announce the beginning of the month." Confucius replies, "Zigong! You regret the loss of a lamb, whereas I regret the loss of the rite" (Slingerland 2003, p. 24). Admittedly, we do not know more about the ritual in question. It does appear evident, however, that Confucius regards the lamb as instrumental to the carrying out of a human ritual, and that he prioritizes the ritual and derides his disciple's concern for the loss of a lamb. Analyzing this passage, Fan (2010) maintains that using animals in certain rituals is *necessary* to show proper reverence. In addition to nodding, bowing, and kneeling, in rituals intended to express reverence, one can offer things of value. "Obviously, the most valuable thing one can offer is life," Fan argues, "and the life of animals serves this purpose exactly in the sacrifice" (Fan 2010, p. 92). Whatever sympathetic love one feels for a lamb ought not detract from one's reverence, which is manifested in carrying out the sacrificial ritual.

In response to this argument, R. Kim (2016) suggests that because there is textual evidence for the revisability of at least some rituals, it is not the case that sacrifice of animals is necessary for preservation of a ritual. For example, in *Analects* 9.3, Confucius allows for the change of fabric used in a ceremonial cap, on account of its being more frugal (while apparently not compromising the reverence inherent to the ritual). Following Kim, "if we take an expanded notion of what sacrifice can involve, the opportunities for sacrifice [are] almost limitless, especially given the multitude of ways in which we can work for justice and peace in this world" (R. Kim 2016, pp. 39–40). Kim's suggestion is compatible with that made by Nuyen (2011) that the social *li* can be seen as continuous with, or incorporating, the ecological *li*, such that a Confucian agent is understood as a "citizen of a biotic community" (p. 560). That Confucius reacts so strongly against the implied suggestion of the revision to *this* ritual suggests that Confucius believes its meaning would be lost without a non-human animal being sacrificed—but this position appears to be taken arbitrarily, or at least not with clear justification. It has been suggested to me that Confucius does not always provide justification for his claims, so the lack of a clear justification here does not imply anything in particular, let alone an exclusivist attitude such as speciesism. I grant that the case for speciesism is not conclusive, especially not on the basis of one or two passages. We have to consider all the data available to us and then make inferences and draw conclusions as far as the data reasonably allows.

The view of non-human animals as property instrumental to human aims does pervade several additional passages, as outlined by Blakeley (2003, p. 139). These passages include references to oxen used for plowing (*Analects* 6.6), horses used for riding and pulling carriages (*Analects* 10.20), fish and other animals used as food (*Analects* 10.8), and animals' fur used for clothing (*Analects* 9.27). Of course, these passages reflect commonly accepted practices in Confucius's context. We can presume that passages such as *Analects* 10.17 and 3.17 are intended to cast Confucius in a favorable light for adhering to these norms, when others might or indeed did challenge these norms.

This is not to say that Confucius does not acknowledge that non-human animals have interests, but he views their interests as coinciding with only the most basic interests of humans. In *Analects* 2.7, another disciple, Ziyou, asks about filial piety. Confucius responds, "Nowadays, 'filial' means simply being able to provide one's parents with nourishment. But even dogs and horses are provided with nourishment. If you are not respectful, wherein lies the difference?" (Slingerland 2003, p. 10). Although it is possible that Confucius mentions dogs and horses only for rhetorical purposes in this passage, such rhetorical purposes are served by acknowledgement that they require nourishment to continue to live. This basic acknowledgment is easy to miss, couched as it is in a statement repudiating what he regards as insufficient filiality toward parents among humans. While dogs and horses are provided with nourishment by their adult owners, the same adults who provide their parents nourishment without an attitude of respect fail to meet their duty. More is owed to parents than to non-human animals. Adults cannot survive childhood without the care of their parents (*Analects* 17.21), but they can make it to adulthood without any care or nourishment from non-human animals.

Just as the case for culturalism in the *Analects* can be complicated by consideration of a sample of apparently inclusivist passages, the same can be done to complicate the case for speciesism. For the most part, I agree with Bai (2009, p. 92), who holds that "it cannot be denied that Confucius…is silent about humane treatment of animals" in the *Analects*. At the same time, Confucius is not silent about the interests of non-human animals, and the authors of the *Analects* are not silent about Confucius's positive regard for non-human animals—even if this voice is less resonant than its opposite. Separating from *Analects* 2.7, Confucius's acknowledgment of dogs' and horses' interest in nourishment is a basic starting point. Additionally, as a counterpoint to *Analects* 10.17, one could invoke *Analects* 14.33, in which Confucius remarks, "One does not praise a thoroughbred horse for its physical strength, but rather for its *de* 德 (character; excellence; virtue)" (Slingerland 2003, p. 167). Here, Confucius appears to imbue horses—albeit those of a particular stock—with excellence distinct from their brute physical prowess. Of course, it is possible that Confucius's remark about horses is not entirely about horses; it may be that he has chosen a poetic way to remark on human excellence. Nonetheless, the analogy from the case of the thoroughbred horse to the case of the virtuous human betokens an appreciation for the horse exceeding its value as property.

As an account of Confucius's behavior as told by an unnamed observer, there is no mistaking *Analects* 7.27 for an analogy or poetic turn of phrase. Here, we are told that Confucius "would fish with a hook, but not with a net" and he "would shoot with a corded line, but would not aim at roosting birds" (Slingerland 2003, p. 73). This passage receives markedly less commentarial treatment than others just discussed. In an unusual case of a scholar finding this passage highly illustrative, Ni (2016) introduces the passage by stating that "nothing works more effectively than setting an example for students to follow" and indicates that the passage offers a "detailed description" of Confucius. Ni interprets the passage succinctly: "Seeing how the Master treated animals, one also learns how he treated humans. The description contains no mention of *ren*, but the Master's behavior speaks louder than words" (2016, p. 128). Ni is right that the passage is intended to teach by Confucius's example, but what precisely is being modeled in the passage is up for debate.

On the basis of the foregoing passages, the connection Ni draws between how Confucius treats animals and how Confucius treats humans is dubious. Confucius clearly regards non-human animals and animals as inhabiting distinct moral planes. Nonetheless, ostensibly this passage *is* intended to point to Confucius's humaneness toward non-human animals, even if it is granted that Confucius fished and hunted, and thus killed non-human animals. Fishing with a hook, rather than a net, may be considered more humane insofar as this method may spare several fish. A popular method for catching large birds from the Zhou dynasty through the Eastern Han dynasty (Fong 1988–1989, p. 18; Wallace 2010, p. 47), shooting with a corded line (*yi she*) involved "the use of a bow or crossbow with a silk cord attached to a special kind of arrow at one end and a weighted mechanism at the other…the line would become wrapped around the neck of the bird and, when the bird flew higher, the weight would then bring it to the ground" (Wallace 2010, p. 47). It is not this *method* of hunting that is the passage suggests to be more humane, but Confucius's opting against hunting birds that are roosting. Fan (2010, p. 94) views this passage as suggesting that "we should not take animals in a wasteful or unsportsmanlike way, we should not take animals in the wrong seasons, and we should not take an animal if it is pregnant." These remarks are at least partially consistent with an inclusivist reading of the passage, in which non-human animals are regarded comparably to humans. Perhaps his not shooting roosting birds is a result of Confucius's recognizing and respecting family relations in the non-human animal kingdom. For his part, Fan does not imagine this possibility, underscoring that for Confucius, "human values are taken to be more important than animal values" (2010, p. 94). Fan's suggestion that Confucius models appropriate adherence to the rituals associated with these hunting activities seems apt. By opting to kill fewer fish and kill non-roosting birds, Confucius exhibits good sportsmanship; however, he does not thereby exhibit humane treatment of animals the likes of which he extends to humans.

Degrees of Exemplarity

It is interesting that the chapter in which Olberding appraises the morality of Confucius is titled "A Total Exemplar: Confucius" whereas the two chapters devoted to disciples of Confucius are titled "A Partial Exemplar: Zilu" and "A Partial Exemplar: Zigong." On the basis of these categorizations, one may surmise that for Olberding, the latter two exhibit moral shortcomings, whereas Confucius—a total exemplar—does not. Olberding does, in fact, highlight shortcomings of both Zilu and Zigong. For Olberding, Zilu is a partial exemplar, as he "lacks proficiency with crafting a formally appropriate demeanor and frequently fails to meet well the conventional standards of propriety" (2012, p. 159). And Zigong is a partial exemplar, as he lacks *shu* (sympathy); he is so enamored of formalities of conduct that he fails to achieve genuine consideration of others (2012, p. 166). Confucius is not, however, free of shortcomings. While Confucius is "the most complete and compelling exemplar presented in the *Analects*" (2012, p. 105), "there is no suggestion that his goodness is total. He is not perfect" (2012, p. 107). For Olberding, the distinction between a total exemplar and a partial exemplar amounts to the difference between a "good person" and a "courageous person"; the former is exemplary with respect to their attitudes and behaviors in general, while the latter is exemplary with respect to a distinct and limited domain (2012, p. 136).

Although it is somewhat curious that a "total" exemplar would not be totally exemplary, one may accept Olberding's terms and still challenge the notion that Confucius is a total exemplar. If Confucius does promulgate pernicious forms of exclusivism, such as culturalism or speciesism in the *Analects*, then he may not be exemplary in general. Confucius certainly does appear to embody much that is good and worthy of admiration and emulation, however, so perhaps these good qualities would far outweigh whatever bad qualities might be attributed to him. Perhaps the question at stake is less a vindication of Confucius's character, but more a line-drawing question for Olberding as concerns total and partial exemplars. At what point does one's faults shift an evaluation of them from "total" or general exemplars to "partial" exemplars?

According to Olberding, Confucius "strikes the occasional discordant note" but "is a good person and from his example we can begin to draw out and abstract what qualities belong to good people" (Olberding 2012, p. 134). What sort of behavior is counted as the "occasional discordant note"? Olberding refers to such "infelicities" as the previously discussed "cutting remark" that Confucius makes regarding Zaiwo (Olberding 2012, p. 131), or Confucius's disparaging a provincial musical performance by likening it to the use of an ox-cleaver to kill a chicken (*Analects* 17.4). Perhaps we should understand incidents such as these as slips—moments of immaturity in what is typically a comportment of composure. Olberding regards some of these lapses, such as the latter incident, as "simply mistakes" (Olberding 2012, p. 133). Confucius's musical commentary, for example, is "but error" committed while "temporarily seduced by the aesthetically obvious—the music is showy and pretentious," failing to appreciate the value of the music by any other measure (Olberding 2012, pp. 133–134). Although she grants that Confucius is imperfect, and cites these passages and others as illustrations of his infelicities, Olberding downplays their significance to the whole picture of Confucius as moral agent. Occasional rude remarks are may strike discordant notes, but they do not interfere with the overall harmony of Confucius's personal style and the processes within him. Rather than "a cleaned up sage scrubbed of those features that do not conform to pristine moral heroism," Confucius is "[left] with something of his humanity" (Olberding 2012, p. 106).

Whatever our estimation of these minor transgressions, Olberding fails to acknowledge forms of exclusivism that could attach to Confucius as described in the *Analects*, such as culturalism and speciesism. She is largely silent about the passages that I have discussed, however, when she does address a pertinent passage, she appears to excuse Confucius rather than appraise him objectively. Consider Olberding's treatment of *Analects* 9.14, in which Confucius proposes to live among the "barbarians" and suggests that the presence of a *junzi* would render them less barbaric. Olberding maintains that, along with other passages in the text, this passage "has about it the taste of a self-deprecatingly bitter humor," and posits that Confucius's "failure to achieve meaningful employ and recognition" induces "regret humorously tempered with a touch of self-satirization" (Olberding 2012, p. 123). Olberding's describing the passage as exuding "a taste of humor" and revealing "a touch of self-satirization" suggests that utterances such as these from Confucius ought not to be taken too seriously when evaluating his character. I contend, however, that any moral evaluation of Confucius demands our squarely confronting the less likeable, and even positively dislikable aspects of his behavior. While Olberding and I agree that Confucius is not perfect, I believe that some of Confucius's flaws may exceed mere "infelicities." Even if they conform to the norms of his day, if Confucius was a culturalist or speciesist, these are moral imperfections that ought not to be minimized. Moreover, even if the authors of the *Analects* do intend to cast Confucius as a moral exemplar, contemporary readers need not accept this portrayal wholesale, even if there is much about him that is worthy of admiration and emulation.

Concluding Remarks

In this chapter, I have focused on two forms of what I have termed "Confucian exclusivism" that appear to be prevalent in the *Analects*, culturalism, and speciesism. I have focused on these, which are linked conceptually by the association of the "barbaric" with animality. I have not attended to other forms of Confucian exclusivism that warrant attention, such as sexism, though scholars have often acknowledged that "the *Analects* appears to endorse, […] pernicious perspectives on gender" (Olberding 2012, p. 9). I have identified Confucian moral exemplarism as a recent interpretative lens that is problematized by foregrounding exclusivist features of Confucius's thought and action as portrayed in the *Analects*. Of course, exclusivist perspectives such as culturalism and speciesism could have been taken for granted in Confucius's context, with no words used then to express these contemporary-isms. His abiding by such social norms would have been viewed by most as either unremarkable or praiseworthy inasmuch as adhering to tradition was regarded as morally proper behavior. Consequently, my foregrounding Confucian exclusivism does not itself challenge the legitimacy of exemplarist readings of the *Analects* as such. However, the acknowledgement of Confucian exclusivism ought to provoke contemporary audiences to critically examine the text and to consider carefully that which ought to be regarded as exemplary and worthy of admiration and emulation in their own lives.

References

Ames, R.T., and H. Rosemont Jr. 1998. *The Analects of Confucius: A philosophical translation*. Ballantine.

Anderson, B. 1983. *Imagined Communities: Reflections on the Origin and Spread of Nationalism*. Verso.

Bai, T. 2009. The Price of Serving Meat—on Confucius's and Mencius's Views of Human and Animal rights. *Asian Philosophy* 19 (1): 85–99.

Berenpas, M. 2016. An Asian Ethics of Hospitality: Hospitality in Confucian, Daoist, and Buddhist philosophy. In *The Routledge Handbook of Hospitality Studies*, ed. C. Lashley, 157–168. Routledge.

Blakeley, D.N. 2003. Listening to the Animals: The Confucian View of Animal Welfare. *Journal of Chinese Philosophy* 30 (2): 137–157.

Fan, R. 2010. How Should We Treat Animals? A Confucian Reflection. *Dao* 9 (1): 79–96.

Fong, M. H. 1988–1989. The Origin of Chinese Pictorial Representation of the Human Figure. *Artibus Asiae* 1/2: 5–38.

Huang, Y. 2013. Perceptions of the Barbarian in Early Greece and China. *CHS Research Bulletin* 2 (1). http://nrs.harvard.edu/urn-3:hlnc.essay:HuangY.Perceptions_of_the_Barbarian_in_Early_Greece_and_China.2013

Kim, M. 2012. *Moral Exemplars in the* Analects*: The Good Person Is that*. Notre Dame Philosophical Reviews. February. https://ndpr.nd.edu/reviews/moral-exemplars-in-the-analects-the-good-person-is-that/

Kim, R.T. 2016. Confucianism and Non-human Animal Sacrifice. *European Journal for Philosophy of Religion* 8 (1): 27–49.

Lai, Y., and K. Lai. 2022. Learning from Exemplars in Confucius' *Analects*: The Centrality of Reflective Observation. *Educational Philosophy and Theory*. https://doi.org/10.1080/00131857.2022.2132936

Li, M. 2020. Reframing Confucianism Epistemology: Exemplarist Morality in the Confucian Analects. *Journal of Arts & Humanities* 9 (9): 45–50.

Liu, Q. 2003. Filiality Versus Sociality and Individuality: On Confucianism as 'Consanguinitism'. *Philosophy East and West* 53 (2): 234–250.

Ni, P. 2016. *Confucius: The Man and the Way of Gongfu*. Rowman & Littlefield.

Nuyen, A.T. 2011. Confucian Role-based Ethics and Strong Environmental Ethics. *Environmental Values* 20 (4): 549–566.

Nylan, M. 2012. Talk About 'Barbarians' in Antiquity. *Philosophy East and West* 62 (4): 580–601.

Olberding, A. 2012. *Moral Exemplars in the Analects: The Good Person is That*. Routledge.

Pines, Y. 2015. Beasts or Humans: Pre-Imperial Origins of the 'Sino-Barbarian' Dichotomy. In *Mongols, Turks, and Others: Eurasian Nomads and the Sedentary World*, ed. R. Amitai and M. Biran, 59–102. Brill.

Poo, M. 2005. *Enemies of Civilization: Attitudes Toward Foreigners in Ancient Mesopotamia, Egypt, and China*. SUNY Press.

Slingerland, E. 2003. *Confucius Analects*. Hackett.

Tan, S. 2005. Imagining Confucius: Paradigmatic Character and Virtue Ethics. *Journal of Chinese Philosophy* 32 (3): 409–426.

Wallace, L. 2010. *Chasing the Beyond: Depictions of Hunting in Eastern Han Dynasty tomb reliefs (25-220 CE) from Shaanxi and Shanxi.* [Doctoral dissertation, University of Pittsburgh].

Zhang, E.Y. 2023. The Ethics of Hospitality: Tracing the Confucian Other. *Journal of Confucian Philosophy and Culture* 39: 5–29.

Mathew A. Foust is Professor of Philosophy and the Chair of the Department of Philosophy and Religion at Appalachian State University. He teaches and publishes in several areas, including American philosophy, Chinese philosophy, ethics, and the philosophy of religion. Among his publications are a monograph *Confucianism and American Philosophy* (SUNY Press), a co-edited volume (with Sor-hoon Tan) *Feminist Encounters with Confucius* (Brill), and several peer-reviewed articles.

Part II

Comparative Studies of Inclusion or Exclusion in Religious Traditions

6

Legitimating the Other's Wisdom for Common Cause: Rev. Dr. Martin Luther King's Palm Sunday Sermon on Mohandas K. Gandhi

John W. Fadden

Introduction

Martin Luther King, Jr.'s oft quoted statement from *Stride Toward Freedom*, "Christ furnished the spirit and the motivation, while Gandhi furnished the method,"[1] remains a profound formulation of the transformation that is possible when otherness is drawn near and one learns from their religious Other. King and his Montgomery congregation did not abandon their relationship to Gandhi's wisdom and the people of India after their efforts desegregated Montgomery's buses. In early 1959, King went on a pilgrimage to India, returning to the pulpit in Montgomery in time to deliver a Palm Sunday sermon on the life of Mohandas K. Gandhi. The sermon exhorted the listener to continue the struggle for a just world by nonviolent methods and the power of agapic love. King was open to the wisdom of his religious others—not to convert them to his way of seeing, but as accomplices co-laboring in the struggle for a just world.

---

[1] Martin Luther King, Jr. *Stride Toward Freedom: The Montgomery Story* (San Francisco: Harper Collins, 1958), 85.

J. W. Fadden (✉)
Religious Studies Department at St. John Fisher University, Rochester, NY, USA
e-mail: jfadden@sjfc.edu

© The Author(s), under exclusive license to Springer Nature Switzerland AG 2024
M. Shafiq, T. Donlin-Smith (eds.), *Inclusion or Exclusion in the Sacred Texts and Human Contexts*, https://doi.org/10.1007/978-3-031-70180-1_6

Part 1: Engaging Scholars

Very few scholars of King have paid attention to this Palm Sunday sermon. By engaging with three scholars who do so, the chapter seeks to help contextualize the sermon and to prepare the reader for the more detailed engagement to follow below.

"I Can Only Imagine": The Speaker, Audience, and Context of the Sermon

In an article concerned with King's interreligious perspectives, interfaith activist and scholar Eboo Patel briefly comments on the sermon, "The lines in there would be challenging to any Christian audience at any time, in any place–I can only imagine how it was received in mid-century Alabama."[2] Patel points out a few places in the sermon that relate to King's interfaith perspective, part of his larger purpose in Patel's article. Patel is correct to find this sermon as an interesting piece of data in support of his position, and the sermon does challenge the Christian audience's relationship with their, in this case, Hindu Other. Yet Patel's brevity on the sermon ignores the audience, its context, and the occasion of King's rhetoric. Paying attention to the audience and the context would help Patel's case with respect to interfaith activities. Sure, "I can only imagine" may be a throwaway line, but we can imagine King's Christian audience.

While speaking about Mohandas Gandhi in a Palm Sunday sermon may seem a strange topic for an African American Baptist church in Montgomery, Alabama, in 1959, Gandhi was not a new topic for King, the congregants of Dexter Avenue Baptist Church, nor African Americans more generally. In their own context, they already knew about Gandhi, his philosophy on nonviolence, and the Indian people's struggle against British colonialism.

Long before Martin Luther King, Jr. arrived on the scene, African Americans had been keeping attention on the man called Mahatma and the nonviolent independence struggle of the Indian people; whether through the African American press, pilgrimages to India, and tours of the United States by Gandhians, African Americans paid serious attention to Gandhi, his philosophy, and his techniques of nonviolent direct action.[3]

---

[2] Eboo Patel, "Martin Luther King Jr. and the Light of Other Faiths," *Cross Currents* 63.3 (2013): 274.

[3] See the foundational work of Sudarshan Kapur, *Raising Up a Prophet: The African-American Encounter with Gandhi* (Boston: Beacon Press, 1992).

Since at least the time of Marcus Garvey, African Americans had been exhorting each other to pay attention to what Gandhi was doing. The African American press covered Gandhi from his time in South Africa and continuing through his struggles in India, and debated Gandhian nonviolence and its relevance for African Americans under Jim and Jane Crow.

African American intellectual leaders helped to connect Gandhian nonviolence to the African American context. Historian Dennis Dickerson argues King's theological perspective "derived directly from a previous generation of black religious intellectuals who in the 1930s and 1940s developed themes and tactics that influenced King's civil rights movement leadership."[4] And further, "The sacredness of human personality, the sinfulness of segregation, and the need to destroy it with morally acceptable methods were among several ideas that informed King's rhetoric."[5] Dickerson focuses on black religious intellectuals who came of age in the 1930s and 1940s: Mordecai W. Johnson, President of Howard University; Benjamin E. Mays, dean of Howard's divinity school and then President of Morehouse College; Howard Thurman, also at Howard, later dean of Marsh Chapel at Boston University; and Morehouse professor George D. Kelsey. All but Kelsey made the pilgrimage to India to meet with Mohandas Gandhi. Besides their positions on college campuses, all were ordained Baptist clergy, and all were on the national and international stage through their speeches, sermons, and publications asserting the sacredness of human personality, the sinfulness of segregation, and advocating nonviolent strategies against Jim Crow.[6]

The previous generation of African Americans' bridge-building with Gandhi and the Indian independence movement helped to introduce King to Gandhi's teachings. King scholar Lewis Baldwin points out that even before arriving at Crozer Theological Seminary, a young King was exposed to Gandhi, likely through the local Black newspaper and Tuesday morning talks by Benjamin Mays. But, it was a lecture by Mordecai Johnson at Fellowship House in Philadelphia that inspired King to study Gandhi more, or at least to buy a stack of books on Gandhi.[7] As historian Peniel Joseph notes, King discovered Gandhi's concept of *satyagraha*

---

[4] Dennis C. Dickerson, "African American Religious Intellectuals and the Theological Foundations of the Civil Rights Movement, 1930–1955," *Church History* 74.2 (2005): 217–218.

[5] Dennis C. Dickerson, "African American Religious Intellectuals and the Theological Foundations of the Civil Rights Movement, 1930–1955," *Church History* 74.2 (2005): 218.

[6] Dennis C. Dickerson, "African American Religious Intellectuals and the Theological Foundations of the Civil Rights Movement, 1930–1955," *Church History* 74.2 (2005): 219.

[7] Lewis V. Baldwin, *The Arc of Truth: The Thinking of Martin Luther King Jr.* (Minneapolis: Fortress, 2022), 28–29.

and found it particularly appealing in the face of Jim Crow, and equated Gandhi's movement with a collective application of Christ's love.[8] Yet, King did not become a proponent of Gandhian nonviolence at this point. It would take the experiences of the Montgomery Bus Boycott to push him further down the nonviolent path.

Indian disciples of Gandhi also participated in bridge-building through their visits and tours of the United States. Notably, in 1951, the Gandhian leader Ram Manohar Lohia toured and lectured in the US for six weeks. Significantly, Lohia lectured on Gandhian nonviolent direct action at Fisk University and at the interracial Highlander Folk School. Notably, Rosa Parks trained at Highlander Folk School in the summer of 1955 and discussed the idea of civil disobedience.[9]

During the period of the Montgomery Bus Boycott and after, disciples of Gandhi visited Montgomery and the Kings. Indeed, it was a visit from R.R. Diwakar, an Indian politician, writer, and proponent of Gandhian nonviolence (and chairman of the Gandhi Smarak Nidhi), in mid-August 1957 who challenged King to set the example of physical suffering.[10] A year later, Kaka Kalelkar, a preeminent Indian follower of Gandhi's philosophy and methods, social reformer, and member of India's upper parliament, visited Montgomery to speak to the Montgomery Improvement Association in August of 1958 (arranged by the cultural committee of Dexter Avenue Baptist Center, where he spoke).[11]

The Montgomery Bus Boycott was a period when Dexter Avenue Baptist Church members and their pastor experienced the power of nonviolent direct action. As Houston Bryan Roberson summarizes in *Fighting the Good Fight*,

> Dexter Avenue Baptist Church was involved in the Montgomery Bus Boycott in three ways: (1) through direct participation of some of its members–namely Mary Fair Burks, Rufus Lewis, and Jo Ann Robinson; (2) through the use of the church facility for the crucial meetings where religious and civic leaders committed to boycott the city buses; and (3) through the leadership of its pastor Martin Luther King, Jr., who became the leader in helping inspire and sustain demonstrators during this long and ultimately successful protest.[12]

---

[8] Peniel E. Joseph, *The Sword and the Shield: The Revolutionary Lives of Malcolm X and Martin Luther King Jr.* (Updated Edition; New York: Basic Books, 2020), 60.

[9] Sudarshan Kapur, *Raising Up a Prophet: The African-American Encounter with Gandhi* (Boston: Beacon Press, 1992), 151.

[10] William D. Watley, *Roots of Resistance: The Nonviolent Ethic of Martin Luther King, Jr.,* (Valley Forge, Penn.: Judson Press, 1985), 57.

[11] Houston B. Roberson, *Fighting the Good Fight: The Story of the Dexter Avenue King Memorial Baptist Church, 1865–1977* (New York: Routledge, 2013 [2005]), 156.

[12] Houston B. Roberson, *Fighting the Good Fight: The Story of the Dexter Avenue King Memorial Baptist Church, 1865–1977* (New York: Routledge, 2013 [2005]), 140.

Yet, it was also a time of learning about nonviolent direct action on the fly.

One of the key individuals for helping Martin Luther King learn to apply Gandhian nonviolence was Bayard Rustin. Rustin influenced the move in the direction of Gandhian nonviolence and became one of King's most trusted advisors. Hoda Zaki claims, "Rustin represents the most direct source of the idea and practice of nonviolent resistance to influence the freedom struggle in the United States."[13] In 1947, after the assassination of Gandhi, Rustin visited India for six weeks and met with the leaders of the Gandhian movement. After racists bombed the Kings' home at the end of January 1956 during the Montgomery boycott, Rustin arrived to advise King. Rustin "shared his experiences as a professional organizer with King, exposing him to the intricacies of nonviolence as a way of life, which would disallow the use of armed bodyguards."[14] Rustin remained an important advisor for the young King on his path of nonviolence. While King may have started studying the wisdom of Gandhi in seminary, Rustin's guidance during the Montgomery movement seems to have helped to transform nonviolence into a way of life, and not just a tactic, for King.[15] Further, according to Peniel Joseph, Rustin helped to arrange King's meetings with key associates of Gandhi on the Kings' trip to India in early 1959.[16]

Indeed, in *Stride Toward Freedom,* King depicted his congregation's context—and all of Montgomery—as one that knew about Gandhi.

> About a week after the protest started, a white woman who understood and sympathized with the Negroes' efforts wrote a letter to the editor of the *Montgomery*

---

[13] Hoda M. Zaki, "From Montgomery to Tahrir Square: The Transnational Journeys of Nonviolence and Utopia," *Utopian Studies* 26.1 (2015): 210.

[14] Peniel E. Joseph, *The Sword and the Shield: The Revolutionary Lives of Malcolm X and Martin Luther King Jr.* (Updated Edition; New York: Basic Books, 2020), 66.

[15] King was not just influenced by African American pacifists who learned from Gandhi. In 1956 he was in correspondence with one of the seminal voices to theorize nonviolence in America, Richard Gregg, a radical white Christian who came to nonviolence via the labor movement and a major figure in Fellowship of Reconciliation. Gregg had spent years in India studying Gandhi's nonviolent theory in practice and wrote numerous books about nonviolence, the most important being *The Power of Nonviolence* (1934). King was introduced to Gregg's work by Glenn Smiley, who along with Rustin helped tutor King on Gandhian nonviolence. According to Joseph Kosek, "Under the influence of Gregg's ideas, the Montgomery bus boycott gradually became a Gandhian project." Joseph Kip Kosek, "Richard Gregg, Mohandas Gandhi, and the Strategy of Nonviolence," *The Journal of American History* 91.4 (2005): 1344.

[16] Peniel E. Joseph, *The Sword and the Shield: The Revolutionary Lives of Malcolm X and Martin Luther King Jr.* (Updated Edition; New York: Basic Books, 2020), 79.

> *Advertiser* comparing the bus protest with the Gandhian movement in India. Miss Juliette Morgan, sensitive and frail, did not long survive the rejection and condemnation of the white community, but not long before she died in the summer of 1957 the name of Mahatma Gandhi was well-known in Montgomery. People who had never heard of the little brown saint of India were now saying his name with an air of familiarity.[17]

King's acknowledgment of Gandhi's name being well known in Montgomery in the summer of 1957 suggests that his audience at Dexter Avenue Baptist Church was also familiar with Gandhi's name well before Palm Sunday in 1959.

In summary, we can imagine King's Christian audience. Congregants of Dexter Avenue Baptist Church were people who were involved in the Montgomery movement and who were among African Americans who for the past generation had already been keeping watch about Gandhi. The congregants had welcomed Gandhian visitors in recent years, such as R. R. Diwakar and Kaka Kalelkar; no doubt they had read about the Gandhi-led freedom movement in India through the African American press; and they had learned from African Americans who had been visitors to the saint of India or had spent time in India learning from Gandhians after Gandhi's death, such as Mordecai Johnson who was an invited speaker to the church in 1957, but also Bayard Rustin. We can imagine that King and the congregants of Dexter Avenue knew each other well enough that his choice of Gandhi would be met not as a surprise nor an uncomfortable challenge, but rather as a hopeful exhortation for the task ahead using an iconic Other with whom the congregation was familiar.

King's Theological and Moral Opposition to Colonialism Abroad and at Home: The Common Cause

Preeminent King Scholar Lewis Baldwin classifies the Palm Sunday sermon on Gandhi as one of King's works on colonialism and connects the Black Freedom Struggle in America to broader international freedom struggles. With respect to King's writings on India's struggle for independence, Baldwin observes, "King spoke to the deep ties between black Americans and the people of Asia, and he saw certain shared values that moved across the cultural boundaries that separated his people in America from both Asians and Africans."[18] Specifically related to the

---

[17] Martin Luther King, Jr., *Stride Toward Freedom: The Montgomery Story*, (San Francisco: Harper Collins, 1958), 85.

[18] Lewis V. Baldwin, "Introduction," in *"In a Single Garment of Destiny" A Global Vision of Justice* (Boston: Beacon, 2014), 54–55.

Palm Sunday sermon, Baldwin comments, "The fact that King devoted a sermon to the memory of Gandhi and India's anticolonial crusade on Palm Sunday 1959 is telling enough, for it highlighted his ability to frame his arguments against colonialism in religious and ethical terms."[19] Baldwin's observations help us to see the common cause being made across international freedom movements.

Besides Baldwin, other scholars have noted the King's budding internationalism, connecting the Black Freedom Movement in America with the freedom struggles around the globe with respect to his trip to India. While King may have imagined himself following in the footsteps of a previous generation of African American theologians visiting Gandhi, the reality of his visit was closer to that of a state visit by an international leader.[20] Sociologist Sean Chabot argues the pilgrimage signaled King's legitimacy and authority as a leader of the movement on the international stage.[21] In addition, King's trip to India, historian Peniel Joseph observes, "introduced him to the ways in which problems of race, poverty, and violence flourished around the world, echoing the civil rights conflicts at home." And further, "He returned to America's domestic civil rights front more aware than ever of the movement's international dimensions."[22]

After a journey to the land of Gandhi, King could not help but see the promise that Gandhian nonviolence (as refracted through his own experience and the mentorship of African American pacifists) offered in transforming a white supremacist colonial state into a place of freedom. This vision is found in the Palm Sunday sermon. King was sharing a global outlook with his audience, in which Gandhi functioned as an icon of the international struggle for freedom.[23] King's iconic Gandhi was a Gandhi for Black America. From Baldwin's brief conversation of

---

[19] Lewis V. Baldwin, "Introduction," in *"In a Single Garment of Destiny" A Global Vision of Justice* (Boston: Beacon, 2014), 55.

[20] Paul Harvey, *Martin Luther King: A Religious Life*, (Lanham, MD; Rowman & Littlefield, 2021), 99–100.

[21] Sean Chabot, "Framing, Transnational Diffusion, and African-American Intellectuals in the Land of Gandhi," *International Review of Social History* 49, Supp (2004): 20.

[22] Peniel E. Joseph, *The Sword and the Shield: The Revolutionary Lives of Malcolm X and Martin Luther King Jr.* (Updated Edition; New York: Basic Books, 2020), 80.

[23] According to Jake Hodder, "When pacifists cast King in the role of America's black Gandhi, therefore, they hardwired him into these global political currents. Moreover, they did so knowingly." These global political currents refer to the pan-African nonviolence anticolonial movements also casting figures in the role of Gandhi. Jake Hodder, "Casting a Black Gandhi: Martin Luther King Jr., American Pacifists and the Global Dynamics of Race." *Journal of American Studies* 55.1 (2021): 63.

King's sermon, we observe: in learning about the struggle of the Other, the audience discovers something about their own struggle.

Agapic-Motivated Nonviolence: The Theme of the Sermon

Finally, the Christian theologian and philosopher Cornel West locates the Palm Sunday Sermon in King's thought on radical love. West situates King's concept of radical love and agapic-nonviolent resistance as a response to the challenges of Marx and Nietzsche.[24] The Palm Sunday sermon, in particular, "lay[s] bare his [King's] profound and poignant hammering out the idea and practice of radical love."[25] West's observations help us to see how the sermon was a development in King's own Christian understanding of nonviolent resistance.

The opening sentences of the sermon direct the audience's attention to the "love of God." King orates, "This is the time in the year when we think of the love of God breaking forth into time out of eternity. This is the time of the year when we come to see that the most powerful forces in the universe are not those forces of military might but those forces of spiritual might." Whatever else the sermon may be about, the sermon, as West points out, is about the power of agapic-motivated nonviolence to transform the world.

In King's study of Gandhian nonviolence, as Peniel Joseph notes, King found Gandhi's concepts particularly appealing in the face of Jim Crow, and equated Gandhi's movement with a collective application of Christ's love.[26] For King, Gandhi's example was proof of the power of Christ's love in a nonviolent freedom movement. King's sermon-focus highlighted the power of love-motivated nonviolent resistance as truly transformative in order to hopefully exhort his audience to follow this path.

---

[24] Cornel West, "Introduction," in *The Radical King* (Boston: Beacon, 2015), 4.
[25] Cornel West, "Introduction," in *The Radical King* (Boston: Beacon, 2015), 4.
[26] Peniel E. Joseph, *The Sword and the Shield: The Revolutionary Lives of Malcolm X and Martin Luther King Jr.* (Updated Edition; New York: Basic Books, 2020), 60.

Part 2: Learning from and Applying Gandhi's Wisdom in the Palm Sunday Sermon

On Palm Sunday 1959, Rev. Dr. Martin Luther King delivered his first sermon in the pulpit at Dexter Avenue Baptist Church in Montgomery, Alabama, since his return from his six-week trip abroad to India with a brief stop in "the Holy Land." Palm Sunday is a significant day in Christianity. It is a remembrance of the "triumphal entry" of Jesus Christ into Jerusalem as depicted in the canonical gospels. In relation to the liturgical calendar, Palm Sunday is the week prior to Easter. All of which is to say that Palm Sunday sermons tend to focus on Jesus and this particular moment in the gospels. On this occasion, however, King expounded on the life of Mohandas K. Gandhi.

King admitted to his audience that he was diverging from the ordinary expectation of the Palm Sunday sermon at the beginning of the sermon. He pleaded with his audience to indulge him to talk about Gandhi. King appealed:

> And I think I'm justified in doing this because I believe this man, more than anybody else in the modern world, caught the spirit of Jesus Christ and lived it more completely in his life. His name was Gandhi, Mohandas K. Gandhi. And after he lived a few years, the poet Tagore, who lived in India, gave him another name: "Mahatma," the great soul. And we know him as Mahatma Gandhi.

Gandhi, their Indian Other, was drawn near to the audience by appeal to the spirit of Jesus Christ. Gandhi in the sermon provided the audience a model to learn how to live as a follower of Christ.

The preacher King was aware of what he "ought" to be preaching and did not wish to stray from the gospel. King anchored his exposition of Gandhi in the biblical text. He moved Gandhi from otherness to Other by use of two verses in the Gospel according to John.[27] King found his justification in talking about Gandhi in John 10:16 and 14:12. The first verse spoke to King's ecumenical "world house" vision and brought Gandhi into alliance with King's Christian audience. The sec-

---

[27] It is not only with the Dexter Avenue Baptist Church that King makes the appeal to John's Jesus. In defending himself against the charge of turning his back on Christianity for a "new kind of American sectarianism" after contributing to the Gandhi Society in 1962, he frames Gandhi as a fulfillment of Jesus's words "I have other sheep that are not of this fold." Lewis V. Baldwin, "Of Their Spiritual Strivings: Malcolm and Martin on Religion and Freedom," in *Between Cross and Crescent: Christian and Muslim Perspectives on Malcolm and Martin*, ed. Lewis V. Baldwin and Amiri YaSin Al-Hadi (Gainesville: University Press of Florida, 2002), 120.

ond verse, King cited prophetically to suggest that Jesus Christ was speaking about the work and result of Gandhi and the Gandhian movement. As one who did greater things than Jesus, Gandhi became the Other from whom the congregation could learn, not just the Hindu independence movement leader in a faraway land they had only read about in the newspaper or in their nonviolence training.

King suggested these two verses apply "more uniquely to the life and work of Mahatma Gandhi than to any other individual in the history of the world." Further, while Gandhi was not a member of a Christian church, King still considered Gandhi "the greatest Christian of the twentieth century." This claim that Gandhi "was a Christian" in a dialogue sense of coming to recognize the "Other" in your terms does not merely reduce the Other to "Christian" but moves an audience to see Gandhi and the Christian audience in common cause. This identification of the Hindu Other in Christian terms is similar to how one of King's interlocutors in India drew him to recognize himself as Hindu and a Dalit.[28]

The wisdom received from the Other is the power of nonviolent resistance to transform the world through the spirit of Jesus and the love of God.

> I would say the first thing that we must see about this life is that Mahatma Gandhi was able to achieve for his people independence through nonviolence means. I think you should underscore this. He was able to achieve for his people independence from the domination of the British Empire without lifting one gun or without uttering one curse word. He did it with the spirit of Jesus in his heart and the love of God, and this was all he had. He had no weapons. He had no army, in terms of military might. And yet he was able to achieve independence from the largest empire in the history of this world without picking up a gun or without any ammunition.[29]

In Gandhi, King suggested—as African Americans had already observed in the previous generation—one struggle against colonial domination becomes a model for another struggle against colonial domination toward freedom. The success of

---

[28] Roy Whitaker provides one more important insight about King's pluralism in the example of King's incorporation of the Indian caste-identity into two sermons. "By intuitively listening and appropriately responding, King transformed into an 'African American Hindu'. Nonetheless, he was neither literally changing religions nor replacing his African American identity with a Hindu-Indian identity." Whitaker continues, "His statement positioned his audience to identify with the African American or Hindu oppressed peoples of the world." Roy Whitaker, "'Our Loyalties Must Be Ecumenical': Martin Luther King, Jr. as a Pluralist Theologian," *Journal of Ecumenical Studies* 51.3 (2016): 412.

[29] All quotes come from "Palm Sunday Sermon on Mohandas K. Gandhi, Delivered at Dexter Avenue Baptist Church," *The Martin Luther King, Jr. Research and Education Institute*, https://kinginstitute.stanford.edu/king-papers/documents/palm-sunday-sermon-mohandas-k-gandhi-delivered-dexter-avenue-baptist-church.

Gandhi gave African Americans proof of concept that a movement could achieve independence through nonviolent means. Even in 1959, after the success of the Montgomery Bus Boycott, questions remained about the efficacy of nonviolence for a broader freedom movement. The sermon offered encouragement to continue with the method of nonviolence. King observed, as did African American religious intellectuals before him, that Gandhi embodied the spirit of Christ and the love of God. Thus, King followed the African American tradition of talking about Gandhi in Christian terms.[30] Christianizing Gandhi had the rhetorical effect of allowing the Christian audience to see their God at work in India, on the side of the people of India against the British Empire. Common cause was made, the Christian audience was invited by King to identify with Gandhi and the people of India.

King was talking to his audience about their own situation through his depiction of Gandhi. Gandhi's method, King suggested, was Christian—based on the Sermon on the Mount section of the Gospel according to Matthew. Further, Gandhi read the same Thoreau that the movement had read and heard about in Montgomery. The challenge, for Gandhi and his followers as well as King and his audience at Dexter Avenue Baptist church, was to resist evil without resorting to violence or to hate—you still needed to love the individual that carries on the evil system.

In King's sermon, Gandhi's first campaign in India became a lesson for the audience about nonviolent resistance and love and understanding. Gandhi was the model for the method, identifying with Gandhi and the Indian people's freedom struggle encouraged the people of Dexter Avenue Baptist Church to adopt the method for the longer struggle, the one after that first victory. As Gandhi's story continued King related how the more well-to-do Indians became involved in the independence movement. It was a challenge to the predominantly Black middle class congregation of Dexter Avenue Baptist Church that there is more to do, perhaps even work that would require the loss of personal power and wealth that comes from their jobs.

King used Gandhi's Salt March as an example of nonviolent resistance in action. In telling the story, King put words into Gandhi's mouth that the African American audience would have been familiar with in their own freedom struggle: "some of us might have to die" and "some of us might be thrown in jail," but "let us just keep moving." For King's sermon, the Salt March illustrated the power of unified nonviolent resistance when a people resist an unjust law. This power defeated the British Empire. As the audience continued to identify with the Indian people and Gandhi, they were being encouraged to struggle against evil in their

---

[30] See Paul Harvey, *Martin Luther King,* for numerous examples of King Christianizing Gandhi for U.S. Christian audiences.

own colonized context. King emphasized the way of love and understanding goodwill as Gandhi's chosen path. This emphasis pointed to the positive ethos of Gandhi's nonviolent philosophy.

In describing the Gandhian philosophy of nonviolence and its effectiveness in transforming society, King offered an idealized version of post-independence India whose resistance to the British Empire did not result in the people of India and the people of Britain remaining enemies but, through the way of love and understanding goodwill, they became friends. The lesson to be learned by the audience: The struggle was not over until a new friendship and reconciliation exists. Such a transformative aim does not skip the steps of the struggle which would allow the oppressor to remain oppressor. Nonviolent direct action is not merely a tactic, it seeks to transform society, with the implication that the enemy is won over and transformed into the friend.

King expounded on the personal character traits of Gandhi to develop a role model for the movement. King seemed to be asking the congregation of Dexter Avenue to be like Gandhi—the man who transformed dominating imperial relations to bring freedom to the people of India. Gandhi as an authoritative icon helped to exemplify the radical characteristics pastor King sought to develop in his audience and himself: self-discipline so that his public and private, his outward and his inward self were not in conflict; identifying with the masses absolutely; renouncing the world with respect to property; and has the capacity for self-criticism.

By painting an idealized picture of Gandhi overcoming the caste system, King provided his audience with a vision of a possible future in America that nonviolent direct action could offer. The vision invited the Dexter Avenue audience to imagine America's Dalits and America's high caste Brahmins singing and praising God together. King used the caste system example to show that Gandhi "was just as firm against doing something about that as he was about doing away with the exploitation of the British Empire." This example may have even challenged the audience to not just see Gandhi's wisdom as how to gain Black freedom in America, but also how to achieve freedom among other marginalized people in society.

While Gandhi was the authoritative Other whose wisdom King drew from, the sermon finished with a focus on Christ. Gandhi, the Other, is not Christ. He must in this moment fade back to otherness, allowing the Christian audience to return their thoughts to Palm Sunday and its significance for them. This was accomplished by King connecting Gandhi's murder to the assassination of Lincoln and the crucifixion of Christ. King finally weaved back in seasonal themes for the Christian audience. The message of the death of Gandhi, or the death of Lincoln, was not one of defeat.

King returned to God's appeal for this present age:

> "He who lives by the sword shall perish by the sword." Jesus said it years ago. Whenever men follow that and see that way, new horizons begin to emerge and a new world unfolds. Who today will follow Christ in his way and follow it so much that we'll be able to do greater things even than he did because we will be able to bring about the peace of the world and mobilize hundreds and thousands of men to follow the way of Christ?

King's exhortation to his audience blended the life of Gandhi and the way of nonviolence he lived, with the wisdom of Christ. So the exhortation was not "who will follow Gandhi and do greater things than he" but who "will follow Christ" with the aim of bringing about world peace.

In the closing prayer of his sermon, King maintained the oneness of God while making connections to other religious traditions:

> O God, our gracious Heavenly Father, we thank Thee for the fact that you have inspired men and women in all nations and in all cultures. We call you different names: some call Thee Allah; some call you Elohim; some call you Jehovah; some call you Brahma; and some call you the Unmoved Mover; some call you the Architectonic Good. But we know that these are all names for one and the same God, and we know you are one.

Where the religion of the Other might seem a barrier, King and his theological understanding of God's oneness allowed him to see commonality amongst humanity's religious traditions. This commonality helped King to share the wisdom of Others, even on Palm Sunday.

In short, the sermon was an exhortation to congregation and pastor alike to learn from and enact Gandhi's wisdom in a world where bussing might be desegregated but white supremacy, capitalist exploitation, and America's imperial desires and bellicose behaviors threatened not just the future of the members of Dexter Avenue Baptist Church, African Americans, and the poor and exploited members of society, but everyone.

Conclusion

In conclusion, King's Palm Sunday Sermon on Mohandas K. Gandhi hopefully exhorted his Dexter Avenue Baptist Church audience to learn from the wisdom and experience of their Hindu Other to struggle for Black Freedom in America. While the Other may be a non-Christian, King's exposition of Gandhi discovered, like an earlier generation of Christian African Americans discovered, a Christian foundation for understanding Gandhi's philosophy of nonviolence. For King, Gandhi's method in practice was evidence of the power of God's agapic love. King was able to legitimize Gandhi's wisdom by appeals to the gospel. The audience was prepared for such a sermon through earlier bridge-building between international freedom movements that paid attention to the struggles against racist oppression in America and British colonialism in India, and the local experience of the Montgomery Bus Boycott.

A transformative event can happen when the Other draws close; knowledge and understanding, while partial, is shared; the two parties are not the same as they were prior to their relationship. King's sermon sought to encourage this sort of relationship between the Gandhians and his community. His aim was not for Gandhi to "be" a Christian; rather, King temporarily brought Gandhi close to show two particular peoples' common cause and to share Gandhi's wisdom in order to develop and strengthen his audience's Christian nonviolent philosophy for the Black Freedom Movement in America. Perhaps there is a lesson for us today: By being in relation with one's Others, one can share wisdom across religious and cultural divides, find common cause, and adapt and apply the Other's wisdom to one's own context and, in the process, be transformed. Such encounters allow for the particularity of one's religious identity to remain (although transformed), while also providing a conception of interreligious collaboration for common cause in a polyreligious world working toward universal liberation.

Bibliography

Harvey, Paul. 2021. *Martin Luther King: A Religious Life*. Lantham, MD: Rowman & Littlefield.
Joseph, Peniel E. 2020. *The Sword and the Shield: The Revolutionary Lives of Malcolm X and Martin Luther King Jr.* Updated ed. New York: Basic Books.
King, Martin L. 2014. *"In a Single Garment of Destiny": A Global Vision of Justice*. Edited by Lewis V. Baldwin. Boston: Beacon Press.
———.2015. *The Radical King*. Edited by Cornel West. Boston: Beacon Press.
Patel, Eboo. 2013. Martin Luther King Jr. and the Light of Other Faiths. *Cross Currents* 63 (3): 270–275.
Roberson, Houston B. 2013 (2005). *Fighting the Good Fight: The Story of the Dexter Avenue King Memorial Baptist Church, 1865–1977*. New York: Routledge.

John W. Fadden earned his PhD in Religious and Theological Studies from the University of Denver Iliff School of Theology through their Joint Doctoral Program. Previously, Dr. Fadden earned an MDiv from Colgate Rochester Crozer Divinity School. Since 2011, Dr. Fadden has been teaching at St. John Fisher University in the Religious Studies Department. It should be noted that Dr. Fadden teaches Martin & Malcolm, which is a course that explores the religious and political lives of Martin Luther King, Jr., and Malcolm X, focusing on their contribution to the Black Freedom Movement. Dr. Fadden has presented papers at numerous national and international conferences, including the annual Society of Biblical Literature meetings and the "Sacred Texts and Human Contexts" conferences.

Encountering God's Grace in Islam: A Christian Reading of the Forty Hadith of Nawawī

Hans A. Harmakaputra

Introduction

As a Christian who grew up in Indonesia, the country with the largest Muslim population in the world, I occasionally heard Christian preachers contrasting Christianity with Islam concerning the mode of attaining salvation. Christians believe salvation comes as God's grace, and that grace enables humans to have faith and do what is good. In other words, one's good conduct would not save the person. In contrast, Islam is portrayed as a religion that teaches salvation as a mechanical procedure where humans must do more good than evil conduct because Allah will determine their status based on what they did. In other words, there is a presumptuous idea among Christians that grace is a foreign concept in Islam. This misleading thought, unfortunately, is not exclusively circulated in Indonesia. There are quite a number of Christians around the world who subscribe to a similar paradigm that divides Christianity and Islam in the matter of grace, particularly among more conservative Christian groups.

Such a comparison is based on a misconception of Muslim tradition stemming from a superficial understanding of Islam. Perception of people of other faiths

H. A. Harmakaputra (✉)
Department of Philosophy, Religion, and Classics, Augustana University,
Sioux Falls, SD, USA
e-mail: hans.harmakaputra@augie.edu

stems from biases, and the lack of knowledge is deplorable, if not dangerous, because it reinforces negative stereotypes and harms interfaith relations. It is also counterproductive to the goal of interreligious endeavors to bring people closer to each other through dialogue. In a pluralistic society today, it is crucial to support interfaith works by dismantling theological perceptions that support an exclusionary stance toward others.

This essay explores the idea of grace in Muslim tradition as a way to rectify the popular misconception about Islam using comparative theology.[1] As a Christian, my engagement with Muslim traditions has convinced me that God's grace is foundational in Islam and is instructive for Muslim practices. Grace might not be a popular word, but different religious aspects are connected to it. Three interrelated aspects of God's grace are elaborated in this essay: salvation, human freedom, and social dimension. As in Christianity, God's grace is related to the notion of mercy and forgiveness of God that intertwined with human faith. Moreover, human freedom and action are not autonomous. Instead, they are rooted in God's grace.

This essay limits its focus to the Forty Hadith of Nawawī, a popular book of selected hadiths derived primarily from the Sunni canonical hadith collections. The following section surveys the idea of grace in the tradition focusing on the Qur'an and several prominent Muslim thinkers. The third section provides a brief explanation of hadith and the place of hadith in the Muslim community from a Sunni perspective. Finally, I will elaborate on several examples from the Forty Hadith of Nawawī and how they are connected to the concept of God's grace.

Grace in Christianity and Islam

The Concept of Grace in Christianity

The illustration at the beginning of this essay portrays how Islam is depicted as having no concept of grace. In other words, for some Christians, Islam is a religion of good work, which is different from Christianity as a religion of grace. This binary concept of good work and grace follows the classical account of Pelagianism versus Augustine of Hippo (d. 430 CE). Augustine, a prominent Church father, rejects Pelagianism's fundamental belief in humans' own capacity to attain salvation through sheer free will. Instead of being complementary, Augustine asserts that grace is the main instrument for human salvation and that this grace is a free gift

---

[1] Comparative theology can generate different types of learning, including rectification. Rectification involves the reestablishment of proper understanding of the other.

from God. Humans have fallen into sin since the time of Adam and sin distorts even humans' free will, making them unable to produce good works. Augustine's basic premise that grace from God is essential in human salvation becomes the foundation for the Christian understanding of human existence. Framing the comparison between Islam and Christianity as similar to the debate between Pelagianism and Augustine is erroneous as it suggests only a caricatural account of grace in each religious tradition. A more rigorous theological explanation of grace is necessary to construct a better comparison. This part briefly explains Christian perspectives on grace before investigating the notion of grace in Islam.

Grace as God's Self-Communication

Karl Rahner formulated one of the most influential views of grace in Christian theology (1904–1984 CE). Rahner understands God's revelation as God's self-communication, which he identifies as grace. The divine communicative action is grace because its very purpose is to bring universal salvation to all. Thus it is clear that the communication of God is the revelation of God's own being and "in this way it is a communication for the sake of knowing and possessing God in immediate vision and love."[2] The universal aspect of God's self-communication is indispensable in Rahner's theological system because God's grace permeates all creation and exists outside the church's boundary.

In this way of understanding grace, Rahner overturned the traditional Scholastic theology of grace that focused primarily on "created grace" over "uncreated grace." Shaped heavily by Thomas Aquinas' idea of grace, "created grace" refers to divine gifts that are not God but are above humans' natural powers, a quality of the human soul infused by God.[3] On the other hand, "uncreated grace" is not a divine gift, but God's self as present in the recipient that initiates and enables a divine-human relationship. Rahner gave priority to the "uncreated grace," which is God's self-communication.

Christian theology always maintains that grace is given as "unmerited" and totally as a gift from God. For Rahner, the "unmerited" feature means that grace is absolutely gratuitous as God's free act is based on love, given even before "any and every sinful rejection of God by a finite subject."[4] As recipients of grace, human

---

[2] Karl Rahner, *Foundations of Christian Faith: An Introduction to the Idea of Christianity* (New York: Seabury, 1978), 117–18.

[3] Roger Haight, "Sin and Grace," in *Systematic Theology: Roman Catholic Perspectives*, Vol. 2, eds., Francis Schüssler Fiorenza and John P. Galvin (Minneapolis, MN: Fortress Press, 1991), 109.

[4] Rahner, *Foundations of Christian Faith*, 123.

beings and their structures of consciousness have been changed so that God will always be their ultimate orientation as the horizon to which they are drawn. This intrinsic process within the human structure is why Christian theology recognizes grace as "supernatural," elevating human beings beyond themselves.[5]

From this perspective, as Roger Haight notes, grace is not a countermeasure of sin to restore the perverse human nature. Rather, "God's gracious and salvific intent precedes creation; God creates human beings because God intends an interpersonal dialogue with creatures who can respond."[6] Against this backdrop, creation is integral to God's grace as an expression of God's self-revelation and love.

Grace and Human Freedom

Christian tradition offers a broad spectrum of positions regarding human freedom. Although the idea of Pelagianism is rejected, God's grace is never understood as completely controlling human freedom. The Christian tradition from Augustine to Aquinas portrays grace as working together with and transforming human freedom. Martin Luther, the Protestant Reformer, prioritizes grace that forgives sin to the extent that human freedom is minimized.[7] However, it does not mean humans are no longer responsible for their deeds. Instead, God's grace empowers human freedom so it no longer operates under the bondage of sin. Haight states that God's grace "expands the horizon of freedom and opens up human creativity to values beyond self, implicitly in the direction of God and divine values."[8] Grace connects humans with God and orients human freedom toward God. As a result, God's grace and human freedom are not necessarily in competition with one another.

Still, God's grace and human freedom are not operating on the same level. Unlike God, who transcends history, humans are finite beings bound to operate on the level of history. Therefore, even though human work results from human freedom and God's grace, the distinction must be maintained. Haight explains,

> On one level, God sustains human freedom in being by creation, while God's presence and influence of love inform its self-transcending character. On another level, what is done in this world on the level of history is manifestly the creation of human freedom. Thus the whole of salvific action is performed by human freedom wholly sustained by grace.[9]

---

[5] Rahner, *Foundations of Christian Faith*, 123.
[6] Haight, "Sin and Grace," 116.
[7] Haight, "Sin and Grace," 120.
[8] Haight, "Sin and Grace," 122.
[9] Haight, "Sin and Grace," 124.

Humans are free to exercise their freedom. Yet, it is not entirely autonomous because of the cooperation with God's grace.

Social Dimension of Grace

The emergence of liberation theology in the twentieth century, along with other theological views from the perspectives of the marginalized, has enriched the discourse on sin to include the notion of social or structural sin. Sin is not only a summative of faulty or wrong things a person does because sin can exist within the social structures of human society. Unjust and oppressive systems are examples of social sin. Transforming such structures requires more than personal repentance. Proponents of liberation theology view grace as more than God's gratuitous gift for salvation of the soul but "as a liberating force in public, social life."[10] The social dimension of grace denotes how human beings mediate grace in the world through transforming society.

Haight defines social grace as "the institutionalization and objectification of the dynamics of grace originating in personal-individual freedom."[11] From this perspective, human freedom has a specific purpose. Since human freedom can potentially be creative and destructive, reflecting human nature's ambivalence, God's grace influences human freedom to create graced social structures. The classical Christian virtue of love of neighbor is at the core of this endeavor. Yet, its interpretation is not limited to interpersonal relations but must also be understood concerning people's social existence. In other words, participation in building social structures that reflect God's will of justice, peace, and love is a form of loving one's neighbor.[12]

Grace in Islam

Revelation as God's Initiative

Grace as God's self-communication in Christianity demonstrates the nature of God as compassionate and caring to the creatures: God works in history to reconcile the primordial relationship between creatures and God. In the Christian tradition, the notion of grace as God's gratuitous gift and not human privilege highlights this foundational belief. Grace is, first and foremost, God's initiative, not humans.

---

[10] Haight, "Sin and Grace," 111.
[11] Haight, "Sin and Grace," 130.
[12] Haight, "Sin and Grace," 131–32.

Similarly, Islam emphasizes God's active presence in history through God's revelation that reminds all humans of their primordial covenant with the Creator. Qur'an 7:172 describes,

> And when thy Lord took from the Children of Adam, from their loins, their progeny and made them bear witness concerning themselves, "Am I not your Lord?" they said, "Yea, we bear witness"—lest you should say on the Day of Resurrection, "Truly of this we were heedless."[13]

In this verse, God called human beings even before they came into existence and created a covenant. This primordial covenant left human beings with an imprint of God and their relationship with God in their soul. It is connected with the concept of *fiṭrah* as the innate nature of human beings with an endowed capacity to recognize God. The *fiṭrah* gives humans moral responsibility, even if they forget this primordial covenant.[14]

The Qur'an mentions different covenants between God and the believers in general, as well as with Abraham, the Israelites, and others. Nevertheless, the covenant in this verse is unique because it is unmediated and universal: God made the pact directly and with all humanity.[15] The verse also suggests that revelation becomes God's initiative to remind people of God and this covenant. All the prophets and messengers sent by God to humankind were instrumental in establishing their relationship with God, retelling them of their obligation, and warning them against disobedience.

Mona Siddiqui, a prominent Muslim scholar, notes that the Qur'an might not reference an intimate relationship between humans and God as in the Christian concept of God as "Father." Instead, God's goodness and compassion lie in God's salvific action for humankind through prophets and "it is ultimately God's grace that reconciles humankind to God."[16] The Quranic phrase "We are nearer to him than his jugular vein (50:16)" poignantly expresses this relationship: God's continuous effort to reach out to humans even if they fail to recognize God and to maintain the connection with God.[17]

---

[13] Seyyed Hossein Nasr, et al., *The Study Quran: A New Translation and Commentary* (New York: HarperCollins, 2015), 466.

[14] Nasr, *The Study Quran*, 467.

[15] Nasr, *The Study Quran*, 467.

[16] Mona Siddiqui, *The Good Muslim: Reflections on Classical Islamic Law and Theology* (Cambridge: Cambridge University Press, 2012), 152.

[17] Nasr, *The Study Quran*, 1267.

Human Freedom and God's Will

In Sunni Muslim tradition, the classical discourse on human freedom focuses on destiny (*qadr*). The Mu'tazilites, who flourished between the eighth and tenth century CE, approach the issue of human freedom from a rationalist position to maintain God's justice. In their view, humans are agents of their actions. If humans are not entirely responsible for their actions, it will jeopardize God's justice. However, this approach undermines the importance of the Divine Command as understood by the majority of Muslim tradition. The defeat of the Mu'tazilites has paved the way for the Ashʿarite school to dominate the discourse. While the Mu'tazilites became notorious as an "unorthodox" position within the Sunni theological schools, the Ashʿarite position remains the standard until now.

Abū al-Hasan al-Ashʿarī (d. 936 CE), the founder of the Ashʿarite school, generated a middle way between the total predeterminism by God's will and the autonomy of human's will through the idea of "acquisition" (*kasb*). According to this idea, God creates human actions, both good and evil, and those actions are "acquired" by humans. However, this position does not diminish the human's responsibility while adhering to divine sovereignty as reflected in the mainstream belief that "there is no power except through God" (*lā hawla walā quwwata illā billāh*).

To illustrate these schools' positions, I will provide an example.[18] X holds a knife and uses it to stab Y. Due to this action, Y is injured and finally dies. Is God responsible for Y's death? Or is X accountable for his actions? From a total deterministic point of view that believes in the totality of divine will, God holds the responsibility because X's action does not belong to the person. If, according to fate, Y's time had been over, he would have died through another means if not for X's action. The Mu'tazilite position holds X liable because humans are the creators of their actions. If X did not stab the knife, Y would not die. According to the Ashʿarite position, if X does not use the knife, we do not know whether Y is still alive or not.

Social Dimension of Grace

Islam regulates human conduct not only on an individual but also on a societal level. Thus, there are different ways to express the social dimension of grace. Here the focus is on hospitality. Siddiqui notes that hospitality in the Qur'ān is not mere "acts of kindness but as moral imperatives and ethical commands .... when two people meet, God is always present."[19] From this perspective, hospitality is not

---

[18] I modified an illustration cited in Salih Sayilgan, *Exploring Islam: Theology and Spiritual Practice in America* (Minneapolis, MN: Fortress, 2021), 120–21.

[19] Mona Siddiqui, *Hospitality and Islam: Welcoming in God's Name* (New Haven, CT: Yale University Press, 2015), 29.

limited to providing guests with food, shelter, and conversation; it can mean different things.

First, hospitality can mean inviting people we want to build relationships with into our house. However, the tradition speaks strongly about welcoming strangers, such as in the story of Abraham receiving an angel in his house.[20] Second, the Qur'ān and *sunna* link hospitality with charity or giving, especially toward people experiencing poverty. Third, the tradition urges people to be hospitable to travelers, especially pilgrims who travel for spiritual purposes.[21] Last, even when someone does not have any means to give or is not in a position to help others, at the least, he can refrain from harming others and it is already considered a charitable act.[22]

The Place of Hadiths in the Muslim Community

Development and Authority

Hadiths (Ar. sing. *hadīth*; pl. *ahādīth*) are highly regarded by Muslim communities, whose authority is only second to the Qur'an.[23] If the Qur'an is considered the word of God, then hadiths display Prophet Muhammad's words and deeds, demonstrating how to live according to God's will. In hadiths, the word of God manifests in human actions. Therefore, following Prophet Muhammad's examples is considered the highest objective of a Muslim, which may lead to the best life a Muslim could ever have.

The importance of hadith as the penultimate authoritative source in the Sunni tradition was formulated gradually. It was Muhammad b. Idrīs al-Shāfi'ī (d. 820 CE), one of the founders of Sunni legal schools (*madhaib*), who argued that hadiths attributed to Prophet Muhammad are superior to other figures and helped to establish the importance of the *sunna*.[24] Al-Shāfi'ī was successful in mediating the debate between the proponents of tradition (*ahl al-hadīth*), who reject any reasoning, and the proponents of reasoning (*ahl al-Ra'y*). According to him, analogical rea-

---

[20] Siddiqui, *Hospitality and Islam*, 25–26, 30.

[21] Siddiqui, *Hospitality and Islam*, 31, 48.

[22] Siddiqui, *Hospitality and Islam*, 66.

[23] Technically, the second most authoritative source for Muslims is the *sunna* or Prophet Muhammad's examples. However, those examples are preserved, transmitted, and understood through hadiths. Jonathan Brown, *Hadith: Muhammad's Legacy in the Medieval and Modern World* (Oxford: Oneworld, 2009), 3.

[24] Brown, *Hadith*, 29.

soning is authoritative only after the Qur'an, hadith, and *ijmā*. James Robson states that al-Shāfiʿī argument was built upon a Qur'anic phrase, "the Book and the Wisdom" (e.g., see *al-Baqara* verse 151), which shows hadiths as not merely records of the Prophet's life but that were subjected to divine guidance. Later on, another issue arose about determining the validity of each hadith that had numerously circulated then.

Muslims have been interested in what Prophet Muhammad did and said since he was still alive. Soon after his death, people circulated traditions about his deeds and sayings through oral transmission. Naturally, many Muslims recorded the traditions about the Prophet in written form for their own use. However, the records were not assembled systematically as in the later time when scholars started to compile hadith collections. There used to be hundreds of thousands of traditions that went through a thorough examination to determine the validity of each tradition. The output of such effort is what today is known as hadith collections. For example, al-Bukhāri said that he had examined 600,000 *ahādīth* and what was included in his *Ṣaḥīḥ* are only 7275 traditions, including some repetitions.[25] One of the criteria for determining the validity of a hadith is an analysis of the chain of transmitters (*isnād*).[26] Generally, there are four categories based on their validation level: sound (*ṣaḥīḥ*), fair (*ḥasan*), weak (*ḍaʿīf*), and fabricated (*mawdūʿ*).[27]

In the eleventh century, the Sunnis recognized six canonical hadith collections as the most authoritative ones. Those are *Ṣaḥīḥ* of Bukhāri (d. 870 CE), *Ṣaḥīḥ* of Muslim (d. 875 CE) and four *Sunan* of Abū Dawūd (d. 888 CE), al-Tirmidhī (d. 892 CE), al-Nasā'ī (d. 915 CE), and Ibn Mājah (d. 915 CE). The two *ṣaḥīḥ* books were quickly accepted by Muslim communities since their beginning, while Ibn Mājah was the last among the six to get recognition.[28]

Divine Sayings (Hadith Qudsī)

Most hadiths record Prophet Muhammad's activities and sayings and this genre of hadith is called hadith *nabawī*. However, there is a distinctive type of hadith that contains God's acts and sayings known as hadith *qudsī* or divine sayings. The *isnād*

---

[25] Aisha Y. Musa, "Ḥadīth Studies," in *The Bloomsbury Companion to Islamic Studies*, ed. Clinton Bennett (London: Bloomsbury, 2015), 80; Brown, *Hadith*, 32.
[26] Different criteria and complexities of early *hadīth* criticism can be seen in Brown, *Hadith*, chapter 3.
[27] Musa, "Ḥadīth Studies," 78.
[28] Musa, "Ḥadīth Studies," 82. For more detailed description Brown, *Hadith*, chapter 2.

of a divine saying goes back to God, not to the prophet. Nonetheless, they are considered as hadith and not of the Qur'ān. The reason is that the wording did not come from God but from Prophet Muhammad; only their meanings are from God. Muslims also believe that while the Qur'ān were directly dictated one word after another from God to Prophet Muhammad through Angel Gabriel, the divine sayings came during the Prophet's ascension to heaven (*Miʿrāj*), in his dreams, or through divine inspiration (*ilhām*).[29]

Divine sayings are scattered in many books, from canonical collections to other hadith compilations. In the later period, some scholars compiled divine sayings in one book, such as Muhammād al-Madanī (d. 1786 CE) or, the more famous one, Ibn al-Arabī (d. 1240 CE), who wrote *Mishkāt al-Anwār*.[30] *Mishkāt al-Anwār* contains 101 divine sayings and has become an excellent resource for Sufis.

The Importance of Hadith

Since the time of Shafiʿī, hadiths have become the second most authoritative source in Islamic jurisprudence (*fiqh*). All aspects of Muslim life use hadiths primarily, from worship to domestic matters, business ethics to dressing code, and others that came under the purview of Islamic jurisprudence.[31] However, even though hadith is mainly read in connection with *fiqh*, one should remember that the Prophet himself was not a legal jurist who established Islamic law. Rather, he was busy with moral and political matters of the people. Therefore, many local customs were accepted and practiced by Muslims during the prophet's time. Looking from this vantage point, hadith plays a significant role in cultivating both the individual and society's moral and ethical aspects.

For ordinary people, who are not jurists, hadiths function as a compass to guide their practical lives regarding morals and ethics. What seems to be a doctrinal or theological matter is always interconnected to moral and ethical obligations as a Muslim. For instance, among Muslims in Indonesia, it is acceptable to allow the

---

[29] Brown, *Hadith*, 62.

[30] Brown, *Hadith*, 62.

[31] The science of Islamic jurisprudence since its very beginning was closely related to the traditions of the Prophet Muhammad and the companions, but the inclusion of written prophetic sayings in the formative period of Islamic law was a complex and gradual process. For a concise explanation of the relationship between hadith and jurisprudence, see Brown, *Hadith*, chapter 5.

use of weak (*ḍāif*) hadiths for the purpose of good deeds, including teaching good morals and virtue, while using weak hadiths for formulating law is prohibited.[32]

Muslims' use of hadith for piety and moral guidance became the reason for the wide popularity of a shorter compilation of hadiths throughout history. Forty hadith collections are one of the most popular genres after the six canonical hadith books were formed. A particular hadith cited to justify the practice of compiling forty hadiths is this: "Whoever memorizes for my community forty hadiths from my *sunna*, I will be his intercessor on the Day of Judgement."[33] Even though many hadith critics ascribe its status as weak (*ḍaʿīf*), it has motivated scholars to collect forty hadith and shaped the hadith culture and scholarship. For instance, most forty hadith collections do not cite whole chains of transmission (*isnād*). Instead, each hadith only has the name of the companion who heard it from the Prophet. This abbreviated style of *isnād* became a distinctive feature of the post-canonical hadith literature, which differs from the canonical hadith period that demanded a full *isnād* per hadith. The development of the forty-hadith genre also influenced the Muslim practice of memorizing certain hadiths for education and piety.[34]

Among many forty hadith collections, al-Nawawī's *Forty Hadith* is arguably the most famous. It was written in the thirteenth century CE by Imām Yaḥyā ibn Sharaf al-Dīn al-Nawawī (d. 1277 CE) and has inspired scholars to produce a large number of commentaries. Jonathan A. C. Brown adds that it is also one of the most widely read books besides the Qur'an among Sunni Muslims.[35]

A Christian Reading of the Forty Hadith of Nawawī

This section comprises a selection of hadiths from the Forty Hadith of Nawawī.[36] The focus is on how they connect to God's grace based on three categories: God's love and forgiveness, human freedom and virtuous deeds, and hospitality.

---

[32] This practice is rooted in the tradition in which the concept *faḍā'il al-ʿamāl* states that using weak hadith for the purposes of virtuous deeds are acceptable.

[33] Brown, *Hadith*, 55.

[34] Brown, *Hadith*, 55–56.

[35] Brown, *Hadith*, 56.

[36] Due to the limited space, I only cited the content of the hadith. The English translation of all hadiths are taken from Ezzeddin Ibrahim and Denys Johnson-Davies, trans., *An-Nawawī's Forty Hadith: An Anthology of the Sayings of the Prophet Muhammad* (Cambridge: The Islamic Texts Society, 1997).

God's Love and Forgiveness

Grace as God's self-communication signifies how salvation is primarily God's initiative that gratuitously invites human beings into a relationship with God, not because of humans' meritorious actions. In Islam, the divine revelation through numerous prophets and messengers to remind human beings of their primordial covenant with their Creator demonstrates grace profoundly. When humans respond positively to the invitation, they enter a personal relationship with God. This personal tone does not mean God and humans are equal, but rather emphasizes the nature of God as compassionate and merciful.

Hadith 31 states: "A man came to the Prophet (may the blessings and peace of Allah be upon him) and said: O Messenger of Allah, direct me to an act which, if I do it, [will cause] Allah to love me and people to love me. He said: Renounce the world and Allah will love you, and renounce what people possess and people will love you."[37] The hadith points out that attachment to this world, i.e., wealth, obstructs one's relationship with God.

The themes of God's love and forgiveness are presented in these divine sayings. Hadith 38 narrates,

> Allah the Almighty has said: Whoever shows enmity to a friend of Mine, I shall be at war with him. My servant does not draw near to Me with anything more loved by Me than the religious duties I have imposed upon him, and My servant continues to draw near to Me with supererogatory works so that I shall love him. When I love him I am his hearing with which he hears, his seeing with which he sees, his hand with which he strikes, and his foot with which he walks. Were he to ask [something] of Me, I would surely give it to him; and were he to ask Me for refuge, I would surely grant him it.[38]

This hadith is well known among Muslims and has generated different interpretations. For instance, it is used among Sufis to refer to the revered status of Friends of God (*awliyā' Allāh*) and their intercessory power. However, for many Muslims, the hadith recommends that Muslims complement the required religious duties with performing supererogatory works to become more intimate with God.

Another rendering theme of a relationship with God is hadith 24:

> O My servants, all of you are astray except for those I have guided, so seek guidance of Me and I shall guide you. O My servants, all of you are hungry except for those I

---

[37] *An-Nawawī's Forty Hadith*, 104.

[38] *An-Nawawī's Forty Hadith*, 118.

have fed, so seek food of Me and I shall feed you. O My servants, all of you are naked except for those I have clothed, so seek clothing of Me and I shall clothe you. O My servants, you sin by night and by day, and I forgive all sins, so seek forgiveness of Me and I shall forgive you.[39]

Besides emphasizing the relationship between a faithful and God, the hadith also speaks about human limitation and disposition toward sinful behaviors while highlighting God's forgiveness. In a similar vein, hadith 42 depicts the vastness of God's mercy in this way:

Allah the Almighty has said: O son of Adam, so long as you call upon Me and ask of Me, I shall forgive you for what you have done, and I shall not mind. O son of Adam, were your sins to reach the clouds of the sky and were you then to ask forgiveness of Me, I would forgive you. O son of Adam, were you to come to Me with sins nearly as great as the earth and were you then to face Me, ascribing no partner to Me, I would bring you forgiveness nearly as great as it.[40]

Humans should not equate God's forgiveness with the freedom to do as one wishes or mistake it for complacency. Instead, a person who responds positively to God's initiative knows her place as God's servant and will not abuse God's mercy and compassion by acting irresponsibly. Teachings on forgiveness are also exhortations so humans will not live in despair amid their imperfections. Instead, they should focus on producing good deeds. Therefore, a general reminder of good conduct, as in hadith 18, is essential: "Fear Allah wherever you are, and follow up a bad deed with a good one and it will wipe it out, and behave well towards people."[41]

Human Freedom and God's Will

A relationship with God does not suggest equality: humans are creations, and God is the Creator. However, a person whose mind is oriented toward God knows her responsibility as a servant of God. As mentioned, the mainstream Sunni tradition favors the Ash'arite position that balances human freedom and God's will. Hadith 37 recounts Prophet Muhammad stating:

Allah has written down the good deeds and the bad ones. Then He explained it [by saying that] he who has intended a good deed and has not done it, Allah writes it down

---

[39] A part of hadith 24. *An-Nawawī's Forty Hadith*, 80.
[40] *An-Nawawī's Forty Hadith*, 126.
[41] *An-Nawawī's Forty Hadith*, 66.

with Himself as a full good deed, but if he has intended it and has done it, Allah writes it down with Himself as from ten good deeds to seven hundred times, or many times over. But if he has intended a bad deed and has not done it, Allah writes it down with Himself as a full good deed, but if he has intended it and has done it, Allah writes it down as one bad deed.[42]

This particular hadith contradicts the misconception of Christians who think Islam is a religion that operates with the cold, mechanic procedure of calculating good and evil deeds, which is perhaps more applicable to the Mu'tazilites position. It also highlights the importance of having good intentions.

Ideally, a person of faith should unite her intention with God's will. However, discerning the will of God is arduous, so following what is prescribed as religious duties is preferable. Hadith 6 explains:

> That which is lawful is plain and that which is unlawful is plain and between the two of them are doubtful matters about which not many people know. Thus he who avoids doubtful matters clears himself in regard to his religion and his honor, but he who falls into that which is unlawful, like the shepherd who pastures around a sanctuary, all but grazing therein. Truly every king has a sanctuary, and truly Allah's sanctuary is His prohibitions. Truly in the body there is a morsel of flesh which, if it be whole, all the body is whole and which, if it be diseased, all of it is diseased. Truly it is the heart.[43]

On the other hand, one's conscience is integral to the discernment. Hadith 20 recounts the Prophet saying: "Among the words people obtained from the First Prophecy are: If you feel no shame, then do as you wish."[44]

Social Dimension of Grace

The relationship with God must also be translatable into a love of neighbors. Hadith 13 resembles the second part of the "Golden Rule" in Christianity: None of you [truly] believes until he wishes for his brother what he wishes for himself.[45] It accentuates how one's faith correlates with one's conduct toward other human beings. Hadith 15 narrates, "Let him who believes in Allah and the Last Day either speak good or keep silent, and let him who believes in Allah and the Last Day be generous to his neighbor, and let him who believes in Allah and the Last Day be

---

[42] *An-Nawawī's Forty Hadith*, 116.
[43] *An-Nawawī's Forty Hadith*, 42.
[44] *An-Nawawī's Forty Hadith*, 72.
[45] *An-Nawawī's Forty Hadith*, 56.

generous to his guest.[46] The hadith also underlines the importance of hospitality, whether to their neighbors or strangers, as discussed earlier in the essay.

An indispensable part of human relationships in society, seen as a core belief in Islam, is preventing injustices and oppression. Some hadiths speak directly about this theme. Hadith 34 reports, "Whosoever of you sees an evil action, let him change it with his hand; and if he is not able to do so, then with his tongue; and if he is not able to do so, then with his heart—and that is the weakest of faith."[47] In some situations, one cannot speak against injustices and oppressions without risking their life, let alone partaking in a physical struggle to change the situation. An example of this situation is when someone lives under a despotic ruler where free speech is prohibited. Even under this extreme duress, a faithful person must do her best to enact justice in whatever capacity. At the least, one must recognize the evil action at heart. In ordinary circumstances, this saying encourages people to participate actively in creating a good society.

Conclusion

The primary purpose of this essay is to study the notion of grace in Islam as a means to counter the misconceived definition of Islam and Christianity as a religion of work and a religion of grace. Such a binary way of dividing the two religions generates a false sense of superiority derived from a shallow, if not distorted, understanding of Islam. I do not claim to solve the issue in its entirety because numerous parts of the Muslim tradition are left unexplored. Rather, this is a humble endeavor to trace the notion of grace, mainly through reading the Forty Hadith of Nawawī. As a Christian, I found that the idea of God's grace in Islam is interwoven with the belief in God's mercy and forgiveness, human freedom and God's will, and the imperative to do good in interpersonal relations and society. The comparison is not meant as just an academic exercise but primarily to rectify the misconception of Islam among Christians. Indeed, distortive understanding of the other remains one of the main obstacles in today's Christian-Muslim dialogues. I hope this essay contributes to better mutual understanding and stimulates more discussion on this topic. God knows best.

---

[46] *An-Nawawī's Forty Hadith*, 60.
[47] *An-Nawawī's Forty Hadith*, 110.

Bibliography

Brown, Jonathan. 2009. *Hadith: Muhammad's Legacy in the Medieval and Modern World.* Oxford: Oneworld.
Haight, Roger. 1991. Sin and Grace. In *Systematic Theology: Roman Catholic Perspectives*, ed. Francis Schüssler Fiorenza and John P. Galvin, vol. 2. Minneapolis, MN: Fortress Press.
Ibrahim, Ezzeddin, and Denys Johnson-Davies, Trans. 1997. *An-Nawawī's Forty Hadith: An Anthology of the Sayings of the Prophet Muhammad.* Cambridge: The Islamic Texts Society.
Musa, Aisha Y. 2015. Ḥadīth Studies. In *The Bloomsbury Companion to Islamic Studies*, ed. Clinton Bennett. London: Bloomsbury.
Nasr, Seyyed Hossein, et al. 2015. *The Study Quran: A New Translation and Commentary.* New York: HarperCollins.
Rahner, Karl. 1978. *Foundations of Christian Faith: An Introduction to the Idea of Christianity.* New York: Seabury.
Sayilgan, Salih. 2021. *Exploring Islam: Theology and Spiritual Practice in America.* Minneapolis, MN: Fortress.
Siddiqui, Mona. 2015. *Hospitality and Islam: Welcoming in God's Name.* New Haven, CT: Yale University Press.
———. 2012. *The Good Muslim: Reflections on Classical Islamic Law and Theology.* Cambridge: Cambridge University Press.

Hans A. Harmakaputra is Assistant Professor of Religion in the Department of Philosophy, Religion, and Classics at Augustana University in Sioux Falls. Previously, Harmakaputra was Visiting Assistant Professor in Comparative Theology and Christian-Muslim Relations at Hartford International University for Religion and Peace in Hartford, CT. He has published articles in various journals, including *The Muslim World* and *Journal of Interreligious Studies,* and a monograph titled *A Christian-Muslim Comparative Theology of Saints: The Community of God's Friends* (Brill, 2022). Currently, he is working on a new monograph titled *Christian-Muslim Relations After Conservative Turn in Indonesian Islam* (forthcoming from the University of Edinburgh Press).

8

From Exodus to Hizmet: Redefining Other and Self in Thought and Action

Ori Z. Soltes

From Religion to Race: Purposes and Complexities

Religion offers a consistent pair of principles: it begins with revelation from the ultimate "Other;" and revelation always requires interpretation. The structure of every religious tradition with a revealed text as its foundation builds its spiritual edifice by means of interpretation. The revealed texts themselves are understood to have a divine source, but it is the human mind and sensibility that interprets.

There are certain truisms for this process. One is that God often speaks in terms not obvious to the human mind. At *best*, when there are still prophets providing the divinely-sourced revelations, they may be able to turn back to God for clarification. Or not. For instance, neither Moses nor his constituents asked God what it means "not [to] seethe a kid in its mother's milk" (Ex 23:19)—perhaps because at that time they all understood that this sort of gastronomic delicacy was considered objectionably cruel to God. (That injunction comes at the end of a succession of prescriptions regarding justice and mercy, keeping the sabbath, and celebrating three primary annual festivals.) It is rabbinic interpretation, developing more than a thousand years after Moses and evolving over the subsequent centuries, which construes this

O. Z. Soltes (✉)
Professor of Theology, Art History, Philosophy, and Political History, Georgetown University, Washington, DC, USA
e-mail: solteso@georgetown.edu

phrase to mean that a traditional Jew cannot mix meat and milk at the same meal. In fact—through interpreting the phrase to "build a fence around the Torah" (itself an interpretation of a Torah verse: Deut 22:8) to mean that one must go beyond a given commandment's prescriptions in order not to abrogate it—not even milk and meat *products* may be consumed together (so cheeseburgers are unacceptable).

Perhaps more significantly, nobody apparently asked God to clarify what *murder* is in the prescription found in the Bible in Exodus 20 and repeated in Deuteronomy 5, that "thou shall not commit murder." That Sixth Commandment provokes the question: If I kill a man in self-defense, is that murder? If I crush a mosquito on my arm, is *that* murder? (and how does this question become more complicated if I am reading the revealed text in, say, an English translation? The King James version translates—*mistranslates*—the Hebrew root *r-tz-h* as "kill," which means that killing a mosquito (or a cow, for food; or my potential killer, in self-defense) is an abrogation of the divine Commandment.

Not surprisingly, within the Abrahamic traditions we may recognize a disturbing ambiguity with regard to interpreting how to understand treating the human "other." Twice (Ex 22:21 and Deut 10:19) the Torah reminds the Israelites not to oppress the stranger, "for you were strangers in the land of Egypt." Jeremiah (7:6) puts oppressing the stranger, widow, and orphan in a category with shedding innocent blood and following false gods. Yet Ezra (10:3) enjoins the Judaean descendants of the Israelites to *send away* their foreign wives and children.

One way to explain this seeming contradiction is through exploring which Hebrew terms are being translated in these different contexts as "stranger/foreign." *Ger* is a term with implications of being a guest and comes, in the subsequent Israelite view, to be understood to refer to any non-Israelite who abides by the seven Noahide Laws. More neutral is the term, *zar*, whereas the term *nokhri* has somewhat more dangerous implications and is more explicit with regard to worshipping foreign gods—an issue that necessarily preoccupies the Israelites and their Judaean descendants, since their God-concept is what most distinctly distinguishes them from all of their diverse neighbors. By far the most commonly used term is *ger*, with its positive implications. This is the term used in Exodus and Deuteronomy and in Jeremiah. The term used in Ezra (in a verbal form) is *nokhri*. So the man desperate to pull together the Judaean community that has become spiritually and culturally chaotic in the century since the return from exile and the rebuilding of the Temple in Jerusalem refers to pushing out those—even family members—whom he sees as undermining Judaean spirituality.

It is not their foreignness in the ethnic or political sense that threatens the community, but those promoting idol worship who are detrimental to the community—in a world in which the Judaeans alone worship a single, imageless God while all of the peoples around them worship diverse, imaged gods and goddesses. That prescription by Ezra is, moreover, delivered in the context of his having redacted the Torah's text that is designed to outline a covenant between the Judaeans and their God in detail. And the Book of Ezra represents him reading out the entirety of the Torah before Jerusalem's Gate of Water at the time of the harvest festival when so many Judaeans were gathered there—and depicts the people weeping upon hearing the divine words and realizing how far they had fallen from keeping the covenant. Ezra 10:2 refers to one individual (Shekhaniah, son of Yehiel) proclaiming that "we have trespassed against our God and taken pagan wives"—where the term that I am here translating as "pagan" is the same term, *nokhri*.

So *otherness* proves to be a complexly nuanced idea in the context of the Hebrew Bible, and the issue of interpreting the revelation a complicated one. As Judaeanism itself gradually bifurcated, yielding twin offspring—Judaism and Christianity—each of these offspring referred to itself as the "True Israel" (*Verus Israel*), as they contended with each other not only theologically, but for political acceptance by the pagan Roman authorities. While earlier Christian writers recognized Jews as siblings versus the pagan "other," later, as the Church achieved hegemony within the Empire, and as late Rome yielded to medieval Europe, its leaders marked Judaism as a most disturbing "other" with increasing frequency.

Thus, Origen in his treatise, *Against Celsus*, (written ca. 248 CE), makes common cause with the Jews against the pagans whose form of faith he is criticizing—which is to say that, in spite of certain disagreements with Judaism (most obviously their not acknowledging the divinity of Jesus), they are still considered "us"—allies over and against the emphatic "others" reflecting the paganism that Celsus is championing. A century later—between the time when the Roman Emperor Constantine's Edict of Milan legalized Christianity (313 CE) and Emperor Theodosius made it the official religion of the empire (ca 380 CE), and in the generations that followed—leading spokesmen for the Church had redirected Judaism toward an intensely othered category.[1]

The arrival of Islam into Europe in the eighth century offered a new "other"—addressed by Christendom through the violence of the Crusades and to a somewhat less severe extent, by the *Reconquista* of Iberia at the other end of the Mediterranean. The conquest of Jerusalem by Christian Europeans in 1099 is particularly notable not only because of the bloodshed that accompanied that conquest, but because of both the ebullience with which the slaughter was referenced by Geoffrey de Bouillon, one of the Christian leaders, and also for the fact that the othering of Jerusalem's defenders so as to legitimize the slaughter included not only Muslims

---

[1] For a good summary of the details, see Peter Brown, "Sorcery, Demons, and the Rise of Christianity from Later Antiquity into the Middle Ages," in Mary Douglas, ed., *Witchcraft Confessions and Accusations*. (London & NY: Routledge. 1970).

and Jews, but even Christians who co-defended the city that they inhabited with fellow Muslim and Jewish Jerusalemites against the outsider Christian invaders who happened to share their form of faith.

In any case, each of the three Abrahamic traditions, in its own way articulated its own primacy and the other forms of faith as lesser "others" over the course of the centuries that follow. We can see this in antithetical ways throughout the medieval and into the modern worlds. Both Christianity and Islam carried religion toward political hegemony. For Christianity, this process took more than 350 years, if one marks the beginning of the new faith from, say, the Crucifixion (ca 30–35 CE) and progresses to its arrival at political hegemony during the Emperorship of Theodosius (379–95 CE). For Islam, uniquely, politics and faith were intertwined from the beginning, since Muhammad was both the commander of the faithful and the commander-in-chief of the troops and then of the polity that he led. In both cases, however, among the key principles that the two religions shared with regard to the idea of peoplehood (together with the principles of God, of revealed and interpretational texts that connect the people and God, and of the notion that certain places on the planet are particularly conducive to that relationship) was *inclusiveness*. Both Christianity and Islam actively sought to convince all others, of whatever religion, ethnicity, or race, to see the true—the only true—light of their respective understandings of God and of how to achieve closeness with God.

By contrast, Judaism—which shared the other three key pillars with the other two Abrahamic traditions—moved eventually in the antithetical direction with regard to the concept of peoplehood.[2] Judaism had no political power—the polity that centered the Judaean community, with its independent history extending from the Seleucid to the Roman periods, was long gone by the time a full morphing into Judaism had occurred. So whereas in its early centuries, Judaism competed with Christianity for new converts—reaching out as its sibling did to pagans (and to Christians who were simultaneously reaching out to Jews)—by the end of the fourth century this had become all but impossible. The consequence was that Judaism evolved toward exclusivity—"We don't wish to convert you to our faith, because we don't think you are truly worthy of it"—also leading gradually to the myth of a specific Jewish ethnicity. The point is that to each form of faith the others

---

[2] To be more precise: Judaism and Islam share more absolutely their God-concept than either does with Christianity; they obviously all look to different texts as primary and secondary, albeit with overlap among them; and all look toward Jerusalem as a center, but each with its own historical and spiritual emphases, and for Islam, of course, Makka and Madina are even more important, while for Christianity, Nazareth and Bethlehem are also of singular importance.

are negatively "othered"—Jews are superior to Christians and Muslims, Muslims are superior to Christians and Jews, and Christians are superior to Jews and Muslims—and inferiority was presumed to carry with it a range of unfortunate traits.

The result was both an ongoing range of violent conflicts, from the Crusades to the *Reconquista* (Christians via-à-vis Muslims and, less so, Muslims vis-à-vis Christians) to expulsions and pogroms (Christians vis-à-vis Jews) that accompanied whatever theological discussions were evolving. Nor was such othering limited to interfaith violence. The issues of heresy and schism—Arianism and Trinitarianism, Sunnism and Shi'ism, Roman Catholicism and Eastern Orthodoxy, diverse Protestantisms and the Church at Rome—and religious wars that accompany those issues punctuate the Christian-and-Muslim-dominated world of Europe and the Mediterranean and Middle East across the centuries. The Jews are typically a group on the receiving end of violence and persecution in various times and places across that world, but rarely in a position to persecute others or each other, simply because they are islands in vast other seas. There would be little opportunity for Rhineland Jews to know how Moroccan Jews were living their lives and thus little chance of being offended or taking action against whatever the offences might be.[3] So the otherness of others had varied implications in the long history between antiquity and modernity.

The theology and politics of self and other found a new tapestry of interweave with the development of anthropology as an academic discipline in the apparently secularizing atmosphere of the nineteenth-century West. The concept of "race" and the notion of othering non-Europeans based on a crude schematic of humanity as contrived of three basic races, expanded the field of exclusionary ideology. The romantic nationalism that was expanding during the same era further particularized this—in part by a frequent identity-association of specific nation-states with specific religions.

Thus, applying terminology derived from Genesis 9 and the reference to Noah's three sons—Sham, Ham, and Japheth—first, in the expanding field of comparative linguistics—led to using the term "Shemite," slightly altered to "Semite." That term came to refer to a group of languages with certain characteristics that were

---

[3] That Jews were just as capable as their Abrahamic siblings of fomenting violence against others becomes evident with the internal tangling between the Mitnagdic (mainstream rabbinic) and Hassidic (mystical) communities in the late eighteenth through early twentieth centuries in parts of Eastern Europe—and such action toward outsider others is all-too-present in the current condition of the State of Israel and its relations with—its oppressive behavior toward—its Palestinian neighbors.

born and developed in the Middle East and East Africa. The same term, appropriated by anthropology, was used to refer to Asians—whereas "Hamites" referred to Africans and "Japhethites" to Europeans—providing a simple schematic for otherizing non-Europeans based on presumed racial category.

On the other hand, the newly shaped political concept of nation-state that emerged through the age of revolutions by the late eighteenth century, which began to shape a distinct new series of polities or ambitions for ethno-political self-definition, based on common language and culture, was harnessed to the romantic idea of associating one's self not only with the land of one's birth but the language that was treated as if it had sprung from that land's very soil, and thus the poetry and prose that emerged from it, as well as the folk music and people- and landscape-focused visual art associated with it. Identity became overlaid both with political sensibility and with an othering of everyone not considered part of one's national group. When, in spite of the secularizing atmosphere in much of Europe, a given nation-state nonetheless claimed a particular national religion (eg, France as secular but Catholic, England as Anglican, Germany as Catholic or Lutheran, Russian as Russian Orthodox), then other groups, even if they had inhabited the land for hundreds or thousands of years, were labelled "other."

The most obvious way in which these ideas met was—again—in the case of the Jewish minority. Thus in Christian Prussia-Germany and Catholic France, by the mid-nineteenth century, the othering of Jews was acquiring a new vocabulary. These theoretically secular states no longer othered Jews based on religion, but in racializing them as "Semites"—on the somewhat fallacious conviction that all Jews derived from the Middle East (therefore, Asia, not Europe) and that, by ethnicity and bloodline they could never be German or French—they could be re-othered for racial reasons.

The actual complexity that besets the human capacity for defining human "categories" spilled into the twentieth century, overladen and interwoven with politics and economics—and the new technology of oil with its potential for affecting both arenas—with a particular consequence for the Middle East that was in the process of being invaded again (without the religious connotations, at least in theory) in a process that led directly into and out of World War I. The Euro-Christian conviction that its moral and scientific superiority gave it the right—and responsibility, as a white man's burden—to colonize the other races in the rest of the world, "civilizing" while plundering them, had particular consequences for and in the Middle East.

Accompanying the political reconfiguration of the entire region, in part for the purposes of obtaining its petroleum most easily, was accompanied not only by othering, but by an othering compounded by a limited interest in understanding the region's inhabitants. One obvious manifestation of this is the profound ignorance—largely still intact a century later—regarding the terms used to refer to its most notable sub-groups. Thus, for example: Arabs as Muslims, Christians, Druze, and Jews; Jews as a religion, race, culture, or nation; Turks and Iranians as non-Arabs; Muslims not only as Sunni and Shi'i but defined by an array of *madhabs* [schools of jurisprudence]; Kurds as an ethnic group. The definitional fog to which we are the heirs helps reinforce the potential for (and actuality of) conflict in and beyond the region in making it easier to relegate diverse segments of humanity to otherness.

Dialogue Solutions

The wide array of consequent complications can, nonetheless, begin to yield to a simple solution: dialogue that is interfaith, interethnic, and international. Such a solution requires a definition of dialogue that includes spiritual humility to acknowledge the co-legitimacy of different interpretations of divine revelation and human need. Put otherwise: it requires the humility to recognize that what we understand regarding our own faiths, to say nothing of the faiths of others, while they may begin with revelation, arrived at the issue of interpretation many generations ago and continue to be shaped by interpretation.

One might recognize a distinct conceptual underpinning to the concept of dialogue in Austrian-born Jewish philosopher Martin Buber's seminal 1923 work, *I and Thou*. Buber (1878–1965) distinguishes two ways of being in the world.[4] In succinct summary: One is "I-it"—in which I *other* everything and *experience* it all as an "it" without its own full-fledged integrity. "I-Thou" bespeaks a perspective in which I have a *relationship* with everyone (and everything) around me—in which, with a full sense of reciprocity, I fully recognize the "I-ness" of others, for whom I am a "Thou." The consequence is a fully reciprocal dialogic mode of being, in which alienity is subsumed into a sense of commonality that embraces and revels in difference rather than being scared by it.

Among contemporary movements rooted in religion and politics that transcend both—and which in different ways put Buberian thinking into action—two might be noted. *Seeds of Peace* and the *Hizmet* Movement.

Seeds of Peace was founded by John Wallach (1943–2002)—a child of survivors of Hitler's Holocaust—in 1993. Wallach's interests in rapprochement between

---

[4] Buber's book, written in German, first appeared in English in 1934. There are currently several translations out there.

hostile, othering factions, particularly in the Middle East, came to a focus shortly after the abortive 1993 World Trade Center bombing. At a reception in Washington for Shimon Peres, the Israeli foreign minister, Wallach suddenly challenged Mr. Peres as well as Egyptian and Palestinian leaders to send teenagers to a summer camp that he would organize later that year. Amazingly—and this must be credited to his charismatic personality—they all responded favorably. The initial group of 45 youths—15 Israelis, 15 Palestinians and 15 Egyptians, who would have to be able to speak English as a *lingua franca* and be 14 to 16 years old—were chosen with the cooperation of their respective governments.

Wallach shaped the organization around the conviction that governments negotiate treaties but only *people* can make peace. *Seeds of Peace* uses the informal format of a summer camp experience, specifically in Otisfield, Maine, in the northeastern United States—far from the homes of its international participants and also from the urban challenges of America—to which participants from areas of perpetual conflict are brought. Typically, three camp sessions of approximately three-and-a-half weeks each take place every summer. The youths are pushed into a range of interactive situations with each other—most often engaging directly with those previously thought of unequivocally as their enemies.[5]

Seeds—as the participants are called—share their personal experiences of conflict, and confront each other directly over competing historical narratives, including othering the other group(s). The intended goal and the inevitable consequence is that kids—brought up to think of those with whom they now intensely interact, as enemies—find themselves becoming aware of other narratives than their own, being newly tolerant of those whom they had formerly regarded as inimical, and even actively embracing each other as friends. By the end of the program, the Seeds have achieved new thresholds for understanding that, for many, go beyond what they could have imagined at the start of the summer.

In 1999, Wallach began to enlarge the Middle East program by founding the *Seeds of Peace Center for Coexistence* in Jerusalem to promote understanding between Israeli and Arab children year-round. Children from around the region (primarily Israelis, Palestinians, Egyptians and Jordanians) work there on various cooperative projects and visit one another's schools.

So, too, within five years of the founding of the first camp program, *Seeds of Peace* began to expand beyond the Middle East: it gradually encompassed young-

---

[5] For more detail, see the article by Ori Z Soltes, "Parallel Educational Paths to Peacebuilding: The *Hizmet* Movement and *Seeds of Peace*," in Abu-Nimer, Mohammed & Timothy Seidel, eds., *The Hizmet Movement and Peacebuilding*; and for still greater detail, the well-written volume by Wallach, *The Enemy Has a Face: The Seeds of Peace Experience*.

sters from the politically divided island of Cyprus, along with smaller delegations from Greece and Turkey proper. It came to include the Balkans, including kids from Albania, Bosnia and Herzegovina, Croatia, Kosovo, Macedonia, Romania, and Serbia. It has brought together young leaders from Mumbai, India, and Lahore, Pakistan. Ultimately it further expanded to shape a sister organization in the United Kingdom, and partnerships with other organizations in the United States that share a similar agenda. It has also worked in American venues to address tensions between American-born populations and immigrant communities from Somalia, Sudan, Vietnam, Iraq, Thailand, and other countries. A Syracuse dialogue program at the Otisfield Camp, for young people in America, focuses mainly on four topics: stereotypes and assumptions, white privilege, institutionalized racism, and the role of allies.

Local *Seeds of Peace* staff in each participating country work to build on the Camp experience through intensive, year-round programs that focus on four of the most important assets and abilities that leaders in conflict regions require in order to create meaningful change: strong relationships across lines of conflict; a sophisticated understanding of core conflict issues; practical skills in communication, critical thinking, and change-making; and the ability to take action on behalf of peace. The processes begun at Camp are then able to flourish at home.

Over time, the number of *Seeds of Peace* participants has expanded; currently about 450 teens spend time at the Otisfield Camp every summer—ten times the initial number. Overall, the program has graduated over 7,300 young leaders and educators from 27 countries across four continents. It has grown from a summer program into a year-round, multi-faceted leadership development initiative, the goal of which is to raise successive generations of leaders who understand in their guts the "usness" of otherness.

The written and oral teachings of Fethullah Gulen (b. 1938) have inspired the *Hizmet* Movement's far-flung constituents to think of how a more perfect world may be brought about by thinking, speaking, and acting dialogically within an interreligious, multi-ethnic, and international framework, and by actions reflecting a broad sense of serving others—*hizmet* means "service" in Turkish—altruistically.

The *Hizmet* Movement is marked by the paradox inherent and logically present in mystical thought, especially as expressed in the Sufi tradition of the twelfth-century Ibn 'Arabi, the thirteenth-century Jalaladdin Rumi, and Gulen. For, in spite of its Muslim underpinnings, the *Hizmet* Movement does not promote a specifically Muslim agenda in the work that it accomplishes. Islam is explored and explained by Gulen and thus within the *Hizmet* movement in civil rather than religio-political terms. It is about being *part of* a world freed of ignorance, poverty, and strife, rather than *dominating* the world through either the word or the sword.

By the 1980s, indeed, Gulen had identified three human problems that *Hizmet* has subsequently evolved to try to help solve: ignorance, poverty, and factionalized social discord. The response of the movement that he has inspired is, accordingly, threefold.[6]

Thus somewhere between 1500 and 2000 schools have been founded, from elementary to university levels, in over 170 countries on six continents, informed by *Hizmet* ideals.[7] These schools have as a primary purpose to create generations of young people who are devoted to altruistic service. They are run by administrators and teachers who are themselves models of altruistic *hizmet*, and offer to their students of diverse ethnic, religious, and racial backgrounds a range of subjects from humanities to sciences to the arts to sports.

Administrators and teachers in the Gulen-inspired schools commit themselves to be available to their students before school hours and after school hours.[8] Their goal is to teach them most effectively to be full human beings in both the Socratic-Platonic sense—asking questions, cross-examining answers, engaging in dialogues within their own minds and with each other—and in the three-dimensional sense of recognizing the value and thus inclusion in the curriculum of a broad range of subjects in order to shape broad perspectives. Their purpose is to train students who are concerned about the world around them and not only about themselves, students who are not only ready but eager to assist in the ongoing process of perfecting the world.

The *Hizmet* Movement and its schools address the matter of peace by *implication*: they are shaping peacemakers because they teach students to embrace a diverse world and to activate their theoretical love for humankind with altruistic actions. The framework out of which the Movement does this is Muslim, yet the schools offer no instruction in, or covert emphasis on, Islam. Students come from diverse religious traditions and are drawn by the principles so actively shaped and their outcome sought by teachers and administrators who exemplify those principles, rather than because a specific parochial course of instruction is offered. On the contrary, a notion articulated by Rumi's poetry that is at the heart of Gulen-inspired schools undergirds them:

---

[6] By now, three decades later, other important issues, such as environmental degradation, have emerged into primacy and are also recognized and encompassed by the thought and action of the *Hizmet* Movement.

[7] The recent complications imposed on the *Hizmet* movement by the current Turkish government and its demagogic leader, Recep Tayyip Erdogan. has included the shutting down of schools wherever Erdogan has been able to do so through bullying or bribery.

[8] This statement is based on personal observation in nine schools in five countries.

> Come, come through the door of love and join us and sit with us. Come, let us speak one to another through our hearts. Let us speak secretly, without ears and eyes. Let us laugh together without lips or sound, let us laugh like the roses. Like thought, let us see each other without any words or sounds. Since all are the same, let us call each other from our hearts, we won't use our lips or tongue. As our hands are clasped together, let us talk about it.

This passion for interfaith, multicultural, interracial, and international dialogue also expresses itself in the social services engaged by *Hizmet* to help alleviate poverty. Sometimes the education and social service programs intersect—as in the Sydney, Australia high school whose juniors and seniors were tasked with raising organic vegetables in the school garden (learning how difficult it is for the farmers who provide vegetables to the market to deal with soil and weather patterns), selling the vegetables to neighbors grateful for otherwise unavailable organic food—and sending the profits to a village in West Africa to help the village build a much-needed water-system. So, too, a steady flow of interfaith and multi-cultural programs creates diverse levels of dialogue and de-othering—from thousands of annual interfaith fast-ending (iftar) dinner programs throughout the month of Ramadan to international cultural festivals in which thousands of kids participate, getting to know each other across dissolving lines of difference.

A Turn to Art

The arts are, in fact, an element of human enterprise that offer particularly rich possibilities for reshaping otherness as embrace. Consider, for instance, the realm of visual art of Siona Benjamin (b 1960). A Jew born in Mumbai, her friends were Hindus and Muslims as she attended Catholic and Zoroastrian (Parsee) schools. Coming to the United States to study art, and in staying here, she developed a unique visual vocabulary that de-otherizes by synthesizing elements from Persian illuminated and Moghul art, Hindu painting, Bollywood posters and Amar Chitra Katha comic books together with Byzantine icons, Jewish and Christian medieval illuminated manuscripts and the pop art of Roy Lichtenstein. She explores feminist issues of recognition and blindness within male-dominated societies—as well as the Western-hegemonic feminist movements within those societies.

Especially in the series begun in the late 1990s and entitled *Finding Home* (*Fereshteh*), her figures have blue flesh. She applies a skin color most frequently associated with a male Hindu god, Krishna, to female figures, forcing the viewer to stop and rethink whatever (s)he thought (s)he *knew* about that association. Moreover, she notes that skin color, even within the context of feminist solidarity, often marks "Otherness." Not only do "well-intentioned Western feminists often direct a Eurocentric gaze at sexual practices and politics elsewhere in the world," but more broadly, "I have noticed and experienced myself that [regarding] non-western women... very often assumptions are made before we can open our mouths: 'Do you speak English?' 'Are you educated?' 'Do you have our level of sophistication?' 'Were you timid, oppressed, uneducated before you came to live in the west?'"[9] So even within the feminist world, race can offer an unwitting marker to those whose perspective is insufficiently—not genuinely—global. "Very often I look down at my skin and it has turned blue. It tends to do that when I face certain situations of people stereotyping and categorizing other people who are unlike themselves."[10] So the color in part responds to—even feminist—Western preconceptions regarding women from elsewhere across the globe; and each figure is also a kind of self-portrait, translating the personal into the universal. Moreover, she has commented often on the idea that blue is also the color of the same sky shared by everyone, underscoring a universalistic, non-othered perspective on human beings.

Her work isn't *about* race—or gender, ethnicity, religion, or nationality—but about *all* of these and whatever other ways in which we pre-judge others as *other*, as *them*, as different and, implicitly (or explicitly) less than *we* are. Nor is it about *her*, in spite of the frequency with which the face of the individual she depicts may be identified as at least a near-self-portrait; it is about all of *us*. The entire *Finding Home* series translates the personal into the universal. Myth and story-telling are universal, only particular details differentiate one tradition from another. Siona's figures are bearers of myth, of story—they entertain as they educate, wrapping the past and its lessons around the future and its hopes.

Let me offer two from among myriad examples from this series that express what she herself consistently refers to as the overall intention of her art: aside from being simply beautiful, it is to be part of fixing the world. Each of the primary figures in *Finding Home: Fereshteh*—meaning "angels" in Urdu—is overtly or covertly female. They are often drawn from the Hebrew Bible—either by way of rabbinic interpretive discussion, with its often phantasmagorical flights of fancy, or by way of her own interpretations (or by both).

A particular branch of the group focuses on Lilith, the legend-based first wife of Adam, who was able to fly and was unwilling to be ground beneath her husband's

---

[9] This last two pair of quotes comes from the artist's remarks before a Morris Museum (New Jersey) audience on May 21, 2007.

[10] From remarks made by the artist in conjunction with a 2007 exhibition of her work—*Blue Like Me: Paintings by Siona Benjamin*—at the Brooklyn Museum of Art.

8 From Exodus to Hizmet: Redefining Other and Self in Thought and Action

dominating heel—for which she was not only exiled from the Garden, but subject to millennia of cruelty. She also came to be viewed, in popular Jewish legend, as a seductress and as a destroyer (particularly of babies).

The artist's 2006 *Finding Home #75 (Fereshteh)* offers Lilith's name in English—but stylized as if it is Urdu. She raises her hands in a *namaste* gesture of prayer, her eyes closed and her brows drawn up in loving concern. The thought-bubble rising from her head begs: "you must save us from their wrath"—the wrath of the demons of division, hostility, and violence within humans. Behind her, in pure Roy Lichtenstein pop art fashion, the colors create a comic-book-style explosion—also visually punning on the sort of flames that, in Islamic art, often rise from the head of the Prophet Muhammad to signify his connection to divinity—and red letters spell out the comic-book word for an explosion: "BLAM!" In these and other images Lilith has become her Hindu divine counterpart, Kali Durga: an aspect of Kali, a consort of Shiva who personifies both creative and destructive forces, male and female divine forces, divine and human forces. Her very Hebrew name, "*Lilit*" ("night creature"), puns, by coincidence, on Sanskrit *lila*: the creative process through which reality is engendered (Fig. 8.1).

In her small 2000 gouache and gold leaf on paper—#46 in the series and entitled "*Tikkun ha-Olam*"—we can find a concise statement of the purpose for her unique output.[11] A traditional Krishna/Kali-style figure dances on a stylized lotus that is also a burst of light, one bare foot raised toward the knee—its toes pointed back so that the foot is a series of curves (rather than a single curve in a slipper, as in Western ballet)—her multiple arms raised upwards (Fig. 8.2).

But there are seven arms—six extending from her two sides and a seventh directly from her head, all raised to the same height so that their termini—as stylized *hamseh* hands yielding to stylized house-shaped flames—create a seven-branched *menorah*, the most persistent symbol in the course of two millennia of Jewish art. In the colorfully spaceless space against which and within which this figure hovers, to one side the words *tikkun ha-olam* ("repairing the world") are written in Hebrew; on the other side they appear again, transliterated into *devanagari* script.

The two primary parts among the many sides of the artist and her multiple worlds are held in perfect, dynamic balance by a figure that is at once self-portrait and the portrait of everywoman—and everyman—in an ideal reality where nobody

---

[11] The phrase is Hebrew and means "repair/fixing the world." It is a rabbinic phrase carried to expanded articulation in the sixteenth-century kabbalistic mystical community in Tzfat (Safed) associated with Isaac Luria, and refers to the obligation of each of us to leave the world a better place than that into which we were born.

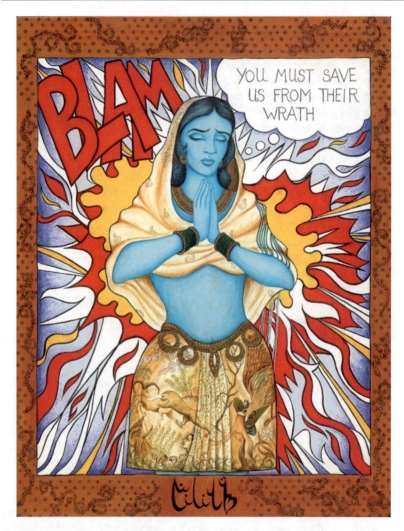

Fig. 8.1 Finding Home: Lilith by Siona Banjamin

8 From Exodus to Hizmet: Redefining Other and Self in Thought and Action

Fig. 8.2 Finding Home: Tikkun ha-Olam by Siona Banjamin

is relegated to "otherness."[12] Her blue skin simultaneously resonates from a personal sensibility, a Hindu visual tradition, and—most of all, as she has often noted, (to repeat)—a universal reality: the same blue sky connecting all of us.

In different ways, the *Seeds* Program and the *Hizmet* Movement, and the visual art of Siona Benjamin, transform the historical problematic of "othering" into a future-shaping, planet-uniting *embrace*.

Bibliography

Buber, Martin. 1958. *I and Thou*. Translated by Gregor Smith, New York: Charles Scribner's Sons.
Pahl, Jon. 2019. *Fethullah Gulen: A Life of Hizmet*. Clifton, NJ: Blue Dome Press.
Soltes, Ori Z. 2022. *Between Thought and Action: An Intellectual Biography of Fethullah Gulen*. Clifton, NJ: Blue Dome Press.
———., ed. 2021. *Growing Up Jewish in India: Synagogues, Customs, and Communities from the Bene Israel to the Art of Siona Benjamin*. New Delhi: Niyogi Books.
———. 2018. Parallel Educational Paths to Peacebuilding: The *Hizmet* Movement and *Seeds of Peace*. In *The Hizmet Movement and Peacebuilding*. Lanham, ed. Mohammed Abu-Nimer and Timothy Seidel. MD: Lexington Books.
Wallach, Jonathan. 2000. *The Enemy Has a Face: The Seeds of Peace Experience*. Washington, DC: United States Institute of Peace.

Ori Z. Soltes is a professor at Georgetown University, teaching across the disciplines of theology, art history, philosophy, and political history. Previously, he was the Director of the B'nai B'rith Klutznick National Jewish Museum and has curated more than 90 exhibitions on history, ethnography, and modern and contemporary art across the country and overseas. Ori Z. Soltes has published over three hundred texts. Among his books, it should be noted that his most recent and relevant to this volume include *Growing Up Jewish in India: From the Bene Israel to the Art of Siona Benjamin* and *Between Thought and Action: An Intellectual Biography of Fethullah Gulen*.

---

[12] For more on Siona Benjamin's work see chapters four and five in Soltes, Ori Z, ed., *Growing Up Jewish in India*.

All Lovers Are Welcome: Rumi and the Spirituality of Hospitality in Fihi Ma Fihi

June-Ann Greeley

> *The Prophet always strove for cohesion, for there are in the binding together of spirits great and weighty effects that do not obtain in individuality and isolation.*[1]
>
> *We must see each other deeply and go beyond those good and bad qualities that adhere to every human being. We must penetrate and see each other's essences because those qualities that distinguish men from another are not their true characteristics.*[2]

Introduction

In one of the commentaries from his compilation of wisdom known as *Fihi ma fihi*, or *Signs of the Unseen* (or, more literally, "in it what is in it"), Mevlana Jalaluddin Muhammad (CE 1207–1273), Sufi mystic and spiritual teacher, known more popularly today as Rumi, shared this parable:

---

[1] Jalaluddin Rumi, *Signs of the Unseen*, trans. by W. M. Thackston, Jr. (Putney, VT: Threshold Books, 1994), 67. All further translated excerpts will be taken from this edition, indicated by page numbers.
[2] Rumi, *Signs*, 39.

J.-A. Greeley (✉)
Department of Languages and Literatures, Middle Eastern Studies Program, Sacred Heart University, Fairfield, CT, USA
e-mail: greeleyj@sacredheart.edu

© The Author(s), under exclusive license to Springer Nature Switzerland AG 2024
M. Shafiq, T. Donlin-Smith (eds.), *Inclusion or Exclusion in the Sacred Texts and Human Contexts*, https://doi.org/10.1007/978-3-031-70180-1_9

An Arabic-speaking poet appeared before a king who not only was a Turk but did not even know Persian. The poet had composed an extremely ornate poem for him in Arabic. When the king mounted his throne with all his courtiers, princes, and ministers in their places, the poet rose and began to recite his poem. In the part of the poem that was to evoke admiration, the king nodded his head; in the part that was to evoke astonishment, he stared wildly, and in the part that was to evoke humility, he paid rapt attention.

The courtiers, bewildered, said: 'Our king never knew a word of Arabic. How can it be that he nods his head at the proper place, unless he can actually understand Arabic and has concealed it from us all these years? If we have said impolite things in Arabic, woe unto us! Now the king had a slave boy... (and) the courtiers went to him... (to ask) if he would find out whether or not the king knew Arabic, or, if he didn't, how he had come to nod his head at the proper place. Was it a miracle or inspiration?... One day... the slave asked. The king laughed and said: 'By God, I do not know Arabic. As for my nodding my head and expressing approval, it was obvious what his intent was in that poem. Therefore, I nodded and expressed approval. It was obvious (what) was intended.[3]

While there are several ways to interpret this engaging story, one possible reading of the narrative is that of a teaching about hospitality in daily living, but hospitality not simply as a gesture of communal convenience or as a practice for civic cohesion, but rather as a spiritual practice and virtuous habit of welcome to the other, whether that other is fully known or is quite unknown. The parable presents, it could be argued, an expression of Rumi's spirituality of hospitality.

Consider the details of the account. The scene opens with a courageous poet who, although unschooled in the language of the court, still presents himself to recite his ode before the king. The esteemed king enters and climbs aloft onto his throne, surrounded by all manner of advisors and subordinates, who are also seated according to their respective ranks. It is a familiar scene of hierarchy and margins but also power. The king, clearly of the highest rank, is beholden to no others and yet has welcomed into his court a foreign poet, one who does not speak the same language as the king, and so the king has two options: he may insist on his own superiority and so dismiss the poet as a stranger as well as someone who does not even speak the language of the king. On the other hand, the king may choose to be hospitable and benevolent and allow the poet to recite his verses, realizing that the poetry is an honorable gift from the poet, generously shared. Someone arrogant, and less magnanimous, and certainly less hospitable, would likely act in the former manner and, governed by the conceit of pride and the animosity of inhospitality,

---

[3] Ibid, 23–24.

9 All Lovers Are Welcome: Rumi and the Spirituality of Hospitality in Fihi Ma Fihi

cast out the poet. However, the king of Rumi's tale decides to do otherwise and acts according to the second option: the king freely chooses generosity and welcomes the poet and encourages him to recite, an act of sincere hospitality. Yet, there is more, for not only did the king welcome the poet to perform, the king also reacted accurately to the emotions the poem seemed to invoke: he "nodded his head" and listened with "rapt attention" to the performance of the poet.

The courtiers of the king, however, represent the other response to the recital: observing the king's emotional behavior during the recitation of the poem, their immediate reaction was not benevolence or sympathy, but rather suspicion and self-interest, only wondering whether the king had deceived them, that is, had actually known Arabic all the time, and, if so, had he understood some of the rude comments they, the courtiers, had made on different occasions. Their greatest concern was how the situation related to them, not how generously the king was reacting to the poem. The courtiers were not able (or willing?) to respond in an equally hospitable manner and, making themselves appear even less honorable, did not even address their concerns to the king directly, but instead imposed on a slave to speak to the king. Rumi notes that the slave was a favorite of the king, but he was nonetheless a slave who had been tasked to question the king about what could have been a very sensitive subject. Again, however, the king demonstrated an abiding attitude of hospitality: he willingly entered into conversation with the slave who had directly asked how he (the king) had been able to respond so positively to the bard, even though the bard had recited in a language unknown to the king. The king replied to the slave most graciously: he (the king) might not have understood the words spoken by the poet but that did not mean that he could not discern what the poet meant, what the poet intended, in his recitation, because he (the king) was able to discern beyond the barriers of language and form and recognize in the poet another human being, not so very different, in essence, from himself. The king was able to welcome the performance of the poet in all sincerity and regard the being of the poet with dignity, as another human being, and not according to labels like "foreigner" or "other", because the king was naturally inclined to the spirit (and virtue) of hospitality. The king recognized in the verses the poet was reciting emotions and feelings which were universal and with which he (the king) could easily identify, and so he was in sympathetic communion with the poet, although they did not understand each other's language. Thus, it is apparent that hospitality, the sincere reception of the full being of another, governed the actions of the king, not inhospitable self-importance or the conceit of status.

Rumi continued with that theme further in that same section: he argued that to negotiate social and public (as well as personal) relationships by focusing only on externals and apparent differences, and rejecting out of hand anything or anyone who are different, foreign, and/or unknown, is a practice both mistaken and hurtful, not worthy of the lover of God. Rather, Rumi taught, people should engage each other much in the same way as the king perceived "the other", looking beyond "duality" and realizing a connection among all people, an interior singularity that transcends difference. Such an awareness should conjure goodwill. As Rumi wrote

> *Duality lies in the branches: the root principle is one... like a breeze blowing through the house: it lifts a corner of the carpet and ruffles the mats, causes the dust to fly into the air... all these things appear to be quite different, yet from the point of view of intent, principle, and reality, they are all one thing, since their movement is all from one breeze.*[4]

It is important to note that Rumi does not deny or reject "difference" or particularity (the dust, the corner of a carpet); rather, he encourages his audience to look with the spirit rather than the physical eye and realize the sameness in all things (people), the same brilliant s(S)ource ("one breeze"), that should invite inclusion, inspire hospitality. However, that consciousness cannot be just a matter of philosophical calculation or impersonal reasoning; it should be also the understanding of the true lover, that is, the sincere devotee, of God.[5] Throughout *Signs*, as Rumi describes, the "lover" of God should always meet the world with love (compassion, generosity) and so endeavor to seek out a common ground with the other, or at least create a space of invitation for communion with the other. That is so, Rumi explains, because

> *form is secondary to love, for without love, form has not value. That which cannot exist without the principal is secondary...(love) is the motivator of form... forms, both representational and actualized, are stirred up by love.*[6]

Love, then, is the guiding principle that excites form, whether that form be an actual material presence or something more abstracted, like an idea or a feeling: the source of every form that is perceived is the same dynamism of love. Wisdom reveals that apparent differences (languages, clothing, hair, eyes, skin, habits of do-

---

[4] Ibid, 24.
[5] For more on Rumi and his mystical rhetoric of 'lover' and 'Beloved', please refer to his own poetry, odes and lyrics, that can be found in *Mystical Poems of Rumi 1: First Selection, Poems 1–200* and *Mystical Poems of Rumi 2: Second Selection, Poems 201–400*, trans. by A. J. Arberry (U Chicago Press, 1991).
[6] Rumi, *Signs*, 144–145.

ing)—all 'forms'—are merely the ephemera of physicality.[7] What is most true transcends the corporeal. Rumi taught that

> we must see each other deeply and go beyond those good and bad qualities that adhere to every human being. We must penetrate and see each other's essences because those qualities that distinguish men from another are not their true characteristics.[8]

Every human being possesses qualities that are positive and negative, yet, such qualities are not important. What is important, argues Rumi, are those "essences" that make each human at once a human being (sameness) and at the same time each human being an individual (difference): the "essences" are the authentic constituents of human nature.

This paper argues that Rumi specifically departed from the familiar exclusivist thinking of individuals in exclusionary religious/political/cultural communities and advocated for a more inclusive ethic in human encounters, based on a spirituality of hospitality that a significant portion of his teachings in *Signs* posit, albeit not systematically, as the essay will demonstrate.[9] Rumi cultivated that spirituality of hospitality and of inclusion from his own mystical discernment that lovers of God must naturally seek companionship and harmony with each other as a symbol of their search for companionship with the Divine. God does not discriminate among lovers, Rumi insisted, so neither should the people themselves. It is incumbent upon the authentic "lover" of the "Beloved" to recognize the common ground of all humanity by transcending apparent differences and perceiving instead with the "eyes" of the loving soul ... *the real being of every beloved thing.*[10] Rumi explained that reorientation of perception with an analogy of a goblet filled with wine. As he described,

> the external forms of all created people and things are like goblets, while such things as knowledge, art, and learning are decorations on the goblet. Don't you see that when the goblet is shattered, none of these 'decorations' remain? The important thing... is the wine... (but) one needs love... to distinguish the wine from the cup.[11]

---

[7] Ibid, ch. 64, 238–239, as an example.

[8] Ibid, 39.

[9] It is worth a brief mention here that Rumi has been described as a Sufi whose mystical spirituality already oriented him toward tolerance and sincere inclusion—which was/is not necessarily true of all Sufis. See Cyrus Masroori, "An Islamic Language of Toleration: Rumi's Criticism of Religious Persecution" in *Political Research Quarterly*, vol. 63, no. 2 (June 2010), 245–246.

[10] Rumi, *Signs*, 75.

[11] Ibid.

The analogy is fairly straightforward but instructive, nonetheless. As Rumi teaches, the physical appearance of a person is like a wine goblet, howsoever fashioned, and the art, history, values, and customs, knowledge and imagination, as well as other cultural effects, of each person are like decorations on the goblet. Too often, Rumi scolds, people fixate on the goblet, its shape and color and adornment, and pay little heed to the wine that is within the goblet, that is the same for each goblet. One day, the goblet might (and usually will) be shattered, and nothing will remain of the unique and ornate glass. However, that should not matter: what was "real" and valuable and meaningful was not the wine glass itself but what it held within, the wine itself. Every wine glass might appear distinctive from every other goblet, but such distinctions matter not at all: the wine that is in the glass is the same for all and is its authentic significance. So also with people, as the analogy intimates: exterior appearances are contextual and arbitrary and so have less significance than what abides internally within each person, the same "wine" that animates each human soul. Love will illuminate that awareness and should embolden each individual to accept another with compassion and care, to opt for hospitality.

Briefly, a Few Words About Hospitality and Islam

It is well known that hospitality was a civic and social virtue in the pre-Islamic cultures of the "Middle East" and "North Africa": the difficult and dangerous geography and weather conditions of the desert argued for goodwill and generosity as mechanisms for survival. Mona Siddiqui, a scholar of Islamic ethics, writes that

> *in a pre-Islamic milieu. Bedouin societies already laid an enormous emphasis on hospitality as central to a noble character. Generosity (karam) is part of hospitality and consists first and foremost in providing food. In its pre-modern and pre-industrial Arabian context, hospitality is regarded as something fundamental to the desert environment and nomadic wanderings.*[12]

As Siddiqui maintains, hospitality was more than simple action: it was "central to a noble character", an indispensable dimension of personal integrity directed to-

---

[12] Mona Siddiqui, "Divine welcome: The ethics of hospitality in Islam and Christianity," posted 29 Jul 2020, updated 3 Apr 2022) https://www.abc.net.au/religion/mona-siddiqui-hospitality-as-welcoming-in-gods-name/12503800 (accessed 5/11/23). See also William Granara, "Nile Crossings: Hospitality and Revenge in Egyptian Rural Narratives" in *Journal of Arabic Literature*, vol. 41, no. 1/2 (2010), 123.

ward the community and for the common good.[13] Hospitality, then, was and remains a virtue, the virtue of invitation, of extending care and compassion (be it food, water, shelter or even tending to animals) to another individual, and notably someone not necessarily within the borders of the family or the tribal unit. Generosity, the sincere extension of the self to the full presence of another, can galvanize the meaning of the public square or "the tribe": the action of engaging hospitably with another alters the dimensions of the shared space, and rather than an area of demarcated boundaries that resist inclusion, one person or group into another, that public space or even tribal place, through the performance of hospitality, becomes an expanded and inclusive area that stimulates fresh opportunities for (new) relationships. As such, each "new" relationship of inclusion alters the dimensions and meaning of the public square or even the tribe or family, and the description of hospitality as a characteristic of "a noble character" resonates with those potential reconfigurations of relationships because sincere hospitality should not impose a hierarchy of power on those newly forged relationships. That is to say, benevolent hospitality to the "other" does not exact a debt of any kind, including gratitude, on the recipient of that generosity, nor should there be any expectation of debt.[14] In that sense, then, hospitality is both act and perception: it is compassionate practice that also perceives the dignity of the other and, in the spirit of equity, receives the other—anyone in need—in all circumstances, whether within living spaces (of humans and animals), at the table, or among the confluence of ideas and opinions. Once another is welcomed into community with others through the agency of hospitality, the space of welcome is transformed by new relationships and new words, conversations, new ideas. A new community emerges.

Mona Siddiqui also affirms that "Islam holds hospitality as a virtue that lies at the very basis of the Islamic ethical system" and, indeed, the *Qur'an* contains several passages that address care for the other (especially the widow, orphan, and the most vulnerable) and generosity in human relationships.[15] All three Abrahamic faiths, in fact, assert the goodness of the virtue of hospitality, the caring welcome

---

[13] See also Khaleel Mohammad, "The Virtues and Limits of Hospitality." *CrossCurrents*. vol. 67, no. 3 (September 2017), 546.

[14] A rich examination of the concept of hospitality, as well as the complications its etymology suggests, can be found in Jayme R. Reaves, "Extending Hospitality: Hospitality as Ethical Practice", ch. 2 in *Safeguarding the Stranger: An Abrahamic Theology and Ethic of Protective Hospitality* (The Lutterworth Press, 2016), 36–71. For a more anecdotal exploration of hospitality in Islamic cultures (and the central place of women in the cultural expression of hospitality), see Moyra Dale, "Generous Hospitality", ch. 9 in *Islam and Women: Hagar's Heritage* (1517 Media/Fortress Press, 2021), 111–120.

[15] See, for example, *Q.* 16:90–92; *Q.* 57:18; *Q.* 2: 261–263.

of the other, in their religious ethics.[16] For example, Judaism, Christianity, and Islam all celebrate a familiar story, that of the patriarch Abraham welcoming three strangers to his table. The *Qur'an* explains

> Hast thou heard tell of Abraham's honored guests? When they entered upon him and said, 'Peace!', he said 'Peace, people unknown to me.' So he turned to his family and brought a fattened calf, and he placed it near them. (51: 24–27)[17]

The context of the Abraham narrative is quite instructive. The general theme of the surah (51, "The Scatterers") teaches that there should be no doubt but that Allah will provide in Heaven, just as Allah has provided everything on earth and that there should be "no doubt" in the soul that such benevolent care is true. The story of Abraham offers a model of how each person should "provide" for each other and any other, that is, displaying kindness and generosity—hospitality—even to those who are "unknown" or strangers. Hospitality is not simply a perfunctory performance of welcome but an attitude of welcome infused with earnest appreciation for the dignity and for the integrity of the other.

Hospitality and Signs of the Unseen

It might seem rather incongruous to consider a mystic, such as Rumi, as a teacher of ethical theory as well as of his more recognized theological and spiritual teachings. However, as Paul L. Heck, a professor of Islamic Studies at Georgetown University, has argued, mystics are indeed well suited to address matters of morality and ethics because

> moral action comes about not simply from knowledge of the outer life (...doctrinal creed and legal ruling) but most fully through the refinement of the inner life whereby concern for self is no longer paramount. Mysticism, then, has something to say to the apparent failure of human reason to establish a framework of common values out of diverse social and legal traditions of morality.[18]

---

[16] Siddiqui, ibid.

[17] Translation of the *Qur'an* used for this paper: *The Study Quran: A New Translation and Commentary,* ed. by Seyyed Hossein Nasr (HarperOne, 2015).

[18] Paul Heck, "Mysticism as Morality: The Case of Sufism" in *The Journal of Religious Ethics*, vol. 34, no. 2 (June, 2006) 253.

9 All Lovers Are Welcome: Rumi and the Spirituality of Hospitality in Fihi Ma Fihi

That statement might seem counterintuitive but it is nonetheless compelling. As Heck argues, reason alone seems to have been (to be) inadequate in the development moral codes or ethical standards that require more than perfunctory assent for their realization. There are occasions when a seemingly moral or virtuous action is simply the performative response to a doctrinal rule or legal requirement, and therefore still self-oriented: the simple completion of an ethical action does not always signify a compassionate or benevolent concern for the other. Authentic morality, Heck avers, must emerge from an internal affirmation of the rightness of the behavior required by the moral teaching, an understanding of the other and an assent of the "inner self" to the absolute correctness of the claims ethical standards make on the individual. The realm of the mystics, like Rumi, is centred most appropriately on the interior life and, in keeping with such mystical consciousness, Rumi emphasizes the necessity of perceiving within and beyond for apt guidance in daily living.

It is important to affirm that throughout his work, *Signs of the Unseen (Fihi ma fihi)*, Rumi remains resolutely Muslim: too often, mystics are mistakenly regarded as outside their religions of origin because they often do not locate their spirituality only on dogmatic teachings and legalisms within the religion. However, mystics are those faithful who turn their religious gaze within, to the soul, as the central focus of spiritual dynamism, and in so doing, diminish the manufactured borders of language, rules, and canon that separate faith traditions and exclude their devotees from each other. Mystics do not deny the value and import of the doctrines and religious obligations within their own faiths: rather, they regard those codes as the basic foundation from which religious faith and spiritual fervor must ascend. Each faith tradition may maintain its own unique language and practices and religious code, mystics explain, but it is vital that believers are able to discern between external distinctions and internal commonalities. Rumi, for example, throughout *Signs,* naturally accords great respect to the *Qur'an* as well as honor to various hadith. However, in his instruction and commentary, he is intent for believers to transform their spirituality and moral discernment from a simple externality that tends toward exclusivity toward a rich internality that embraces inclusivity, that is, from a faith of the intellect and reason alone to a faith of the soul and of revelatory truth. Thus, it makes little sense (and does not accord with true piety) to emphasize the differences in manners of prayer, for example, rather than to recognize the similar devotion that nourishes prayer in any religion. Such recognition promotes engagements of inclusion and hospitality, rather than incidents of discord and hostility. Rumi elaborates on that idea by explaining that

> *prayer (salat) does not exist only in outward form: that is just the 'shell' of prayer because it has a beginning and an end... anything that... has a beginning and an end is a 'form', a 'shell'; its 'soul'... is unqualifiable and infinite, without beginning and without end... the 'soul' of prayer is not only its external form but also a state of total absorption... during which all these external forms... remain outside.*[19]

Rumi speaks not just with mystical passion: he also offers a description of the mystical understanding of the actuality of anything. For Rumi (and other mystics), the "fact" of anything, even an observable practice like prayer, possesses an internal dynamism that its external form might not demonstrate. Using the analogy of an entity encased in a shell, Rumi maintains that prayer is not only its "external form", like the visible or corporeal exterior of a shell, and thus, movements, words, and other effects; rather, prayer consists also of an internal dynamism, its imperceptible or incorporeal "soul", that is "unqualifiable and infinite", transcending the material and mundane. In so doing, Rumi is of course not discounting the value of the exterior presentation; rather, he is underscoring the spiritual necessity of the interior status of being for prayer to be authentic.

To move from that mystical perception of reality to a spirituality of hospitality is not very difficult. Rumi sought to correct people from relying on differences among individuals, based on "external forms", and then exploiting those differences as pretexts for exclusion, refusal or rejection. He taught, as mentioned above, that the outer "shells" only demonstrate divergences or display distinctions: within, in the realm of the soul, Rumi insisted, human beings are alike, connected, neighbor and companion to each other, even with regard to disparate religious affiliations. Therefore, acceptance and inclusion—the attitude of hospitality—not refusal and exclusion, must mold human relationships.

Yet, his teaching transcends pure ethics: Rumi's understanding of hospitality is grounded in a spiritual encoding of human nature. As Rumi explained:

> *let us consider humans: inwardly, in the depths of their hearts, they all love God, search for Him, and pray to Him... such... is neither infidelity nor faith. Inwardly, it has no name, but when the 'water' of that idea flows toward the 'drain spout' of the tongue, it congeals and acquires form and expression. At this point, it becomes 'infidelity' or 'faith'... (but) when 'believers' and 'infidels' sit together, as long as they say nothing expressly, they are in accord... there is an inner world of freedom where thoughts are too subtle to be judges...God creates those thoughts within you.*[20]

---

[19] Rumi, *Signs*, 12–13.
[20] Ibid, 102.

9 All Lovers Are Welcome: Rumi and the Spirituality of Hospitality in Fihi Ma Fihi

Rumi believed that a yearning for God, a desire to be in some kind of communion with the Divine, is present in the core of every human being as a feeling of love, a love illumines the very "depths" of every human heart. It is a love that is a yearning for the one true Reality, a fervent devotion to reclaim a connection that seems to have been weakened during the passage of human existence. That devotion, that desire, (should) excite and motivate every "lover" (of God) to prayer, and Rumi insists that by "prayer", he alludes not just to the *salat* of Islam but to the prayers of other religions as well. As he stated, such pious devotion "is neither infidelity nor faith". The longing to connect to the Divine is universal: *Although the way may differ, the goal is one.*[21] That semblance among all peoples, Rumi argued, is what should guide human interactions and relationships, and inspire hospitality and inclusion in human interactions. It is important to note that Rumi does concede that there are different "ways" among and within communities of people, nor does he wish to discount or refute such differences; however, his preference is to counteract the predilection in so many individuals to engage the other from a place of disagreement and refutation and so to encourage those aspects of connection and correspondence that find expression in hospitality and amiability.

In the passage, Rumi describes the common love of God (in a word, "faith") as the living "water" of humanity, the delicate but requisite nourishment of every human soul. The "water" of faith sustains the human body and soul, affirms life and nurtures complete being. However, when that vital "liquid" "drains out", that is, when "faith" is expressed by the "drain spout" of the tongue—that is, becomes locally verbalized—then what is common within all humanity becomes destabilized and diminished ("congealed"), and exclusionary. Because of language, artificial concepts such as "infidel" or "believer" emerge and incite inhospitable and destructive actions. Rumi then portrays a scene in which two people who love God and yearn for that connection easily sit together, bonded in sympathy by the same desire, by the same interior ardor, "as long as they say nothing" or speak to each in distinctive languages expressing categories of value and meaning. Rumi warns that such categorization usually leads to faulty judgment, to concepts of "believer" and "infidel" being spoken, to separation and division and exclusion. It is rather ironic: even though human beings (likely) developed language in order to facilitate communication, humans have also weaponized language so that each group may communicate separately within demarcated boundaries and exclude anyone external to those boundaries (as in the story that began this paper).[22] Language, which the

---

[21] Ibid, 101.
[22] See also Ibid, 113.

mind and not the heart generates, has been a means to deny the dignity of the other and to refuse compassion and hospitality.

Indeed, in another teaching from *Signs,* Rumi described words, the elements of language, as 'shadows' of reality, as 'pretexts' of communication. He states that

> *it is the element of sympathy that attracts one man to another, not words. If a man should see a thousand or saintly miracles, it will profit him nothing if he does not have sympathy with the prophet or saint.*[23]

Words may foster community with some but may also deter meaningful connections to others, especially if the individual infuses great value not only in words but also the range of images such words generate, such as "infidel" or believer' or even "saint". Images, and the language that engineers them, are the "shrouds" that conceal the reality lying beneath those coverings, and so it is incumbent upon each person to listen "beyond" the actual words that another speaks (or another writes), to see beyond the actual images that the words create, and to be present to the other "in sympathy", with a loving heart. Rumi challenges every person to become vulnerable enough to identify with the other—any other—with generosity and gracious feeling, that is, hospitality.

However, the question may remain whether anyone should care about hospitality, why it should even matter, apart from perhaps as an activity to maintain a kind of perfunctory cordiality in human relations. Hospitality is not always straightforward, compassion and care for the other, especially the stranger or even the adversary, can be daunting. As Rumi suggested, if every person were accessible to ideas ("thoughts") of communion and sympathy, it is probably that the habit of judgment would fall away and the individual as well as social communities would be vastly enriched by turning away from censure and toward the ideal of peace and an evolving harmony. Yet Rumi also insisted that any thoughts of generosity and kindliness, hospitality, are so "subtle" and profound that the source of those ideas (and ideals) can only be God and God alone. The moral and ethical capacity of humanity is admirable but because of its very humanness, it cannot initiate such daunting and counterintuitive thoughts as dissolving barriers of ideology and belief, culture and custom, that separate people, only God is capable. God is the merciful creator of all thoughts in the human mind, notably the dynamic of the subtle understanding that deflects judgment and exclusion, and favors sympathy and benevolence, explained Rumi, and God provides the subtle insight in every person to privilege inclusion

---

[23] Ibid, 7.

and hospitality. The virtue of hospitality originates from the will of God and thus hospitality is more than an ethical standard, it is an evident spirituality.

Conclusion

Human beings have always acted in ways that are either pleasing or displeasing to God, even though humans have always been conscious of what actually is pleasing or displeasing to God. As Rumi explains,

> the human being is an astrolabe of God... when God makes a person to know himself, through the astrolabe of the person's own being, he can witness the manifestation of God and His unqualified beauty moment by moment and glimmer by glimmer.[24]

To describe the human being as the astrolabe of God is to imagine the human being as the keeper of knowledge of heavenly rhythms and astral points of temporal information (particularly for prayer): more generally, the metaphor of "the astrolabe of God" to identify human beings implies that the human has the knowledge (from God) of how the world should work, how the passage of time should move, which behaviors and which actions should occur where and when. Therefore, each person can become a witness to the "manifestation" of the Divine in the world—to God as the Beautiful—at every moment of activity and each glimmer of inner awareness that finds external expression in actions inspired by those "subtle ideas" that defy language. Engaging the other in hospitality—in compassion, welcome, integrity, honesty, benevolence, lack of judgment, amiability, and justice—that emerges from the interior spirit, and not just as a consequence of obligatory demand, becomes then a "manifestation" of God in the world and an expression of the truly (B)beautiful in mortal existence.

Bibliography

Chak, Farhan Mujahid. Winter 2009. La Convivencia: The Spirit of Co-existence in Islam. *Islamic Studies*. 48 (4): 567–590.
Dale, Moyra. 2021. Generous Hospitality. Ch. 9. In *Islam and Women: Hagar's Heritage*, 111–120. Fortress Press.
Masroori, Cyrus. June 2010. An Islamic Language of Toleration: Rumi's Criticism of Religious Persecution. *Political Research Quarterly*. 63 (2): 243–256.

---

[24] Ibid, 11.

Mohammed, Khaleel. September 2017. The Virtues and Limits of Hospitality. *Cross Currents* 67 (3): 546–554.
Reaves, Jayme R. 2016. Extending Hospitality: Hospitality as Ethical Practice. Ch. 2. In *Safeguarding the Stranger: An Abrahamic Theology and Ethic of Protective Hospitality*, 36–71. The Lutterworth Press.
Werbner, Pnina. 2016. Vernacular Cosmopolitanism as an Ethical Disposition Sufi Networks, Hospitality, and Translocal Inclusivity. In *Islamic Studies in the Twenty-First Century: Transformations and Continuities*, ed. Léon Buskens and Annemarie van Sandwijk, 223–240. Amsterdam University Press.

June-Ann Greeley is trained in Classical languages and literature and Medieval Studies. She is the Director of the Middle Eastern Studies Program at Sacred Heart University. As a scholar, she has studied the literature of medieval women, medieval mystics (Christian and Sufism), sacred art and architecture, medieval and modern Celtic authors, and the emergence of Islam in medieval Christian Europe. Her other scholarly interests include religion, genocide, and memoir; Holocaust and twentieth-century genocide studies; the intersectionality of religion, spirituality, and literature; magical realism in world literature; and the "weird" in modern humanities. Currently, Dr. June-Ann Greeley is a professor in the Department of Languages and Literature at Sacred Heart University and the Director of the Middle Eastern Studies Program.

Part III

Contemporary Approaches to Inclusion or Exclusion in Religious Traditions

Searching for Belongingness: A Social Rhetorical Reading on Migration in the Bible

10

José-David Padilla

Introduction

The instinct for survival has moved individuals and family groups to move from one place to another, seeking food and shelter for themselves and future generations. This reality is as ancient as the history of humankind. The Bible is a witness of it. Its major figures like Abraham, Moses, and Jesus himself were, at some point in their lives, migrants moving from one place to another. And just like today, those ancient migrants experienced an anthropological, social, and cultural phenomenon: Xenophobia. It is a tension of acceptance or rejection of those with a different language, culture, religion, and opinions considered dangerous to the community, a reaction based on fear and prejudices to the unknown, especially when the unknown is closer to one's home. This has converted us, immigrants and refugees, into some of the most vulnerable members of society, relying on the charity of others while seeking shelter from the whims of nature and protection from those who despise us, abuse us, and even kill us.

Even today, immigrating is not an easy thing to do. One shall leave behind one's home, language, and culture, fleeing injustice and oppression. However, the dream to live in a land that offers a possibility of a better and dignified life for oneself and

---

J.-D. Padilla (✉)
Department of Theology and Philosophy, Barry University, Miami, FL, USA
e-mail: jpadilla@barry.edu

© The Author(s), under exclusive license to Springer Nature Switzerland AG 2024
M. Shafiq, T. Donlin-Smith (eds.), *Inclusion or Exclusion in the Sacred Texts and Human Contexts*, https://doi.org/10.1007/978-3-031-70180-1_10

one's family makes immigrants bear with courage and hope all the dangers and hardships they pass during their journey. Does the Bible have something to say about the correct treatment of immigrants? Has the Word of God something to say to our contemporary issue of migrants and refugees? In this article, I would like to present the different words used in the Jewish Scriptures to describe strangers, foreigners, and sojourners. Then, I will examine what it meant to be a foreigner during the Roman Empire and why the Christian Community freely chose to be identified as citizen of Heaven.[1] My goal is to clarify the different terms used for immigrants in the Bible. This could bring some insights on understanding the moral relevance to the complexity of immigration issues today in the United States of America, a country founded by immigrants. It is impossible, then, not to reflect upon this human issue because, after all, God is ever present in the dramatic stories of people and invites us to protect the dignity and well-being of every person.[2]

A People on the Move in the Jewish Scriptures

Ancient Egypt has records of a group of people coming into Egypt to reside there for the commercial prosperity of seeking food and other goods to bring back to their homes. Among them were the Hyksos from an area stretching from present-day Syria in the north to Israel in the south. Ancient artwork depicts them wearing long, multicolored clothes, unlike normal Egyptian white attire.[3]

---

[1] I will read these texts through the lenses of the Social-Rhetoric analysis for biblical studies and apply their principles to today's reality. This analysis combines the rhetorical use of words, phrases, and images presented in one discourse or a narrative with the social and anthropological context in which the texts were conceived and the social impact that such discourse had on its implied recipients. A Social-Rhetoric analysis combines rhetorical studies with human sciences to help reconstruct the cultural and social parameters that regulated the social systems in which an ancient text emerged (language, art, clothing, ideas about home, religion, state, social relations, etc.), and gives to contemporary readers new insights into the theological dialogue on migration. Cf. Vernon Robbins, "Socio-rhetorical Interpretation," in Aune, David (ed.), *The Blackwell Companion to the New Testament*. Oxford, Blackwell Publishing, 2010, 192–219.

[2] "It is a faith that transcends borders and bids us to overcome all forms of discrimination and violence so that we may build relationships that are just and loving." United States Conference of Catholic Bishops, *Strangers No Longer Togethe*r, 14, 19.

[3] Egyptologist Orly Goldwasser at the Hebrew University of Jerusalem thinks most of the immigrants probably travelled to Egypt in peace. About 3600 years ago, the pharaohs briefly lost control of northern Egypt and the Egyptian-born Hyksos rose up and grabbed power ruling for 100 years in Egypt. Cf. Collin Barras, "'Invasion' of ancient Egypt may have actually been immigrant uprising" in Science Magazine, July 15, 2020. Retrieved at: https://www.sciencemag.org/news/2020/07/invasion-ancient-egypt-may-have-actually-been-immigrant-uprising.

Abraham's family could probably be among those groups migrating from Syria (Haram) to Egypt (Gen 11:31–32; 12:1–20), and some foreign servants acquired by him left Egypt together with Abraham (Gen 12:16. 20). Later, Jacob's tribe moved into Egypt, escaping the hard drought in Canaan (Gen 46–47), and also some foreignness left Egypt with them during the exile (Ex 12:37–38). In Canaan, more foreigners were among the Israelites because they did not wipe out the local people (Josh 17:12; Jdgs. 3:5) or because they brought in more foreigners by taking people captive in war and bringing them back to work as slaves and laborers (Num 31:9; Jos 9:22–24; Josh 17:13; 1Kings 9:21).

All this indicates that the Hebrew people had their origin in a situation of migration.[4] It is not a surprise, then, to find stories and laws concerning foreigners among the Sacred Texts of the Hebrew people because they also had their origin in a situation of migration (Deut 26:5). In a study realized by Dr. Hans-Georg Wuench, an Old Testament Professor, ancient Hebrews used three terms when speaking about strangers, sojourners, or foreign residents ancient Israel was acquainted with.[5]

The first was the neutral term *zar* (translated as "stranger") applied to anyone present in an area where they do not belong or live in a place that is not their own. Today we may call that person "unauthorized." However, *zar* had a negative sense when referring to those "strange" attitudes, behavior, or people that needed to be avoided or religious practices "alien" to the cult of YHWH or foreign gods. In short, *zar* was used in an overly broad sense, but with a common reference to otherness, different, alien, or distant.

The second term, *nokhri*, translated as "sojourner," applied to anyone retaining their ties to their original home and seeking to stay that way. In a negative connotation of the term, *nokhri* signified the idea that the dominant culture had of a stranger that sojourned temporarily in the land more as dangerous because they could implant foreign practices that went against their religious contexts. Nevertheless, not all sojourners were viewed negatively. From a positive perspective, they were sojourners who entered the land to pursue trade and other commercial ventures or from contractual arrangements between the Israelites and their Canaanite neighbors. Solomon specifically requested that God listen to their prayers, indicating the prominent position some sojourners occupied during the age of the monarchy.

---

[4] vănThanh Nguyễn, S.V.D, *What Does the Bible Say About Strangers, Migrants, and Refugees?* Hyde Park, New City Press, 2021, 14–16.

[5] Hans-Georg Wünch, "The stranger in God's land - foreigner, stranger, guest: what can we learn from Israel's attitude towards strangers?" in *Old Testament Essays* (vol.27 n.3), Pretoria, 2014. Retrieved at: http://www.scielo.org.za/scielo.php?script=sci_arttext&pid=S1010-99192014000300019.

However, they were barred from the Passover meal, were not bound by ritual laws, and were forbidden from ascending the throne as a king.

Any *nokhri* was protected by the sacred tradition of hospitality and folk traditions concerning their proper treatment. The description of Abraham's entertainment of his three mysterious visitors was the perfect example of how a nomad tribe received travelers arriving at their camp (Gen 18:1–8). In addition, a sign of the Messianic Age will be when countries far away will come as sojourners to pray at the house of YHWH (Isa 2:2–4).

The third term, *ger*, is translated as "foreigner." It appeared over 200 times in the Jewish Scriptures. A *ger* detonated a person residing permanently among Israelites from another country or ethnicity, followed many of the stipulations and benefits of Torah, and practiced all cultic and religious activities. In fact, they were under special protection by YHWH; they could not be exploited or oppressed. Israel was reminded that they were foreigners when they lived in Egypt. Hence, God asked the Hebrew people to love the foreign resident as they loved themselves (Lev 19:34), because God loves them equally (Deut 10:18).

Their integration may be led completely to conversion to the faith in YHWH and to becoming a proselyte. A good example is Ruth. She was considered a *nokhri*, but she received protection and blessings as a *ger* (Ruth 2:11). Ruth acted exactly how was expected from an immigrant in Israel: the stretch link to an Israelite family, the readiness to leave their own family, nation, and religion to live in a permanent way with the Hebrew People.

Since their return from their Babylonian exile, the Jews have experienced a constant confrontation with the *nokhrim* (sojourners) from Assyria, Persia, and Greece.[6] Their presence reminded Jews of the loss of their political unity and independence. Clear proof of this sentiment is shown in their disdain for the Samaritans, people of mixed Israeli and foreign descent. These factors, coupled with the relentless persecution of Antiochus IV Epiphanes who aspired to Hellenize the Jewish culture and the installation of Greek cults in Jerusalem (1Mac 1:10–14, 41–61), engendered an uprising of an exacerbated nationalism centered in the practice of religion as a Jewish identity (1Mac 2: 6–41). The sojourners, or the others, or simply "the Greeks" were used to identify someone who was not a Jew.

---

[6] After returning from the Babylonian exile, many Jews were married and had families with non-Jews, something that was not well seen by some Jewish leaders seeking to restore an identity as a people. Ezra and Nehemiah have a definite and strong rejection of intermarriage for fear of Israel falling into idolatry, demanding that those marriages be nulled and sending foreign women and children back to their land (Neh 13:26–27; Ezra 10).

Let me sketch a few things that could be applied from the Hebrew Scriptures to our present-day situation. First, every large community that enjoys some prosperity comprises people who are considered foreigners by the majority. The Hebrew people are witnesses of it because they were the descendants of a foreign ancestor (Dt 26:5), foreigners in another land (Ps 136), or foreigners residing among them (2Chr 2:17). More importantly, Israel should consider itself as a stranger before God, having the status of a stranger (1Chr 29:15). Since a stranger could not possess the land, this was also, in a sense, true for Israel. The land of Israel did not belong to the Israelites but to God (Lev 25:23) because all nations belong to God (Ps 42:1). Therefore, let us not forget that if everything belongs to God, then some developed human communities' social and economic prosperity is a gift from God that motivates those who receive it to share it with others in need. Welcoming others (strangers, sojourners, or foreigners) also means welcoming God, and rejecting others would destroy our own nation (Gen 18–19).

Finally, in a multiethnic community, it is typical to find some sort of interethnic relations.[7] The same phenomenon could be seen between a majority and minority ethnic group within a specific society or between neighboring countries, each having an ethnic diaspora in the other country.

A People on the Move in the Christian Scriptures

During the Roman occupation of Palestine, foreigners (non-Jews) were considered dangerous. Not only had they come to rule and exploit the land that God gave exclusively to the Hebrew People, but they also marred the Holy Land's sanctity with their idolatrous cults. Due to the influence of their religious leaders, Jews of the first century C.E. came to have an attitude of isolation and exclusivity. All of this contributed to their departure from the liberal attitude toward foreigners that permeated the Hebrew Scriptures. For the most pious Jews, these foreigners will not have a share in the world to come (2Mac 7:14). 35–36; Wis 14: 22–27; Philo of Alexandria, *Sacr.*, 32). However, gentile nations are not entirely without hope. God demonstrated that Israel and all nations were included in Abraham's covenant (Gen 22:18; Isa 49:6).

Group membership was the essential ingredient of social identity to the Greco-Roman world around the turn of the first century BCE. For them, a person's source

---

[7] Nicholas S. Timasheff, "The Comparative Study of Inter-Ethnic Relations," in *The American Catholic Sociological Review* (vol. 5, no. 4, 1944), 224–237. Retrieved at: www.jstor.org/stable/3706604.

of identity was the group itself.[8] The dyadic character, the close relationship of identity between two or more people belonging to a particular community, responded to the education given by the same ethnic group in which it was born and from which a reading of reality was made. From this conception, prejudices arose towards everything alien, strange, or "other than" what is part of the group to which one belonged.[9] The best way to ensure their survival was to maintain and protect the concrete identity of their group, making clear distinctions between them and others who were considered potential enemies. In addition, they were endocentric groups because they considered their ethnic groups to be better to those around them. People were identified not by their individuality, but by the community they belonged to or from which they came.[10]

Romans divided people into two major groups: Roman citizens or slaves at the service of the Roman Empire. A Roman citizen, either by birth or acquisition (Acts 22:28), was a free person who pledged allegiance to Rome. They could travel anywhere while being protected by law with all their rights and responsibilities. Those people conquered by Rome, depending on the agreement between Rome and their leader, could live and travel safely and securely inside the Empire's borders. They were considered sojourners or pilgrims in the eyes of law (the Greek word was '*paroikos*').

Becoming a Roman citizen was a highly coveted prize throughout the Mediterranean world because, otherwise, one was considered a "nobody," an object of the law, never a subject. Finally, anyone living outside the Roman Empire was considered uncivilized, dangerous, opposed to Roman civilization, and labeled as alien or "*xenos*" (a Greek term identifying anyone outside the Hellenistic culture as a barbarian). Nonetheless, they also had an intricate immigration system. Some foreigners had the chance to receive legal documentation that allowed them to settle in Rome legally. They were grouped into small organizations called "*collegia*" (colleges) depending on their national heritage. However, many immigrants migrated to the Roman Empire without documentation, as illegal immigrants.

---

[8] Cf. Henri Tajfel and John Turner, "An Integrative Theory of Intergroup Conflict", in Dominic Abrams y Michael A. Hogg (eds.), *Intergroup Relations: Essential Readings*. Hove, Psychology Press, 2001, 94–109.

[9] John Elliott, *Social-Scientific Criticism of the New Testament and Its Social World* (Semeia 35), Atlanta, SBL, 1986, 44–45; Bruce J. Malina, "The Social Sciences and the Biblical Interpretation", in Normal K. Gottwald (ed.), *The Bible and Liberation: Political and Social Hermeneutics*, Maryknoll, Orbis, 1983, 22.

[10] Cf. Esther Miquel, *El Nuevo Testamento desde las ciencias sociales*, Estella, EVD, 2011, 98–102.

This was the social and political context in which Jesus of Nazareth began to proclaim the reign of God here and now. God's ruling in this life consisted of restoring everyone's dignity, giving a sense of identity, and belonging to those who were considered "nobodies" for the Roman Empire or the ruling class of any society: the unprivileged poor, the outcasts (Luke 6:17–26). The difference between the reign of God and the Roman Empire or any other earthly empire (cf. John 18:36) was that God's ruling was happening at a deeper level at the heart of every human being (cf. Luke 17:21). God's ruling was available to everyone who was considered alienated from the life of God, including the gentile men or women, slaves or citizens. Nobody was considered an alien from the commonwealth of Israel or strangers from the covenant of promise, but as fellow citizens of God's kingdom (Ephesians 2:12, 19; 4:18).[11] The cross and resurrection of Christ gave a "letter of citizenship" to the outcasts, marginalized, and foreigners that an Empire like that of Rome denied them (Jn 17:4–16). Loving them through concrete acts marked a before and after in the meaning of life to assume it authentically through donation and service. This was the example of Jesus of Nazareth, and the first Christian communities lived in it that way.

For this reason, the day of their baptism, Christians associated themselves as members of the kingdom of God and "citizens of Heaven." These "fellow citizens with the saints" had "pledged allegiance" to the kingdom of God.[12] If someone was a Roman citizen, it implied abandoning their former identity as a person with privileges and rights and not acting according to the standards of Roman society.[13] The new group, the followers of Christ, created a community or association (*collegia* in Latin) in Roman society.

The members of the reign of God, or "citizens of Heaven," were perceived by others as not integrated into the community at large because they behaved according to their own moral rules under the authority of Heaven. In other words,

---

[11] Cf. Adi Ophir and Ishay Rosen-Zvi, *Goy: Israel's Multiple Others and the Birth of the Gentile*, Oxford University Press, 2018, 167–178.

[12] Baptism was the rite of entry to God's chosen people can be compared to the rite of circumcision that identified every Jew and was probably required for proselytes who fully accepted Judaism. Paul does not consider that circumcision was necessary for the Gentiles who believed in Christ, since, in baptism, a new identity has been granted to all believers, not according to the flesh but according to the Spirit.

[13] Cf. Peter Garsney, *Social Estatus and Legal Privilege in the Roman Empire*, Oxford, Clarendon, 1970; John Anthony Crook, *Law and Life of Rome 90 B.C.–A.D. 212*, London, Thames & Hudson, 1967; Santiago O. Guijarro, "El Nuevo Testamento y la cultura Mediterránea," in *Reseña Bíblica* (3) 1994, 13–21; Wayne A. Meeks, *Los primeros cristianos urbanos. El mundo social del apóstol Pablo*, Salamanca, Sígueme, 1988.

Christians thought of themselves as being in the world and yet being citizens of another kingdom that was not of the world. The First Letter of Peter addresses his Christian audience as "aliens and sojourners in the world" (2:11) and urges them not to live according to the morals of the Roman Empire, because they were "a peculiar people... the people of God" (2:9–10). But the core of being a "citizen of Heaven" was the commandment of agape, that is, unconditional love manifested in the service to others anywhere and at any time, including those considered enemies (Romans 13:8–10).

Another crucial factor in Greco-Roman society, attached to the concept of identity, was family honor, given by the household's authority (the oldest living male or *paterfamilias* in Latin).[14] This authority figure had complete control over all family members' businesses, religions, and lives, including slaves. For a Roman, breaking any relationship with the *paterfamilias* would have brought about dishonor, risking being excluded from family protection and left out of their inheritance.[15] In many instances, Christians, who no longer acted as if they belonged to the Roman world, cut off their relationships with their *paterfamilias* when they were baptized. Their baptism was their "naturalization ceremony," making a "pledge of allegiance" to a new authority, God, the Father, and one Lord, Jesus Christ (2Cor 1:3; Eph 1:2, 4:5–6).

If Christians were dishonored when they rejected the authority of their original *paterfamilias*, the Father of Jesus Christ restored their honor by making them his children and their heavenly *paterfamilias*. Thus, Christians saw themselves not only as subject to the law of the reign of God but also, they saw themselves as children of God. Being children of God was their new honor, and as God's children, they were also members of the household of God.

Christians were not naïve and knew that this radical change in attitude and identity was difficult for many, especially if they enjoyed some rights and privileges of Roman citizenship.[16] Some members, for instance, continued to live according to the ideologies of the Roman Empire, considering themselves to be better than other members of different origins and religious, social, or economic backgrounds. Preventing this situation, the authors of the New Testament made it noticeably

---

[14] Cf. José David Padilla, OP, "Aliens, Sojourners, and Heavenly Citizens; The Inclusive Household of God", in *The Bible Today* (Vol 56, n. 1) 2018, 29–34.

[15] David A. DeSilva, *Honor, Patronage, Kinship & Purity: Unlocking New Testament Culture*, Downers Grove, IVP Academic, 2000, 23.

[16] Cf. Bruce J. Malina, *El mundo del Nuevo Testamento. Perspectivas desde la antropología cultural*, Estella, EVD, 1995, 86–128. Rafael Aguirre, *La mesa compartida. Estudios del Nuevo Testamento desde las ciencias sociales*, Maliaño, Sal Terrae, 1994, 57.

clear: when a believer labeled another person as inferior and outcast, abused or discriminated against, they proved that they were still living under the ruling of this world and did not belong to God (Mt 10:37; 1Cor 6:9).

The New Testament has given us incredible insights to apply to the way the immigration phenomenon works today. First, any discriminatory approach towards the stranger was completely unacceptable for Christians. The members of the reign of God saw themselves as aliens and sojourners in this world (citizens and non-citizens alike) looking forward to Heaven, their real homeland where they could truly belong because it was not built by human will but as an act of God who had prepared a home for all (Heb 11:9–10).

Secondly, this inclusivity in God's home was possible now because of their baptism in the death of Christ, they died to their old ways, and in his resurrection, they were born again. Anyone who called God "Abba, Father" considered themselves attached to God, as their *paterfamilias*, not as slaves under his rule, but as children in Christ. This new identity made them all brothers and sisters, without considering their origins. In their doing, they reflect that Christians were true citizens of Heaven (Jn 13:35; 1 Pe 2:9–10).

Finally, those who treated other aliens and sojourners (believers or not) with no dignity or respect were in the position of estranging themselves from the eternal reality of God's kingdom (Lk 13:28–30). More stunning is the notion that the Son of Man, Christ, identifies himself as a foreigner seeking hospitality on our doorsteps. What we did or neglect to do to the least of foreigners, immigrants, and refugees or any of those Jesus identifies with would determine the goal of our life as blessed or cursed.

Conclusion

Immigration in the Bible is an important topic to consider when discussing immigration today. It is a reality that has accompanied human history from its beginnings and, undoubtedly, it has become an increasingly complex and pressing phenomenon. Modern societies have consistently experienced migration to different degrees and expressions, enriching the society to which they migrate. To deny this reality is to reject the fact that our contemporary societies are the result of diverse cultures and traditions that have been intrinsically and patiently woven over time. Those men and women searching for belonging, for a better life for themselves and their families are the human face of our current globalized world, and yet, they are the face of the most vulnerable members of our society.

Any serious study of the Bible recognizes the plurality of its content. It is a collection of books written in different times and places and by different authors, making it a tapestry woven from a gigantic family, descendants of Abraham, who were migrants at different moments in their history. It was written for and about strangers, migrants, and refugees. And in its pages, it is clearly perceived that, for God, immigrants, exiles, and refugees were not strangers with no identity. God not only entered in solidarity with them, but becomes a God on the move, a *Deus Migrator*, a God that migrates with his people.

Furthermore, the experience of God in the person of Christ has given humanity a new identity and dignity: being a member of God's own home. This revelation is the Good News that needed to be proclaimed worldwide and put into practice by believers who have a "pledge of allegiance" to God's reign, even if they must temporarily move from place to place. Human life is sacred and endowed with dignity, which cannot be trampled. Therefore, to stop any discrimination against migrants, we must begin by restoring the dignity of migrants living with us.

The Bible is the book of a humanity in constant motion, until they rest in God, as Saint Augustine would express it. All of us are the eschatological "citizens of Heaven" because we all live here like foreign visitors, for the world is only our temporary dwelling place (1Ch 29:15; Ps 39:12).[17] Anywhere God reigns, there is no distinction between the citizens and foreigners. This is a notion equally true for believers on both sides of the border, whose real dwelling place is Heaven. Many of the conflicts and problems we have on the table are due to the inequality that underpins today's world. Therefore, a society with a Judeo-Christian spirituality at its core shall create an atmosphere where people want to live and prosper. Thus, despite our origin, gender, race, sexual orientation, and civil laws, we have come to live together as the newborn humanity, long-awaited by the creation. All this shall awaken in us a spirit of solidarity and compassion towards any immigrant and refugee, especially if our societies are grounded on a faith and life values learned from the Judeo-Christian spirituality.

Finally, any poverty, injustice, religious persecution, or war that causes people to immigrate needs to be addressed and stopped so they can remain in their homelands and build a better society and a brighter future for their families. If they immigrate, the larger community shall help in their capacity all those who want to become permanent residents with rights and responsibilities instead of a stranger to be afraid of.

---

[17] "Life is but a sojourn should cause us to be more sympathetic with those immigrants who are displaced from their home and trapped at the borders." vănThanh Nguyễn, S.V.D, *What Does the Bible Say About Strangers, Migrants, and Refugees?* 12.

Bibliography

Batalova, Jeanne, Mary Hanna, and Christopher Levesque. (2021, February 11). Frequently Requested Statistics on Immigrants and Immigration in the United States. Migration Policy Institute. https://www.migrationpolicy.org/article/frequently-requestedstatistics-immigrants-and-immigration-united-states-2020

DeSilva, David A. 2000. *Honor, Patronage, Kinship & Purity: Unlocking New Testament Culture*. IVP Academic: Downers Grove.

Nguyễn, vănThanh, S.V.D. 2021. *What Does the Bible Say About Strangers, Migrants, and Refugees?* Hyde Park: New City Press.

Ophir, Adi, and Ishay Rosen-Zvi. 2018. *Goy: Israel's Multiple Others and the Birth of the Gentile*. Oxford University Press.

Padilla, José David. 2018. Aliens, Sojourners, and Heavenly Citizens; The Inclusive Household of God. *The Bible Today* 56 (1): 29–34.

United States Conference of Catholic Bishops. 2003. *Strangers No Longer Together on the Journey of Hope. A Pastoral Letter Concerning Migration from the Catholic Bishops of Mexico and the United States*, Washington.

José-David Padilla a member of the Order of Preachers in the Catholic Church, was born and raised in the city of Medellín, Colombia. Padilla received the MA and the MDiv from the Aquinas Institute of Theology in St. Louis, MO. He studied Hebrew and Greek at the Biblicum of Rome. Then, he completed his License Degree (STL) in Sacred Scriptures at L'Institut Catholique in Paris. During this time, he also had the opportunity to explore biblical geography and archeology at the École Biblique of Jerusalem. He completed his Doctorate (SThD) at the Pontifical School of Theology of San Esteban of Salamanca, Spain. Currently, Reverend José-David Padilla serves as a professor of New Testament and Director of the Master of Arts in Practical Theology and Ministry at Barry University in Miami, Florida. He is a member of the Academic of Catholic Hispanic Theologians of the United States (ACHTUS), the Society of Biblical Literature (SBL), the Catholic Biblical Association of America (CBA), and the Institute for Biblical Research (IBR). Reverend José-David Padilla actively offers conferences nationwide on different topics concerning the New Testament, especially for Hispanic communities. He has focused his studies in the historical, social and cultural milieu of the first fifty years of Christianity and the figure of Paul.

Al-Walā' Wa-Al-Barā': The Principle of Loyalty to Muslims and Disavowal of Non-Muslims

Theorized by Ibn Taymiyya, Adopted and Developed by Early Wahhabism

Abdoul Aziz Gaye

Introduction

For political, ideological, and other motivations, certain Muslims have utilized Islam to promote a clash between Muslims and non-Muslims and foster animosity and discord within the Muslim community. This chapter examines the interpretations of two Muslim scholars who formulated the principle of *Al-Walā' Wa-Al-Barā'* (Loyalty to Muslims and Disavowal of non-Muslims, or Loyalty to some Muslims and Disavowal of others). These interpretations contradict numerous Quranic verses, Prophet Muhammad's traditions (*Hadith*), and his practical example. Both scholars employed this principle against different adversaries in distinct time periods.

During the thirteenth and fourteenth centuries, Ibn Taymiyya gained notoriety for his theological works that fueled discord among Muslims. Driven by political

---

Abdoul Aziz Gaye died before publication of this work was completed.

A. A. Gaye (✉)
Department of Religious Studies, Nazareth University, Rochester, NY, USA
e-mail: sarwatrumi.lac@gmail.com

© The Author(s), under exclusive license to Springer Nature Switzerland AG 2024
M. Shafiq, T. Donlin-Smith (eds.), *Inclusion or Exclusion in the Sacred Texts and Human Contexts*, https://doi.org/10.1007/978-3-031-70180-1_11

motivations, he devised several principles to exclude numerous Muslims from Islam.[1] Through a fragmented, literal, and exclusivist interpretation of Quranic texts, he formulated the *Al-Walā' Wa-Al-Barā'* principle to incite conflict between Muslims and non-Muslims.

Five centuries later, the founder of Wahhabism, Muhammad Ibn Abd al-Wahhāb, and his descendants adopted and expanded upon the Loyalty and Disavowal principle. They primarily directed its application against Muslim populations in the Arabian Peninsula who did not conform to their religious doctrines and those who opposed the expansionist agenda of their political allies. The Wahhabi scholars devised a new definition of this principle, employing successful religious methods. While this contributed to the establishment of three successive Saudi states, they encountered substantial challenges in implementing the principle originally theorized by Ibn Taymiyya in the thirteenth century.

Ibn Taymiyya and the Principle of Loyalty and Disavowal

Shaykh Taqī al-Dīn Ibn Taymiyya (1263–1328) was a profoundly contentious Islamic scholar renowned for his radical, polemical, and sectarian doctrines. Consequently, he endured multiple incarcerations in Egypt and Syria until his death within the confines of a prison in Damascus in 1328.[2]

In contrast to most of the Muslim scholars who have espoused notions of tolerance and interfaith dialogue deeply rooted in Islamic teachings, Ibn Taymiyya posited the concept of religious confrontation through the principle of Loyalty and Disavowal. According to Ibn Taymiyya, human interactions should be founded upon faith in Allah, as there exist two distinct poles. The Muslim adherents, who align themselves with God, are obligated to cultivate camaraderie and allegiance among one another. The second pole encompasses non-Muslims, who are deemed adversaries of both God and Muslim believers.[3] He subsequently asserted that the principle of unwavering allegiance to fellow Muslims and the dissociation from non-Muslims (*Al-Walā' Wa-Al-Barā'*) constitutes a fundamental tenet of faith in Allah.[4] Ibn Taymiyya quoted several fragments of Quranic verses out of context to support this thesis.[5] These texts mainly forbid Muslims from committing high trea-

---

[1] Ibn Taymiyya, A.A.Ḥ., "Kitāb al-ğihād", in *Mağmū' Al-Fatāwā*, vol. XXVIII, p. 227.
[2] Laoust, H., *Essai sur les doctrines sociales et politiques de Taḳi-d-Dīn Aḥmad B. Taimiya*, Le Caire, Imprimerie de l'Institut Français d'Archéologie Orientale, 1939, p. 34.
[3] Ibn Taymiyya, A.A.Ḥ., "Kitāb al-ğihād", in *Mağmū' Al-Fatāwā*, vol. XXVIII, p. 87.
[4] Ibid.
[5] Ibid.

son during war or conflict against non-Muslims by making alliances with them to fight Muslims. However, Ibn Taymiyya theorized the Disavowal of non-Muslims even in times of peace.[6]

Furthermore, Ibn Taymiyya emphasized the necessity for Muslims to form alliances with fellow Muslim believers, whether they are oppressors or not. He also emphasized the importance of harboring feelings of hatred toward non-Muslims and severing ties with them, even if they happen to be benefactors. According to his views, a Muslim must exhibit love and alliance toward their co-religionists, even if they harm him, as they are considered Allah's allies. Conversely, a Muslim must hold feelings of animosity toward non-Muslims and distance themselves from them, even if they offer assistance to him, as they are seen as enemies of God.[7]

Moreover, Ibn Taymiyya strongly advised Muslims against establishing any kind of relationship with polytheists and the People of the Book (Christians and Jews). According to his teachings, it is not enough for a Muslim to avoid adopting their beliefs and thoughts that contradict the Quran and Hadith; they must also abstain from harboring love and admiration for them, irrespective of whether these non-Muslims are deceased or alive. Ibn Taymiyya argued that if a Muslim forms any kind of closeness with such individuals, he deserves to be blamed, chastised, and considered a hypocrite.[8]

Following this warning, Ibn Taymiyya argued that many Muslims of his time had formed alliances with non-Muslims, whom he referred to as infidels. He asserted that prominent Muslim scholars, devout individuals, and political leaders held admiration for non-Muslims and blended the teachings of Prophet Muhammad with non-Muslim values. Ibn Taymiyya cited the adoption of non-Islamic laws by certain Muslim rulers as an example of such alliances with non-Muslims. Ultimately, he accused these Muslims of hypocrisy due to their failure to comply with his particular interpretation of the Islamic teachings.[9]

Thus, Ibn Taymiyya's theory of the principle of Loyalty and Disavowal rejects the validity of other religions, encourages animosity toward non-Muslims, and labels Muslims who do not adhere to this principle as hypocrites.

Fortunately, during Ibn Taymiyya's time, most Muslim scholars rejected his principle of Loyalty and Disavowal. They pointed out that there are numerous Quranic verses that emphasize the unity of Muslims as brothers, while there is no single Quranic verse that instructs Muslims to sever all ties with non-Muslims and

---

[6] Ibid.
[7] Ibid., p. 95.
[8] Ibid., p. 92.
[9] Ibid., p. 93.

harbor hatred toward them solely based on their non-Islamic beliefs.[10] In addition, Islam permits a Muslim man to marry a Christian or Jewish woman without requiring her conversion to Islam. In such cases, it would be contradictory for the Muslim husband to disavow his non-Muslim wife or her family. Furthermore, throughout history, Muslims have coexisted with non-Muslims for centuries without disavowing them. Finally, the Prophet Muhammad himself had interactions with non-Muslims. These examples highlight the reality that the principle of Loyalty and Disavowal, as proposed by Ibn Taymiyya, was not widely accepted by Muslim scholars and rulers for many centuries.

Regrettably, in the eighteenth century, the Wahhabi movement adopted and developed Ibn Taymiyya's principle, which had been introduced in the thirteenth century. This movement played a role in promoting the notion of Loyalty and Disavowal, which deviated from the long-standing tradition of coexistence and tolerance practiced by Muslims throughout history.

Wahhabism and the Principle of Loyalty and Disavowal (*Al-Walā' Wa-Al-Barā'*)

In 1744, Muḥammad Ibn 'Abd al-Wahhāb, the founder of Wahhabism, formed a political and theological alliance with Emir Muḥammad Ibn Sa'ud. Together, they planned to use armed violence against non-Wahhabi Muslims in order to establish a state based on Wahhabi ideology.[11]

As their targets were all Muslims, Ibn 'Abd al-Wahhāb accused the Shia Muslims, who lived mainly in the East of the Wahhabi's town of Dir'iyya, and Sufi Muslims, who lived in Hijaz in the West, of being polytheists because (according to him) they claimed to worship God, but at the same time they prayed, respectively, to the Prophet Muhammad's son-in-law, 'Ali b. Abi Talib, and to Muslim saints. To fulfill his initial plan, Ibn 'Abd al-Wahhāb adopted the principle of Loyalty and Disavowal but gave it a new definition.

According to Ibn Taymiyya, this principle entailed demonstrating loyalty toward fellow Muslims while disavowing non-Muslims. However, for the founder of Wahhabism, this principle called for love and alliance with Wahhabi Muslims (*Ahl at-tawḥīd*), who (according to him) worship God exclusively, and hatred of non-

---

[10] As in chapter 2, verse 220; chapter 3, verse 103; chapter 9, verse 11; and chapter 49, verse 10.

[11] Ibn Bāz, A.A., *al-Imām Muḥammad b. 'Abd al-Wahhāb da'watuh wa sīratuh*, Riyadh, 1412H, p. 35.

Wahhabi-Muslims (*Ahl aš-širk*), whom he accused of being polytheists. The founder of Wahhabism proclaimed, "The most crucial elements of faith in Allah are the affection bestowed upon those who uphold the oneness of God and the enmity expressed toward polytheists. These sentiments serve as the supreme methods through which the servants of God worship their Lord."[12]

Here, Ibn 'Abd al-Wahhāb used Ibn Taymiyya's principle of Loyalty and Disavowal but gave it a new meaning. Furthermore, he asserted that a Muslim's faith is imperfect if he is worshipping God exclusively without manifesting hatred toward the polytheists (non-Wahhabi Muslims). Ibn 'Abd al-Wahhāb wrote: "A person who adheres to the oneness of God and renounces polytheism cannot tread the righteous path of Islam without harboring hostility and openly displaying animosity and hatred toward polytheists."[13]

Thus, the principle of Disavowal toward fellow Muslims became the fundamental pillar of Wahhabi Islam, rooted in the Wahhabi principle of the Oneness of God.[14] Once the adherents of Wahhabism grasped the significance of the principle of Loyalty and Disavowal, they were obligated to put it into practice.

The Application of the Principle of Loyalty and Disavowal on Non-Wahhabi Muslim Populations

The application of the principle of Loyalty and Disavowal, as advocated by Shaykh Ibn 'Abd al-Wahhāb, is a central tenet of Wahhabism, and it involves two specific categories of non-Wahhabi Muslims: the "ignorant people" (*ğāhiliyūn*) and "false deities" (*Ṭawāġīt*).[15]

"Ignorant people" refer to the non-Wahhabi Muslim masses. Ibn 'Abd al-Wahhāb criticized them for practices that he likened to polytheistic customs during the time of Prophet Muhammad. He argued that they engaged in polytheism by associating virtuous Muslims with Allah in their supplications and worship. This

---

[12] Ibn 'Abd al-Wahhāb, M., al-Risāla al-ṯāniya fī al-kalām 'alā ba'ḍ fawā'id sūrat al-fātiḥa" in *Mağmū'at al-tawḥīd*, p. 127.

[13] Ibn 'Abd al-Wahhāb, M., «al-Risāla al- al-ṯāniya fī sitta mawāḍi' manqūla min al-sīra al-nabawiyya", in *Mağmū'at al-tawḥīd*, p. 99.

[14] For more details on the principle of Oneness of God, please read, Gaye, A.A., "The Violent Wahhabism and the Use of Islamic Texts to Justify Armed Violence Against Muslims and Non-Muslims" in The (De)Legitimization of Violence in Sacred and Human Contexts, Palgrave Macmillan, 2021, p. 200.

[15] Ibn 'Abd al-Wahhāb, M., " Risāla fī ma'nā al-ṭāġūt wa-ruʾūs anwā'ih" in *Mağmū'at al-tawḥīd al-nağdiyya*, pp. 117–118.

led him to declare them disbelievers destined for Hellfire, advocating their treatment as enemies.[16]

Importantly, Ibn ʿAbd al-Wahhāb stressed that Disavowal of non-Wahhabi Muslims should be unwavering, even when dealing with their own family members. Wahhabis were encouraged to seek out new brothers among their fellow Wahhabis, as they were obligated to love those who worshipped God exclusively and consider them their own brothers, even if there was no blood relation between them.[17]

This principle led later to the formation of a Wahhabi movement known as "Al-Iḫwān" ("The Brothers") within the third Saudi state, where Wahhabis lived in separate villages, distinct from the broader muslim population, as will be explored in subsequent pages.

The Application of the Principle of Loyalty and Disavowal on Muslim Leaders (*Ṭawāġīt*)

The principle of Loyalty and Disavowal also extended to what Ibn ʿAbd al-Wahhāb perceived as "false deities" (*Ṭawāġīt*). These included non-Wahhabi Muslim religious leaders and political rulers who did not adhere to strict Wahhabi beliefs and practices. Ibn ʿAbd al-Wahhāb viewed the rejection of *Ṭawāġīt* as a primary commandment from Allah.[18]

He Wahhabis instructed to renounce any attachment to entities other than Allah, and to display hostility toward Muslims who followed these beliefs.[19] He also recommended them to cut ties with those who did not excommunicate non-Wahhabi leaders and rulers, even if they were family members.[20] Finally, Ibn ʿAbd al-Wahhāb asserted that Wahhabis must use armed violence until these Muslim people worshipped God exclusively.[21]

---

[16] Ibn ʿAbd al-Wahhāb, M., «al-Risāla al-ūlā: massʾil al-ǧāhiliyya" in *Maǧmūʿat al-tawḥīd*, p. 89.

[17] Ibn ʿAbd al-Wahhāb, M., ʿal-Risāla al-ṯāliṯa fī tafsīr kalimat al-tawḥīd", in *Maǧmūʿat al-tawḥīd*, p. 108.

[18] Ibn ʿAbd al-Wahhāb, M., «al-Risāla al-sābiʿa fī maʿnā al-ṭāġūt wa-ruʾūs anwāʾih", in *Maǧmūʿat al-tawḥīd*, p. 117.

[19] Ibid.

[20] Ibn ʿAbd al-Wahhāb, M., «al-Risāla al-ṯāliṯa fī tafsīr kalimat al-tawḥīd", in *Maǧmūʿat al-tawḥīd*, p. 108.

[21] Ibn ʿAbd al-Wahhāb, M., "al-Risāla al-ṯāliṯa fī nawāqiḍ al-islām", in *Maǧmūʿat al-tawḥīd*, p. 131.

This rigid interpretation of the principle of Loyalty and Disavowal resulted in violent acts committed by Wahhabis during their invasions of various cities, including Riyadh, Qasim, Qatif, Al-Aḥsā', Taif, and Karbala. These conquests ultimately led to the establishment of the First Saudi State in 1745. The principle of Loyalty and Disavowal persisted in the First State until the Ottoman Empire annihilated this state in 1818, through its governor in Egypt.

The Development of the Principle of Loyalty and Disavowal in the Second Saudi State

The principle of Loyalty to Wahhabi Muslims and Disavowal of non-Wahhabi Muslims theorized and applied by Muhammad Ibn 'Abd al-Wahhāb during the First Saudi State was adopted during the Second Saudi State (1819–1889). While this principle played a significant role in establishing the first Wahhabi regime, fostering solidarity among the Wahhabis and animosity toward their Muslim enemies, this principle led to theological and political challenges in the Second Saudi State.

Unlike the expansive First Saudi State, the Second State was significantly smaller, confined to Najd in the desert, marked by frequent power struggles and coup d'états within the Saudi ruling family, and the difficulties to apply this principle. Several questions arose about its application from Wahhabis who resided in non-Wahhabi Muslim territories, and the case of the Saudi ruler who sought Ottoman military aid, while Wahhabi doctrine considered Ottomans to be polytheists.

Shaykh 'Abd al-Laṭīf b. 'Abd Raḥmān b. Ḥassan b. Muhammad Ibn 'Abd al-Wahhāb, the senior religious leader of the Second Saudi State, faced inquiries about the Loyalty and Disavowal principle. He upheld the necessity of maintaining hostility toward Muslims he accused of being polytheists for Wahhabis.[22]

Addressing the issue of Wahhabis taking up temporary residence in Al-Aḥsā' during Ottoman rule, Shaykh 'Abd al-Laṭīf proclaimed that Ottomans were disbelievers and advised Wahhabis to avoid living in this impure territory; in addition, he extended this to Shiite cities and areas where Western positive laws were enforced.[23]

---

[22] Ibn 'Abdal-Rahmān, A.L.,'*Uyūn Al-rasā'il wa-Al-ağwiba 'lā al-Masā'il*, vol. II, p. 610.

[23] Ibn 'Abd al-Rahmān, A.L., '*Uyūn al-rasā'il wa-al-ağwiba 'lā al-masā'il*, vol. I, pp. 210–211.

On seeking military support from alleged polytheists, Shaykh 'Abd al-Laṭīf discouraged it, even in the face of oppression.[24] To illustrate his unwavering commitment to this viewpoint, Shaykh 'Abd al-Laṭīf referenced the case of Imam 'Abdallāh b. Faisal, a Wahhabi political leader who sought armed support from the Ottoman Empire after experiencing a military defeat against his brother, Sa'ūd. Shaykh 'Abd al-Laṭīf viewed this act as a severe violation of the Disavowal principle by Imam 'Abdallāh.[25]

In the Second Saudi State, applying the principle of Loyalty and Disavowal was challenging due to its small size and political instability. Some Wahhabis deviated by residing in non-Wahhabi areas or forming alliances with non-Wahhabi Muslims, raising questions about the principle's implementation. These challenges persisted into the early Third Saudi State.

The Development of the Principle of Loyalty and Disavowal in the Third Saudi State

In 1902, Imam 'Abd al-'Azīz b. 'Abd al-Raḥmān established the Third Saudi State. He aimed to use the nomadic Bedouin population to build a Wahhabi army and reclaim the territories of the First Saudi State.[26] Embracing Wahhabism and its principle of Loyalty and Disavowal, Imam 'Abd al-'Azīz sought the assistance of the Wahhabi religious clergy to segregate the Bedouin population from the broader Arabian Peninsula. The Bedouins were relocated to distant villages, a move designed to facilitate the capture of territories through armed violence.

To enforce this isolation, Wahhabi scholars expanded the principle of Loyalty and Disavowal by prohibiting Wahhabi Bedouins from interacting with non-Wahhabi Muslims in the Arabian Desert. This development raised questions about *Al-Walā' Wa-Al-Barā'* (Loyalty and Disavowal). Shaykh Muḥammad b. 'Abd al-Laṭīf, son of the senior religious leader of the Second Saudi State, faced inquiries regarding greeting, eating, or social interactions with Shiites and other Muslims who were labeled as polytheists. The Shaykh invoked the principle of Loyalty and Disavowal to forbid Wahhabis from engaging with Shiites and other non-Wahhabi Muslims. He argued that the Islamic greeting ("Peace be upon you") should only be exchanged among true Wahhabi Muslims.[27] Greeting Shiites and others was

---

[24] Ibid., pp. 281–283.
[25] Ibn 'Abd al-Rahmān, A.L., *'Uyūn al-rasā'il wa-al-ağwiba 'lā al-masā,il,* vol. II, p. 920.
[26] Besson, Y., *Ibn Sa'ud roi bédouin*, p. 47.
[27] Ibn 'Abdal- Laṭīf, M., « Kitāb al-ğihād » in *al-Durar al-Sunniyya*, vol. VIII, pp. 437–440.

seen as affection toward God's enemies, an act of great evil.[28] To avoid these actions, the Shaykh advised Wahhabis to isolate themselves in Wahhabi territories and distance themselves from non-Muslims.[29] These developments led to the new principle of exile, which became significant during the early years of the Third Saudi State (1902–1932).

The Exile Concept

The principle of exile involved leaving areas inhabited by non-Wahhabi Muslims and settling among Wahhabis. According to Shaykh Sulaymān b. Saḥmān, this was a religious obligation, driven by the command to be hostile toward Muslim polytheists.[30]

The principle of exile facilitated Imam ʿAbd al-ʿAzīz in establishing approximately two hundred designated villages exclusively for Wahhabi residents, known as ḫuğar (Exile Places). These settlements housed devoted Wahhabi combatants called "Iḫwānu Man Tāʿ Allāh" ("The Brothers Who Obey Allah"), commonly referred to as Al-Iḫwān ("The Brothers"). Through their involvement in over fifty battles,[31] the Iḫwān played a pivotal role in the conquest of extensive territories of the current Saudi State. However, the principle of Loyalty and Disavowal created challenges to the political leader.

The Incompatibility of the Principle of Loyalty and Disavowal with Politics: Theological Confrontations and Wars Between Wahhabis

Although the application of the principle of Loyalty and Disavowal contributed to the formation of the Iḫwān movement, leading to Imam ʿAbd al-ʿAzīz b. ʿAbd Raḥmān's territorial conquests, it also gave rise to several ideological problems and armed rebellions among Wahhabis.

Being absent from Riyadh for more than two years, Imam ʿAbd al-ʿAzīz b. ʿAbd Raḥmān stayed in Ḥiğāz (the Western part of Arabia) to establish his power after

---

[28] Ibid.
[29] Ibid.
[30] Ibn Saḥmān, S., « Kitāb al-ğihād » in *al-Durar Sunniyya fi-al-ağwiba al-nağdiyya*, vol. VIII, p. 463.
[31] Riedel, B., Kings and Presidents: Saudi Arabia and The United States Since FDR, Brookings Institute Press, 2018, p. 20.

his army occupied the cities of Mecca, Medina, and Jeddah. This absence raised concerns among Wahhabi leaders and scholars in Naǧd, fearing his exposure to what they considered immoral Ḥiǧāzi behaviors.[32] However, the Imam maintained his moral character during this time, even with exposure to technological advancements like the telephone and radio, both invented by non-Muslims. In a display of modernity, upon his return to Riyadh in 1926, 'Abd al-'Azīz chose a motor vehicle over the traditional camel for his journey.[33] This decision sparked discontent among a fringe group within the Iḫwān,[34] who criticized him for adopting non-Muslim inventions, such as the telephone, radio, and telegram, which they deemed forbidden in Islam.[35] They also reproached the Imam for his alliance with the British, viewing it as a violation of the principle of Loyalty and Disavowal.[36] It's important to note that the Iḫwān strictly adhered to the Taymiyyan interpretation of the principle, which prohibited any association with non-Muslims. In contrast, Wahhabism primarily discouraged association with non-Wahhabi Muslims, as mentioned earlier.

In response to the initial reproach from the Iḫwān, Imam 'Abd al-'Azīz sought the legal opinion of scholars regarding the permissibility of utilizing these new technologies of that time.[37] The scholars deemed their use lawful. Furthermore, the Imam expressed his willingness to ban these Western inventions only if the Iḫwān agreed to destroy their weapons, which were also manufactured in Western factories[38]

The scholars addressed the second criticism raised by the Iḫwān rebels. Shaykh 'Abdallāh b. 'Abd al-'Azīz al-'Anqarī wrote a letter to them, contending that Imam 'Abd al-'Azīz had not violated the principle of Disavowal by engaging with the British. To support his argument, the Shaykh redefined this Wahhabi principle, stating that forbidden alliance with non-Muslims entailed accepting their beliefs, loving them, obeying them, justifying their actions, and assisting them militarily in fighting against Muslims. The Imam, however, had not committed any of these forbidden acts. The scholar further emphasized that Imam 'Abd al-'Azīz was the ruler of the Muslims, and it was his duty to safeguard their interests. Therefore, he

---

[32] Besson, Y., *Ibn Saʿud roi bédouin*, p. 179.
[33] Ibid., p. 198.
[34] Ibid., p. 200.
[35] 'Aṭṭār, A., *Ṣaqr al-Ǧazīra*, p. 418.
[36] Ibid., p. 414.
[37] Ibid.
[38] Besson, Y., *Ibn Saʿud roi bédouin*, p. 202.

needed to keep his eyes open to foreign countries to protect the welfare of those under his authority and ensure the continuity of his power.[39]

The response given by Shaykh ʿAbdallāh b. ʿAbd al-ʿAzīz al-ʿAnqarī was not accepted by the Iḫwān protesters, who were led by three tribal leaders: Sulṭān b. Biğād of the ʿUtaybah tribe, Fayṣal al-Duwayš of the Muṭayr tribe, and Daydān b. Ḥiṯlīn of the ʿAjmān tribe. They publicly declared that their rebellion aimed to restore the true Islamic religion, which they believed had been undermined by Imam ʿAbd al-ʿAzīz's alliance with the infidels.[40]

The radical stance of the Iḫwān prompted the Wahhabi scholars to send multiple letters to persuade them to remain loyal to Imam ʿAbd al-ʿAzīz's authority. However, the Iḫwān disregarded the advice of the Wahhabi scholars. Furthermore, the Iḫwān declared their territories to be truly Islamic and encouraged the inhabitants of Naǧd to relocate to their lands. This claim raised concerns among the residents of Naǧd, who sought the opinion of the scholars regarding this matter. Consequently, the Wahhabi scholars criticized the Iḫwān for their ignorance in believing that their territories were the sole haven of exile. Additionally, Shaykh Sulaymān b. Saḥmān expressed surprise and anger that the Iḫwān no longer considered Naǧd territories to be part of the Islamic lands.[41] As a result, he referred to the Iḫwān as Bedouins and accused them of excessively enforcing the principle of Loyalty and Disavowal. He believed that their extremism had led them to view the entire territory of Naǧd as a land of disbelief or immorality.[42]

In his conviction that the religious uprising of the extremist Bedouins stemmed from their indoctrination into Wahhabism, the Wahhabi scholar ʿUmar b. Muḥammad b. Sulaym wrote a letter to the insurgent Iḫwān of Arṭāwiyya, led by Fayṣal al-Duwayš. In the letter, he advised them to refrain from reading the Wahhabi book, *Maǧmūʿat Al-tawḥīd*, without seeking guidance from the authorized clergy for its interpretation.[43] The rebels dismissed this suggestion as they firmly believed in the validity of their stance. They persisted in their rebellion against the authority of the Imam and criticized the scholars for their perceived

---

[39] Ibn Abd al-ʿAzīz al-ʿAnqarī, A., « Kitāb al-ǧihād » in *al-Durar al-Sunniyya fī-al-aǧwiba al-naǧdiyya*, vol. IX, pp. 156–158.

[40] ʿAṭṭār, A., *Ṣaqr al-Ǧazīra*, p. 419.

[41] Ibn Saḥmān, S., « Kitāb al-ǧihād » in *al-Durar al-sunniyya*, vol. VIII, p. 478.

[42] Ibid., p. 480.

[43] Ibn Sulaym, U.M., « Kitāb al-ǧihād » in *al-Durar al-Sunniyya fī-al-aǧwiba al-naǧdiyya*, vol. IX, p. 166–169.

complacency. In response, the Wahhabi scholars issued a collective fatwa, declaring the Wahhabi rebels to be disbelievers and apostates.[44]

Following the expulsion of the Iḫwān rebels from Islam, the scholars addressed another collective letter to Imam 'Abd al-'Azīz, urging him to safeguard the Islamic territories against those who posed a threat to them.[45]

With the approval of the scholars, Imam 'Abd al-'Azīz assembled an army consisting of forty thousand fighters.[46] In March 1929, he launched a surprise attack on the Iḫwān camps situated in Rawḍah al-Sibla, which is presently located in Zulfa Province. In this battle, 'Abd al-'Azīz emerged victorious, inflicting significant casualties on approximately four thousand of his former comrades. Fayṣal al-Duwayš sustained injuries, and at his request, the Imam granted him mercy and allowed him to return to his village. However, due to the perceived threat he posed, Sulṭān b. Biğād was imprisoned on the orders of the Imam.[47]

King 'Abd al-'Azīz's Renunciation of the Principle of Loyalty and Disavowal

In September 1932, three years after the defeat of the Iḫwān rebels, King 'Abd al-'Azīz merged the Ḥiğāz Kingdom with the Nağd Kingdom, establishing the Kingdom of Saudi Arabia.[48] Eight months later, he appointed his son Sa'ūd to be the crown prince.[49] With the cessation of territorial expansion, the principle of Loyalty and Disavowal was abandoned. Non-Wahhabi Muslims were henceforth recognized as true Muslims through a decree issued by King 'Abd al-'Azīz, endorsed by the official religious clergy, and communicated to the remaining members of the Iḫwān movement.[50]

The rehabilitation of non-Wahhabi Muslims and the abandonment of the principle of *Al-Walā' Wa-Al-Barā'* was a significant turning point for the Kingdom of Saudi Arabia, as it solidified its sovereignty and gained international recognition. As a testament to this transformation, King 'Abd-al-'Azīz played an active role in

---

[44] Nağd Scholars' Collective Fatwa, « Kitāb al-ğihād » in *al-Sunniyya*, vol. IX, pp. 209–210.
[45] Nağd Scholars' Collective Letter, « Kitāb al-ğihād » in *al-Durar al-Sunniyya*, vol. IX, pp. 94–96.
[46] 'Aṭṭār, A., *Ṣaqr al-Ğazīra*, p. 420.
[47] Ibid., p. 424.
[48] Ibid., p. 449.
[49] Ibid., p. 451.
[50] Al--Rayḥānī, A., *Tārīḫ Nağd*, pp. 435–436.

the establishment of the Arab League in 1945.[51] He further emphasized his friendly relations with the United States of America through a landmark meeting with US President Franklin Roosevelt on February 4, 1945, aboard the *Quincy Cruiser*.[52] The King also maintained his relations with Great Britain, as evidenced by his meeting with British Prime Minister Winston Churchill three days after his meeting with Roosevelt.[53] Following King 'Abd-al-'Azīz's death eight years later, his son Sa'ūd ascended the throne. However, Saud was deposed by the royal family in 1964 and was succeeded by his half-brother Faisal, who was tragically assassinated in 1975. King Faisal's half-brother, Khalid, then assumed the throne until his passing in 1982, after which his half-brother, Fahd, became the king from 1982 to 2005. Subsequently, King Abdallah took the helm from 2005 to 2015, and the current King Salman b. 'Abd-al-'Azīz assumed the destiny of the Kingdom. Since 1932, the principle of *Al-Walā' Wa-Al-Barā'* has officially remained abandoned in the Kingdom of Saudi Arabia.

Conclusion

This chapter reveals that Ibn Taymiyya theorized the principle of *Al-Walā' Wa-Al-Barā'* through a fragmented, literal, and exclusivist interpretation of Qur'anic texts. This principle recommended that Muslims exhibit love and alliance toward their fellow Muslims, even if they were victims of oppression, as they are considered allies of God. On the contrary, non-Muslims were to be despised, and all ties with them were to be severed, regardless of their potential benevolence, as they were deemed enemies of God. This interpretation sowed the seeds of conflict between Muslims and non-Muslims. Fortunately, this exclusive theory formulated by Ibn Taymiyya, seven centuries after the advent of Islam, did not gain traction, as it was dismissed by Muslim scholars of that era. Regrettably, five centuries later, this theory found resonance when it was embraced and expanded upon by the founder of Wahhabism. It was employed against Muslim communities residing in the Arabian Peninsula and their religious and political leaders who did not conform to Wahhabism, and to Emir Muḥammad Ibn Sa'ūd's expansionist agenda, as he stood as a political ally of Ibn 'Abd al-Wahhāb.

The approach employed by Ibn 'Abd al-Wahhāb entailed several steps. Firstly, he sought to equate the non-Wahhabi Muslim populace of the eighteenth century

---

[51] 'Aṭṭār, A., *Ṣaqr al-Ǧazīra*, pp. 484–486.
[52] Redissi, H., *The Pact of Najd*, p. 205.
[53] 'Aṭṭār, A., *Ṣaqr al-Ǧazīra*, p. 495.

with the idolaters of Mecca during the time of Prophet Muhammad in the sixth century. Subsequently, he likened their religious and political leaders to false deities. Lastly, he utilized the principle of Loyalty and Disavowal to instigate Wahhabis to harbor hatred toward the non-Wahhabi Muslim populations and their religious and political leaders, encouraging hostility even toward their own parents, children, and siblings, as they were perceived to be enemies of God. Conversely, Wahhabis were urged to seek kinship solely among their fellow adherents, as they were deemed allies of God. Through this strategy, Ibn 'Abd al-Wahhāb succeeded in dividing the Muslim populations of Arabia, employing the principle of Loyalty and Disavowal, thereby facilitating his political ally, Muhammad b. Sa'ūd, to indoctrinate followers who were prepared to fiercely combat and even eradicate their fellow co-religionists, family members, and tribal kin as God's enemies. This is how the principle of Loyalty and Disavowal contributed to the establishment of the First Saudi State that occupied almost the entire Arabian Peninsula.

The utilization of the principle of Loyalty and Disavowal extended to the Second Saudi State, where it was adopted. Shaykh 'Abd al-Laṭīf, the religious leader and grandson of the founder of Wahhabism, maintained stringent adherence to disavowing non-Wahhabi Muslims and those who did not renounce them. He characterized the Islamic Ottoman Empire, which had overthrown the First Saudi State, to be an apostate empire. Additionally, he prohibited Wahhabis from seeking military support from the Ottomans and from temporarily residing in territories under Ottoman authority within Arabia.

However, during the establishment of the Second State, confined to a small territory primarily in Nağd, the principle of Loyalty and Disavowal was violated by the Wahhabis. Many former adherents of the First State found themselves residing in regions controlled by non-Wahhabi Muslims. Due to political instability and internal conflicts within the Saud family vying for power, it became arduous for them to relocate to the new state. Imam 'Abd Allāh b. Faisal also contravened the Wahhabi principle of *Al-Walā' Wa-Al-Barā'* when he engaged with the Ottomans, seeking military aid in his struggle against his brother. This transpired at a time when Wahhabis accused the Ottoman Muslims, due to their Sufi Islam, of engaging in polytheism.

The principle of Loyalty and Disavowal was employed by the founder of the Third Saudi State, in collaboration with religious scholars, to fulfill his primary objective of establishing an army predominantly comprised of illiterate Bedouins to reclaim the territories previously held by his forbearers during the First State. Through the implementation of the principle of *Al-Walā' Wa-Al-Barā'*, the official Wahhabi religious clergy effectively isolated the Bedouins from their families and tribes, utilizing them as a force to conquer extensive Muslim regions of Arabia through a series of over fifty violent battles.

While the principle of Loyalty and Disavowal played a pivotal role in the establishment of the third Saud political regime, it also gave rise to theological, political, and security challenges for Imam 'Abd-al-'Azīz. Imam 'Abd-al-'Azīz violated the principle of disavowing non-Muslims by allying with the British and using non-Muslim technology. This upset the Iḫwān rebels, causing wars among Wahhabis. After defeating the rebels, the Imam abandoned the principle, officially welcoming non-Wahhabi Muslims through a religious decree.

Thus, the application of *Al-Walā' Wa-Al-Barā'* from the individual sphere to the public, and then to the state level throughout three Saudi states, resulted in the accumulation of power and development of religious and political policy; however, its very exclusionist nature led to its own demise and ultimate rejection by King 'Abd-al-'Azīz, who reversed its orders and promoted more inclusive religious and state policies, which continue to ameliorate the divisions created by this principle among individual and international relations.

Bibliography

Al-Rayḥānī, A. 1972. *Tārīḫ Naǧd wa-mulḥaqātuh*. Beyrouth: Mu'assasat Dār al-Rayḥānī.
'Aṭṭār, A. 1384 H. *Ṣaqr al-Ǧazīra*, Djeddah, Maṭābi' al-mu'assasa al-'Arabiyya.
Besson, Y. 1980. *Ibn Sa'ud roi bédouin: la naissance du Royaume d'Arabie Saoudite*. Editions des Trois Continents: Lausanne.
Bin Ali, M. 2016. *Roots Of Religious Extremism: The Understanding The Salafi Doctrine Of al-Walaʾ Wal Bara*. London: Imperial College Presse.
Cook, M. 2003. *Forbidding Wrong in Islam*. Cambridge: Cambridge University Press.
———. 2000. *Commanding Right and Forbidding wrong in Islamic Thought*. Cambridge: Cambridge University Press.
Goldziher, I. 2005. *Le dogme et la loi dans l'Islam*, 2ème édit., Paris, Geuthner & L'Eclat.
Ibn 'Abdal- Laṭīf, M. 1995. Kitāb al-ǧihād. In *al-Durar al-Sunniyya*, vol. VIII, n.e.
Ibn 'Abdal-Rahmān, A.L. 2000.*'Uyūn Al-rasā'il wa-Al-aǧwiba 'lā al-Masā'il*, volumes I, II, Riyad, Makaba al-Rušd.
Ibn Abd al-'Azīz al-'Anqarī, A. 1995. Kitāb al-ǧihād. In *al-Durar al-Sunniyya fī-al-aǧwiba al-naǧdiyya*, vol. IX, n.e.
Ibn 'Abd al-Wahhāb, M. 1391H. al-Risāla al-ṯāliṯa fī tafsīr kalimat al-tawḥīd. In *Maǧmū'at al-tawḥīd*, Makkah, Maṭba'at al-Ḥukūma.
Ibn 'Abd al-Wahhāb, M. 1391H. al-Risāla al-sādisa. In *Maǧmū'at al-tawḥīd*, Makkah, Maṭba'at al-Ḥukūma.
Ibn 'Abd al-Wahhāb, M. 1391H. Risāla fī ma'nā al-ṭāǧūt wa-ruʾūs anwā'ih. In *Maǧmū'at al-tawḥīd al-naǧdiyya*, Makkah, Maṭba'at al-Ḥukūma.
Ibn 'Abd al-Wahhāb, M. 1391H. al-Risāla al-ṯāliṯa fī nawāqiḍ al-islām. In *Maǧmū'at al-tawḥīd*, Makkah, Maṭba'at al-Ḥukūma.
Ibn 'Abd al-Wahhāb, M. 1391H. al-Risāla al- al-ṯāniya fī sitta mawāḍi' manqūla min al-sīra al-nabawiyya. In *Maǧmū'at al-tawḥīd*, Makkah, Maṭba'at al-Ḥukūma.

Ibn ʿAbd al-Wahhāb, M. 1391H. al-Risāla al-ūlā: massʾil al-ğāhiliyya.In *Mağmūʿat al-tawḥīd*, Makkah, Maṭbaʿat al-Ḥukūma.
Ibn ʿAbd al-Wahhāb, M. 1391H. al-Risāla al-ṯāniya fī al-kalām ʿalā baʿḍ fawāʾid sūrat al-fātiḥa. In *Mağmūʿat al-tawḥīd*, Makkah, Maṭbaʿat al-Ḥukūma.
Ibn Bāz, A.A. 1412H. *al-Imām Muḥammad b. ʿAbd al-Wahhāb daʿwatuh wa sīratuh*, Riyadh.
Ibn Saḥmān, S. 1995. Kitāb al-ğihād. In *al-Durar Sunniyya fī-al-ağwiba al-nağdiyya*, vol. VIII, n.e.
Ibn Sulaym, U.M. 1995. Kitāb al-ğihād. In *al-Durar al-Sunniyya fī-al-ağwiba al-nağdiyya*, vol. IX, n.e.
Ib Ibn Taymiyya, A.A.H. 2000. Kitāb al-ğihād. In *Mağmūʿ al-fatāwā*, vol. XXVIII,1ᵉ édit. Beyrouth, Dār al-Kutub al-ʿilmiyya.
Ibn Taymiyya, A.A.H. 2000. Kitāb tawḥīd al-ulūhiyya. In *Mağmūʿ al-fatāwā*, 1ᵉ édit. Beyrouth, Dār al-Kutub al-ʿilmiyya.
Ibn Taymiyya, A.A.Ḥ. 1966. *al-Siyāsa al-šarʿiyya fī-iṣlāḥ al-rā ī wa-al-raʿiyya*. Dar al Kutub al Arabiyah.
Ibn Taymiyya, A.A.H. 2005. *al-Ṣārim al-maslūl ʿalā shātim al-Rasūl*. Dār al-Kitāb al-ʿArabī: Beyrouth.
Ibn Taymiyya, A.A.Ḥ. 1986. *Minhāğ al-Sunna fī naqḍ kalām al-šīʿa wa-al-qadariyya*, vol.V, 1ˢᵗ Edition, n.e.p.
Ibn Taymiyya, A. A. Ḥ. 2000. *Mağmūʿ al-fatāwā*, édit. intro et comment. par Muṣṭafā ʿAbd al-Qādir ʿAṭā, Beyrouth, Dār al-Kutub al- Ilmiyya.
Laoust, H. 1939. *Essai sur les doctrines sociales et politiques de Taḳi-d-Dīn Aḥmad B. Taimiya*. Le Caire: Imprimerie de l'Institut Français d'Archéologie Orientale.
Redissi, H. 2007. *Le pacte de Nadjd: ou comment l'islam sectaire est devenu l'islam*. Paris: Seuil.
Riedel, B. 2018. *Kings, and Presidents: Saudi Arabia and The United States Since FDR*, 20. Brookings Institute Press.
Shiraz, M. 2016. *Salafi Jihadism: The History of an Idea*. Oxford: Oxford University Press.
Sirriyeh, E. 1989. Wahhabis, Unbelievers and the Problems of Exclusivism. *British Society for Middle Eastern Studies* 16 (2): 123–132.
Wagemakers, J. 2012. The Enduring Legacy of the Second Saudi State: Quietist and Radical Wahhabi Contestations of Al-Walaʺ wal Baraʾ. *International Journal of Middle East Studies* 44 (1). Cambridge University Press.
Wagemakers, J. 2014. The Transformation of a Radical Concept: Al-Walaʺ wal Baraʺ. In *The Ideology of Abu Muhammad Al Maqdisi*. Oxford Academic. https://doi.org/10.1093/acpr of:oso/9780199333431.003.0004

Abdoul Aziz Gaye spent 12 years in Europe to receive a BA, MA, and PhD in Arabic & Islamic Studies from the University of Geneva, Switzerland. Dr. Abdoul Aziz Gaye earned his BA in Arabic Language from the University of Medina. He earned a Postgraduate Diploma in Teaching Arabic for Non-Native Speakers from King Saud University in Saudi Arabia. Dr. Gaye received his PhD on Wahhabi ideology in Arabic and Islamic Studies. His teaching and research interests are Arabic, Islamic Studies, Sufism, and Religious Fundamentalism. Dr. Gaye has taught Arabic Language and World Religions at Nazareth College in Rochester, NY, and at Penn State University.

Multiple Political Discourses in the Islamic Tradition

Ahmet Celik

Introduction

Linda Tuhiwai Smith, in her well-known work *Decolonizing Methodologies,* argues that "we have a different epistemological tradition which frames the way we see the world, the way we organize ourselves in it, the questions we ask and the solutions we seek."[1] The pre-modern *Muslim Community*, I argue, became a self-governing actor by framing the way Muslims see the world and organizing themselves through embracing certain ways of knowing and moral ways of living. These epistemic and moral principles define and limit the political authority of government. Thus, I contend that it was not the political power of rulers, but the *Muslim Community* whose will and values determined the Islamic conceptions of sovereignty, according to pre-modern Muslim thinkers. For them, a *community*[2] is

---

[1] Linda Tuhiwai Smith, *Decolonizing Methodologies: Research and Indigenous Peoples*, Second edition (London: Zed Books, 2012), 190.
[2] Alexander Orwin, *Redefining the Muslim Community: Ethnicity, Religion, and Politics in the Thought of Alfarabi* (Philadelphia: University of Pennsylvania Press, 2017).

A. Celik (✉)
Department of Religion, University of Syracuse, Syracuse, NY, USA
e-mail: acelik@syr.edu

© The Author(s), under exclusive license to Springer Nature Switzerland AG 2024
M. Shafiq, T. Donlin-Smith (eds.), *Inclusion or Exclusion in the Sacred Texts and Human Contexts*, https://doi.org/10.1007/978-3-031-70180-1_12

a group of people that share the same ways of knowing and moral values. Rather than a detached ruler imposing laws on the community, communities themselves defined and organized their lives. Similar to Aristotle's polis (city-state), a *community* consists of people who come together for the sake of a common good through certain epistemological assumptions and normative prescriptions.[3]

In this chapter, my approach is largely philosophical. I engage with the themes and concepts in the political writings of al-Fārābī, al-Māwardī, and al-Juwaynī. al-Fārābī is considered the first political philosopher and presents an Islamic political theory from a philosophical perspective, while al-Māwardī is introduced as the first theorist of Islamic constitutionalism and presents a distinct political theory from a juristic perspective. Alternatively, al-Juwaynī, whose political theory has not been examined widely by contemporary scholars, articulates a more theology-based political theory. Therefore, rigorous re-reading and close engagement with their writings on politics will help us to demonstrate that Islamic political thought can better be defined as a discursive tradition that consists of multiple layers of political discourse through different political genres. Through thematic textual descriptions and analysis, I will attempt to present their conceptualizations of political authority, lawgiving, and administrative power.

Sovereignty has been a fundamental concept in modern political theory. From Bodin and Hobbes to Enlightenment philosophers and post-modern political theorists, sovereignty has been articulated in different ways within distinctive historical contexts. However, its hallmark is the will to representation: the modern state, as the embodiment of the nation, is the only author of the nation's will because collective and popular will can be best represented in the acts and words of representatives who are entitled to rule. Popular will, as the ultimate sovereign, actualizes itself through the laws established by the representative agency, that is, the modern state.[4] Therefore, the modern conception of sovereignty is related to legitimate authority, lawgiving, and the government of the state, which is considered the only representative of collective will. Unlike the modern state, which legitimates for itself the authority to legislate and govern people, Islamic governance (caliphate or sultanate) is legitimate as long as it implements Shariʿa, whose laws and norms are not produced by the government itself.[5] The legitimacy, lawgiving (legislation), and the function of government are domains defined, regulated, and limited by the

---

[3] Aristotle and Carnes Lord, *Aristotle's Politics*, Second edition (Chicago: The University of Chicago Press, 2013), 1.

[4] Wael B. Hallaq, *The Impossible State: Islam, Politics, and Modernity's Moral Predicament*, Paperback edition (New York: Columbia University Press, 2014), 25–26.

[5] Hallaq, 64.

Shariʿa. Therefore, sovereignty is limited to preservation and guardianship of the Community through implementation of the moral and legal principles derived from Islamic sources. In this chapter, I trace three components of sovereignty (legitimacy, lawgiving, and government) in the political treaties of Muslim thinkers to demonstrate that although they developed distinct political theories, they share that sovereignty is dependent on the Community and its Shariʿa.

In order to achieve that, I first define Islam as a discursive tradition that allows for diversity and pluralism. Second, I attempt to explain how this discursive tradition allowed for the construction of multiple layers of Islamic political discourse through various intellectual orientations and different hermeneutic engagements with authoritative sources of Islam in pre-modern Islamic history. Finally, I excavate the traces of sovereignty on which the legitimacy of political authority, legal decision-making, and administrative power of government depends. In the three domains of authority, lawgiving, and government, I argue, one can best find the traces of the Islamic conceptions of sovereignty as well as the elaborations of Islamic political thought.

Islam as Discursive Tradition

The way one conceptualizes Islam usually determines the way one defines and articulates all other areas related to Islam, such as Islamic politics, Islamic economics, Islamic philosophy, and Islamic law. Hence, accurate and coherent conceptualizations of Islam (or the Islamic) are the foundational aspect of all contemporary studies of Islam.[6] Contrary to many other attempts at conceptualizing Islam and the Islamic, I argue that Islam can be defined as a discursive tradition that allows diverse schools of thought and preserves multiple discourses and interpretations of the authoritative texts (the Qur'an and the Sunnah/Hadith) and sacred foundation (historical context and practices of the Prophet and his companions) of Islam. Discursive tradition, to me, refers to rationally oriented discourses aimed to relate the human to the divine at epistemic and moral ground on which the Muslim Community hinges on. The Quranic text and the Prophetic tradition are not only at the center of this relation but also engender a unifying force of the Community (*ummah*).

---

[6] Frank Griffel, "Contradictions and Lots of Ambiguity: Two New Perspectives on Premodern (and Postclassical) Islamic Societies," *Bustan: The Middle East Book Review* 8, no. 1 (July 1, 2017): 2–3, https://doi.org/10.5325/bustan.8.1.0001.

Tradition, unlike the concept of religion that is a modern construct of the European West, "consists essentially of discourses that seek to instruct practitioners regarding the correct form and purpose of a given practice that, precisely because it is established, has a history."[7] Although they begin with a history, these discourses within the tradition are not only about history. Traditional discourses are related to the future (how the point of that practice can best be secured in the short or long term or why it should be modified or abandoned) as much as they are related to the past (when the practice was instituted, and from which the knowledge of its point and proper performance has been transmitted) through the present (how it is linked to other practices, institutions, and social conditions). "An Islamic discursive tradition is simply a tradition of Muslim discourse that addresses itself to conceptions of the Islamic past and future, with reference to a particular Islamic practice in the present."[8] In this regard, the Islamic discursive tradition has its own rationalities and types of reasoning couched in its texts, practices, history, and institutions. Islamic tradition, unlike some Orientalist presentations of Islam that place reason in opposition to tradition, always contains rational argumentation and modes of reasoning surrounding traditional practices.[9] Tradition includes multiple discourses and various forms of practice. Religion, when considered a universal category, "is a reflection of the liberal demand that religion be separate from the sphere of real power and reason such as politics, law, and science."[10] Therefore, a study of Islam "should begin, as Muslims do, from the concept of a discursive tradition that includes and relates itself to the founding texts of the Qur'an and the Hadith. Islam is neither a distinctive social structure nor a heterogeneous collection of beliefs, artifacts, customs, and morals. It is a tradition."[11] Hence, it can be argued that the central domain around which all different discourses emerge and take their shape is the foundational texts of Qur'an and the Prophetic tradition.

A discursive tradition is made up of language and reason. Muslim thinkers accept many different interpretations and schools of Islam. There is no one absolute truth in the realm of human understanding; there can be multiple expressions of the truth.[12] The main force behind the existence of multiple schools in law, philosophi-

---

[7] Talal Asad, "The Idea of an Anthropology of Islam," *Occasional Papers*, Center for Contemporary Arab Studies, Georgetown University, 1986, 20.

[8] Asad, 20.

[9] Asad, 22.

[10] Talal Asad, *Genealogies of Religion: Discipline and Reasons of Power in Christianity and Islam* (Baltimore: Johns Hopkins University Press, 1993), 28.

[11] Asad, "The Idea of an Anthropology of Islam," 20.

[12] Hallaq, *The Impossible State*, 58–59.

cal theology, spirituality, and philosophy is the legitimacy of disagreement. The second component is that tradition connects all of these discourses to a sacred foundation, which is the normative origin of Islam. This is the Divine Revelation and Prophetic tradition of Muhammad. Hence, Islamic discursive tradition is the constitutive dynamic of Muslim Community. The common denominator of these varying rational orientations and discourses is both the acceptance of Divine Revelation and the Prophetic tradition as authoritative sources and the reference to a certain historical past as the origin of Islamic tradition. As Muhsin Mahdi states:

> Since the Islamic community owed its origin, its law and its character to a revelation and a prophet, it is natural that the central problem of practical philosophy or political philosophy in Islam would be that of understanding the phenomenon of prophecy, i.e. the rational explanation of the nature and source of the prophet's knowledge, and the nature and the source of the powers through which he performs miracles, convinces the multitude and induces them to carry out his commands.[13]

Political Genres in the Islamic Tradition

The three Muslim thinkers, whose works on politics I am going to excavate, represent distinct genres of politics and preceding rational engagement with political subjects in the Islamic intellectual history. They, to put it simply, are representatives of three modes of reason or discourses: rhetorical (*khatābah*), dialectical (*jadal*), and demonstrative (*burhān*). "Rhetorical and dialectical reasoning are associated with the multitude of human beings and are the modes of reasoning adopted in popular disciplines, whereas demonstrative reasoning is the province of an elite class of philosophers, who use it to achieve certainty."[14] These three rational discourses are differentiated based on the premises on which the rest of the argument is built. The premises or axioms, from which these discourses begin, justify the conclusion of the argument. As Ibn Rushd (Averroes) states in his Decisive Treatise (*Fasl al-Maqal*):

> For the natures of men are on different levels with respect to [their paths to] assent. One of them comes to assent through demonstration; another comes to assent through dialectical arguments, just as firmly as the demonstrative man through demonstration,

---

[13] *Muhsin Mahdi Ibn Khaldun's Philosophy of History*, 84–85, accessed May 8, 2023, http://archive.org/details/MuhsinMahdiIbnKhaldunsPhilosophyOfHistory

[14] Muhammad Ali Khalidi, ed., *Medieval Islamic Philosophical Writings*, 1st ed. (Cambridge University Press, 2005), https://doi.org/10.1017/CBO9780511811050.

since his nature does not contain any greater capacity; while another comes to assent through rhetorical arguments, again just as firmly as the demonstrative man through demonstrative arguments. Thus since this divine religion of ours has summoned people by these three methods, assent to it has extended to everyone.[15]

Islam as a discursive tradition implies multiple theoretical articulations and various practical implications of Islamic sources and history. Muslim thinkers could produce a variety of schools and rational orientations in philosophy, philosophical theology (Kalām) law (Fiqh), and spiritual paths (Sufi orders) that could shape diverse theoretical and practical expressions of Islamic tradition. The emergence of a variety of political genres within Islamic political thought is the direct result of the nature of the Islamic tradition, which allows multiple claims of truth and methodological investigations within the discipline of political theory. Each one of the political genres is built on specific modes of reasoning and methodology. While philosophers examine political phenomena from the perspective of pure rational premises, jurists use legal premises of Sharīʿa to explain political phenomena. Multiple truth claims had emerged and were represented by particular thinkers and texts according to diverse reasoning and methodology. This is the distinctive characteristic of Islamic discursive tradition that not only allows but also preserves the diversity of philosophical, legal, and moral orientations and schools.

Al-Fārābī (d.930), who is considered the first Muslim political philosopher, is committed to philosophical method and conceptualization, problematizes political matters through demonstration (*burhān*), which is a mode of reason that starts from first principles or self-evident premises of intellect and proceeds to prove everything else from them, either directly or indirectly. This rational method interprets and understands any religious phenomena upon premises of pure intellectual faculty. Al-Māwardī (d.1058), as jurist, is introduced as the first legal theorist of Islamic constitutionalism and approaches political subjects from a rhetorical (*khatābah*) mode of reason that bases its conclusions on persuasive opinions of Sharīʿa. Finally, al-Juwaynī (d.1085), as a philosophical theologian, articulates his political perspective through a dialectical (*jadal*) mode of reason that begins from commonly accepted opinions within Islamic theological (epistemic) framework. Although all three thinkers are Muslims and lived in the fourth and fifth centuries of Islamic history, they had developed diverse political theories by embracing distinct methods to examine political subject matters. These three figures laid down the foundation of Islamic political thought by writing books on politics. They de-

---

[15] Averroës, *The Book of The Decisive Treatise*, Islamic Translation Series (Provo, Utah: Brigham Young University Press, 2001), 8.

fined politics in a comprehensive manner for the first time. Through investigating their different approaches to politics, the rest of this article aims to explore multiple political discourses and diverse conceptions of sovereignty in Islamic political thought.

Tracing the definitions of sovereignty can lead us to see how these thinkers defined the central domain of Muslim Community, which shaped and determined, in their writings, all other secondary domains of sociopolitical life.[16] Although discussions on the caliphate/imamate constituted a significant portion of political writings, Muslim thinkers across the generations have insisted that the source of legitimate authority was the Community and their adherence to a particular epistemic and moral system to which all political powers had to depend. Hence, the Muslim Community, which was defined and shaped by the metaphysical premises of Divine Revelation and the particular human (sociopolitical) expressions of its truth, can be claimed to be a self-governing actor in the political theory of Muslim thinkers.[17] In this regard, the general will of the Community and the abstract universal laws of Divine Revelation that were embraced by the Muslim Community took the shape of legal and theological schools (madhhab) and Sufi orders (mystic groups). The function of the caliphate or sultanic power was to guard the pluralism of Muslim Community and establish order and stability by protecting each group without supporting any of them or imposing one over the other.[18]

Multiple Political Discourses in the Islamic Tradition

Many thinkers such as Leo Strauss and Muhsin Mahdi have argued that Islamic law, philosophical theology, and philosophy on key questions of political theory cannot be reconciled. Most of the Straussian interpreters of the political works of al-Fārābī have argued that his construction of Plato's theory of the perfect state as in "On the Perfect State" (*Mabādi' Ārā' Ahl al-Madīnat al-Fāḍilah*) did not have any roots in either Islamic legal theory or philosophical theology. They argued the same about his theory of prophecy and the different roles of the prophet versus the

---

[16] Hallaq, *The Impossible State*, 63.
[17] Hallaq, 49.
[18] Ahmed Abdel Meguid, "Reversing Schmitt: The Sovereign as a Guardian of Rational Pluralism and the Peculiarity of the Islamic State of Exception in Al-Juwaynī's Dialectical Theology," *European Journal of Political Theory* 19, no. 4 (2017): 12, https://doi.org/10.1177/1474885117730672

philosopher as possible legislators (*Shari'an*) and rulers.[19] The central problem of the role of the prophet as a lawgiver and a ruler constitutes one of the key strands of the discussions of sovereignty and the role of the caliph in Islamic history. I disagree with the argument of irreconcilability.[20] On the contrary, I contend that al-Fārābī's theory shares certain similarities with al-Māwardī and al-Juwaynī's perspectives.[21] For instance, moral and legal norms of Shariʿa produced by the Prophet and developed by the successors of the Prophet is one of the key features of all three thinkers.[22] Therefore, after close examination of the political treaties of these three figures, I argue that although they are committed to a particular methodological attitude and mode of reasoning, their political theories can be considered "Islamic" based on common patterns and shared conclusions of their political theories. The rest of the chapter will focus on three major topics in the political writings of these thinkers: 1) legitimate political authority; 2) law, the lawgiver, and the rule of law; and 3) sovereign ruler and limited government.

al-Fārābī; Philosophical Political Science

Legitimate Political Authority

For al-Fārābī mankind is social by nature. Their association and communal life necessitate laws that will organize their worldly affairs and lead them to moral and intellectual perfection, which is the ultimate happiness.[23] The ultimate purpose of human existence is attaining happiness. Such happiness can be achieved by con-

---

[19] Charles E. Butterworth, "Alfarabi's Goal: Political Philosophy, Not Political Theology," in *Islam, the State, and Political Authority: Medieval Issues and Modern Concerns*, ed. Asma Afsaruddin, Middle East Today (New York: Palgrave Macmillan US, 2011), 54, https://doi.org/10.1057/9781137002020_4

[20] Massimo Campanini, "Alfarabi and the Foundation of Political Theology in Islam," in *Islam, the State, and Political Authority: Medieval Issues and Modern Concerns*, ed. Asma Afsaruddin, Middle East Today (New York: Palgrave Macmillan US, 2011), 35–52, https://doi.org/10.1057/9781137002020_3

[21] Andrew March, "Falsafa and Law," in *The Oxford Handbook of Islamic Law*, by Andrew March, ed. Anver M. Emon and Rumee Ahmed (Oxford University Press, 2018), 148–54, https://doi.org/10.1093/oxfordhb/9780199679010.013.57.

[22] Abdel Meguid Ahmed, "Prophecy," in *The Princeton Encyclopedia of Islamic Political Thought*, ed. Gerhard Böwering, Patricia Crone, and Mahan Mirza (Princeton, N.J: Princeton University Press, 2013).

[23] Alfarabi, "The Attainment of Happiness," in *Medieval Political Philosophy: A Sourcebook*, ed. Joshua Parens and Joseph C. Macfarland (Ithaca, N.Y.: Cornell University Press, 2011), 56–57.

necting with the Active Intellect (emanating from God) who delivers the first principles of reasoning and the theoretical knowledge of universals related to God, cosmos, and human nature.[24] In addition, one needs to have a rational capacity to extend the first principles of reasoning and apply them to particulars. However, the vast majority of humanity is not able to achieve this connection without the help and guidance of someone who is perfect in his understanding of universals and in how they correspond to the particulars of all aspects of life.[25] Governance of the city, al-Fārābī says, is thus natural and necessary for the sake of the majority who need someone to lead them to happiness. He uses the analogy of a healthy body whose parts fulfill their functions and help each other in hierarchical order to keep the body, as a whole, healthy; a virtuous city is the city whose citizens fulfill their functions and assist each other according to the order established by the first ruler.[26] Once every citizen performs their individual task in harmony with others, they will reach the ultimate happiness according to their inner nature, rational capacity, and fulfillment of their task in appropriate order. The virtuous city resembles the cosmos, which is organized and ruled by the Supreme Being (God) in a hierarchical order.[27] Political authority is a natural and essential part of human life. Although the necessity of a political authority is natural, the legitimacy of any political authority comes from its acquisition of theoretical knowledge, practical skills, and moral perfection of character.[28] Such a political rulership can lead the community to true happiness. All in all, the community and individual take precedence over the political authority, whose legitimacy derives from them.

Law, Lawgiver, and the Rule of Law

According to al-Fārābī, the prophet, like the philosopher, is the one who has perfect rational and imaginative faculties. They enable him to convey universal principles and ideas to the common people by articulating them in accordance with the particularities of their contexts. Therefore, he is the one who can lead his community to perfection. He represents Divine Revelation, which corresponds to universal rational ideas, in an immediate and practical way the entire community can under-

---

[24] Fārābī, *On the Perfect State: Mabādi' Ārā' Ahl al-Madīnat al-Fāḍilah*, trans. Richard Walzer ([S.l.] : Chicago, IL: Great Books of the Islamic World ; Distributed by KAZI Publications, 1998), 241.

[25] Alfarabi, "The Political Regime," in *Medieval Political Philosophy: A Sourcebook*, ed. Joshua Parens and Joseph C. Macfarland (Ithaca, N.Y.: Cornell University Press, 2011), 40.

[26] Fārābī, *On the Perfect State*, 231–35.

[27] Fārābī, 237.

[28] Alfarabi, "The Political Regime," 42.

stand.[29] As the political leader of the community and God's prophet, the first ruler governs according to universal rational truth, albeit articulated through the particularistic expressions of law, rituals, and virtues.[30] Rational capacity and strong imagination are the essential dimensions of prophethood in al-Fārābī's political theory. Therefore, the source of Law is as divine as it is human in the sense that universal and abstract truths are adapted into concrete, practical, and particular contexts.[31] In this way, all members of the community can understand and practice divine truth in their life in order to reach the perfection of their capacity and attain happiness.[32]

The lawgiver is a prophet who can issue particular laws, addressing all details of the legal/moral and socioeconomic lives of people for the establishment of a virtuous city and community. The divine characteristic of law does not preclude human interference and interpretation.[33] Philosophers (people of knowledge) are the true successors of the prophet who can infer new laws and rulings based on what the Prophet had established before.[34] Even the Prophet, who was an ordinary man, represented the human understanding and application of revealed law. Therefore, the rule of law was not only above and over all political powers but was also the standard by which all ruling powers derived the legitimacy requisite for rule.

Sovereign Ruler and the Limited Government

al-Fārābī considers the first ruler of the community as the prophet, who led people in all kinds of affairs that required the intervention, regulation, and execution of a political leader. He presents a detailed account of the role of the Prophet in establishing the virtuous city or community. He requires very high standards and qualifications for someone to be elected as the successor of the prophet or/and the ruler of the community.[35] Only the Prophet Muhammad and the first rightly guided caliphs of Muslims could fulfill those qualifications. By keeping these qualifications a prerequisite for a virtuous rulership, al-Fārābī aimed to preserve the epistemic and moral foundations of the Islamic conception of sovereignty. If these qualifica-

---

[29] Fārābī, *On the Perfect State*, 245–47.
[30] Alfarabi, "The Attainment of Happiness," 63.
[31] Alfarabi, "The Enumeration of the Sciences," in *Medieval Political Philosophy: A Sourcebook*, ed. Joshua Parens and Joseph C. Macfarland (Ithaca, N.Y.: Cornell University Press, 2011), 19.
[32] Fārābī, *On the Perfect State*, 237–39.
[33] Alfarabi, "The Enumeration of the Sciences," 21.
[34] Fārābī, *On the Perfect State*, 249–51.
[35] Fārābī, 247.

tions, especially ones regarding knowledge and moral perfection, are not possible to find in one person, then sovereignty can be divided between more than one person.[36] People of knowledge are the best-suited candidates for taking the responsibility of rulership over the community. Because they are equipped with all sorts of knowledge inherited from their successors up until the prophet, al-Fārābī argues that philosophers are the true heirs of the prophet-lawgiver. They are the only group who has legitimate authority to derive rulings from the laws laid down by the first ruler. They produce new laws regarding newly emerging cases through analogical reasoning and interpretation of existing laws. In this way, they preserve the laws and political order against outer enemies of the virtuous city and protect against misinterpretations/misapplications of the truth and virtuous religion.[37] Therefore, if a ruler is not qualified to be a philosopher, he needs to rule with the help of a philosopher who has the appropriate knowledge of laws established by the first ruler and can help the current ruler apply them. Furthermore, it is only the philosopher who can help to preserve the virtuous religion and city through maintaining certain laws and adopting new laws.[38] In this sense, the governance of the city and community is dependent on the laws and their rational interpretation by scholars/philosophers, not the coercive power of the government.

al-Māwardī; Juristic Political Science

Legitimate Political Authority

Most of studies on al-Māwardī's political thought are predicated on his seminal work *al-Aḥkām al-Sulṭāniyya* (the Ordinances of Government), in which he brings together, from a wide range of literature, opinions of jurists on the institution of caliphate, appointment of viziers and amirs, judicial systems, taxation, land market, and so forth.[39] Therefore, this work can be considered as a simplified administration and constitutional handbook. However, his social and political theory can be fully captured when his other works, such as *Tashīl al-Naẓar (Facilitating Administration)*, are examined.[40] In this book, al-Māwardī highlights the reasons

---

[36] Fārābī, 253.
[37] Alfarabi, "The Enumeration of the Sciences," 20.
[38] Fārābī, *On the Perfect State*, 253.
[39] ʿAlī Ibn-Muḥammad al-Māwardī, *The Ordinances of Government: = Al-Aḥkām al-Sulṭāniyya w'al-Wilāyāt al-Dīniyya*, ed. Wafaa Hassan Wahba, 1. paperback ed, Great Books of Islamic Civilization (Reading: Garnet, 2000).
[40] Eltigani Hamid, "Al-Māwardī's Theory of State: Some Ignored Dimensions," *American*

why political systems are instituted, maintained, and declined. He argues that mankind is social by nature; however, what brings them together is religion, wealth, and force. For him, the most effective driving force of human association is religion (not necessarily Islam), which also requires its believers to choose a political leader that can organize their life.[41] Thus, the source of legitimate political authority is religious obligation, not some basic rational premise dictating the formation of human association as philosophers contend. Hence, it is a religious obligation upon the Muslim Community to elect a caliph (ruler) to take care of the public affairs of people.[42] In al-Māwardī's approach, rulers have a contract ('aqd) with the Community to apply Shariʿa norms and protect them in an exchange of allegiance and obedience.[43] Rulers, in the Sunni doctrine of caliphate, do not have any divine rights of kings, instead they have the duties of establishing justice through Sharīʿa norms and the responsibility for the people's protection.

Law, Lawgiver, and the Rule of Law

In the very introduction of *al-Ahkam*, al-Māwardī states that the reason he compiled his book is to help the ruler (caliph) know his duties and rights with respect to laws, administration, and the other public affairs of people that are found in the books of jurists dispersedly. By writing this book, he aimed to collect the scattered rules regarding all aspects of government from a variety of legal corpus.[44] al-Māwardī, in his introduction, expresses the role of jurists in determining not only the very details of laws regulating the public and private lives of the Muslim Community but also the boundaries of the political authority of the caliphate and the assessment of the legitimacy of political regulations. Although the sources of law are the Quran and Prophetic tradition, which can (and should) be studied by rulers, only jurists are, argues al-Māwardī, qualified with the necessary legal knowledge and training to deduce the norms of Sharīʿa. The ruler, who is not qualified regarding the knowledge of the Sharīʿa, must depend on scholars (jurists/theologians) to implement the norms of Islam and adjudicate legal issues.[45] Therefore, it is quite clear that legal reasoning (ijtihād), to preserve, interpret, and

---

Journal of Islam and Society 18 (October 1, 2001): 1–18, https://doi.org/10.35632/ajis.v18i4.1979.

[41] Hamid, 5.
[42] Māwardī, *The Ordinances of Government*, 3.
[43] Māwardī, 17.
[44] Māwardī, 1.
[45] Hallaq, *The Impossible State*, 52; Māwardī, *The Ordinances of Government*, 72–87.

produce the law, is the exclusive domain of scholars.[46] Although they mostly apply law non-officially through mediation or the issuance of legal opinions as a response to the questions they are accustomed to be asked, scholars always need the ruler to appoint them to apply law within the judicial system. The rulers' lack of legal capacity enables scholars to establish their epistemic, moral, and legal authority in public affairs of the Muslim Community.

Sovereign Ruler and the Limited Government

According to al-Māwardī, rulership (caliphate) is a succession to the Prophet regarding the protection of religion and management of the Muslim Community's affairs.[47] It is a religious and collective duty of the Muslim Community to elect a political leader. Thus, the sovereignty of a ruler is dependent on his capacity to apply religious norms and the consent of the Community expressed through ahl al-ḥall wa al-ʿaqd (electors/representatives of the Community).[48] The Shariʿa, as law and jurisprudence developed by scholars and as a moral/spiritual guideline for the Muslim Community, must be the basis of any claim to power if it is to be legitimate.[49] The political and military powers of usurper sultans were usually considered legitimate when they declared their allegiance to the Shariʿa norms.[50] al-Māwardī's acceptance of local usurpers as legitimate, if they acknowledge the authority of the caliphate and supremacy of the Shariʿa, has been taken by some contemporary scholars as the main mission behind his political writings.[51] However, when other works of al-Māwardī are examined, one can easily discover that he acknowledges the tensions and relations between power (ruler) and religion (scholars).[52] Both rulers (holders of power and guardians of order) and scholars (epistemic and moral leaders of the Community and the main actors of the legal system) are mutually in need of help from each other. Therefore, one can claim that a political regime will not be as important as the legal system in which the law is not produced by rulers, who, to the contrary, owe their legitimacy to their concession to the rule of law.[53]

---

[46] Hallaq, *The Impossible State*, 58.
[47] Māwardī, *The Ordinances of Government*, 3.
[48] Māwardī, 3–4.
[49] Hallaq, *The Impossible State*, 50.
[50] Māwardī, *The Ordinances of Government*, 36–37.
[51] Erwin I. J. Rosenthal, *Political Thought in Medieval Islam: An Introductory Outline* (Cambridge: Cambridge University Press, 1958), 30–31.
[52] Hamid, "Al-Māwardī's Theory of State," 6.
[53] Hallaq, *The Impossible State*, 63.

al-Juwaynī: Theological Political Science

Legitimate Political Authority

al-Juwaynī has a unique approach in his political theory. He does not only present a theory of the caliphate but also theorizes its absence.[54] He attempts to defend that the caliphate or the caliph is not the foundation of the Muslim Community. With the collapse of the caliphate and absence of a ruler, the Muslim Community will continue to survive, depending on the leadership and guidance of scholars (mujtahids) who are considered the epistemic and moral leaders of people. They have the knowledge of Sharīʿa whose norms can help the believers to organize their lives. The continuity of law and society depends on the Sharīʿa, not the power of the ruler (caliph). Community's adherence to Sharīʿa norms and scholars' authority is the foundation of sociopolitical order and the stability of the Muslim Community.[55] For him, humans are social by nature; however, it is the epistemic ground of Sharīʿa accepted by the whole Community that is the unifying dynamic and drawing force of Muslim polity. The legitimacy of political authority is rooted in the commitment of rulers to Sharīʿa norms that were adhered to by the political subjects of the caliphate.

Law, Lawgiver, and the Rule of Law

The role of imâm/caliph (ruler of Muslim Community) is either concerned with religion or the worldly affairs of the people.[56] As the guardian of the Muslim Community, according to al-Juwaynī, the ruler should neither impose absolutist intellectual assumptions that are beyond common sense even though they are regarding the principles of religion, nor support one school of Islamic law against the other. Hence the ruler, as functional guardian, does not have absolute power, and his role "consists in securing a public domain for political subjects of different rational orientations to function."[57]

According to Muslim jurists and theologians, the true lawgiver is God and His Messenger; thus, only those who are equipped with the knowledge of Sharīʿa—the

---

[54] Sohaira Siddiqui, "Power vs. Authority: Al-Juwaynī's Intervention in Pragmatic Political Thought," *Journal of Islamic Studies* 28, no. 2 (May 1, 2017): 199, https://doi.org/10.1093/jis/etw057.

[55] Siddiqui, 199.

[56] Wael B. Hallaq, "Caliphs, Jurists and the Saljuqs in the Political Thought of Juwayni," *The Muslim World* 74, no. 1 (January 1984): 36, https://doi.org/10.1111/j.1478-1913.1984.tb03447.x.

[57] Meguid, "Reversing Schmitt," 9.

true understanding and practice of Divine Revelation and Prophetic tradition—are able to interpret and implement the law or deduce laws for new cases emerged after the Prophet. Both al-Māwardī and al-Juwaynī argue that the ruler, who is not qualified with the knowledge of Shariʿa, has to depend on scholars to implement laws and adjudicate legal issues.[58] Therefore, it is quite clear that the legal reasoning, to preserve, interpret, or produce the law, is a peculiar domain of scholars (jurists/ theologians). However, scholars always need the appointment of a ruler to apply law in the judicial system, although they mostly apply law unofficially through mediation or by issuing legal opinions in response to questions they are asked. According to al-Juwaynī, even in the absence of a ruler, as the functional guardian, that is called the state of exception, each political subject should follow the independent scholars of any school of law they endorse.[59] This is explicitly showing that legal and intellectual pluralism of Islamic society is protected not only under normal political conditions but also during states of exceptions when there is no qualified ruler or no ruler at all.[60]

Sovereign Ruler and the Limited Government

al-Māwardī and al-Juwaynī, I argue al-Fārābī as well, identify the rulership of Muslims (and non-Muslims) as a *niyābat al-nubuwwah* (succession to the Prophet) in all kinds of affairs that required the intervention, regulation, and execution of a political leader. While al-Fārābī presents a detailed account of the role of the Prophet to establish the city or unite the community, al-Māwardī and al-Juwaynī require very high standards and qualifications for someone to be elected as the leader (caliph) of Muslim Community in such a way that only the Prophet and the first rightly guided caliphs could fulfill. By keeping these qualifications, a prerequisite for election of caliph, Muslim jurists and theologians (and philosophers) aimed to preserve the epistemic foundation of Islamic conception of sovereignty. If these qualifications, especially the one regarding knowledge and piety, are not possible to be found in one person, according to al-Juwaynī (al-Fārābī and al-Māwardī as well), then it can be divided between a ruler and scholars.[61] Throughout their equipment with all sorts of knowledge inherited from previous successors up until the Prophet, scholars have already been the true heirs of the Prophet.[62] They are the only group who had a legitimate authority to drive rules from basic sources of

---

[58] Hallaq, "CALIPHS, JURISTS AND THE SALJ," 34.
[59] Siddiqui, "Power vs. Authority," 211.
[60] Meguid, "Reversing Schmitt," 10.
[61] Siddiqui, "Power vs. Authority," 210–11.
[62] Hallaq, *The Impossible State*, 53.

Islam (Qur'an and Prophetic tradition), produce laws regarding newly emerging cases through legal reasoning, interpret the verse of Qur'an and traditions of the Prophet, and finally defend community and religion against outer enemies and inner misinterpretations/misapplications of Islamic sources.[63] On the other hand, caliphs are the only ones who can facilitate scholars to fulfill their mission and execute some legal rules left exclusively to the authority of political leaders, such as laws related to taxation, criminal, and military areas.[64]

Conclusion: Epistemic Foundation of Islamic Political Thought

Islamic conceptions of sovereignty can be best articulated as follows: the protection of pluralism of particular forms of rationality was the foundation of a well-ordered body politic at the height of Islamic civilization.[65] Sovereignty from the Islamic perspective was defined in terms of protecting rational pluralism and diverse schools, which originate from various interpretations of Qur'an and the Prophetic tradition. The ultimate task of the sovereign ruler in Islamic political thought and within Muslim Community was to preserve a rationally pluralistic community through the implementation of norms and rulings of Shariʿa.[66] The protection of multiple philosophical, theological, spiritual, and legal schools and groups was one of the main characteristics of Islamic conceptions of sovereignty, grounded on Islamic epistemic and moral principles. The Ruler (imām/caliph) governs the community in terms of not imposing his laws upon individuals but allowing each particular school of law to practice their rational system in harmony and well-ordered society.[67] The general principles and limits of reasoning underlying the production of the normative and prescriptive claims of Shariʿa determine the powers and obligatory tasks of the ruler. In the Islamic conception of sovereignty, sovereign power consists neither in following a singular rational norm dictated by the government nor in deciding on the exceptions to such norms; rather, it consists in defending a finite multitude of possible rational norms derived from Islamic sources.[68] In the Islamic conception of sovereignty, there is not such an absolute

---

[63] Hallaq, "CALIPHS, JURISTS AND THE SALJ?," 41.
[64] Hallaq, *The Impossible State*, 66–68.
[65] Meguid, "Reversing Schmitt," 20.
[66] Hallaq, *The Impossible State*, 58–59; Meguid, "Reversing Schmitt," 10.
[67] Hallaq, *The Impossible State*, 73.
[68] Meguid, "Reversing Schmitt," 9.

will of the sovereign state; instead, every and each particular rational school is protected by Islamic governance through the epistemic and moral grounds provided by Shariʿa.

Bibliography

Alfarabi. 2011a. The Enumeration of the Sciences. In *Medieval Political Philosophy: A Sourcebook*, ed. Joshua Parens and Joseph C. Macfarland. Ithaca, N.Y: Cornell University Press.
———. 2011b. The Political Regime. In *Medieval Political Philosophy: A Sourcebook*, ed. Joshua Parens and Joseph C. Macfarland. Ithaca, N.Y: Cornell University Press.
Asad, Talal. 1986. The Idea of an Anthropology of Islam. *Occasional Papers*. Center for Contemporary Arab Studies, Georgetown University, 1–22.
———. 1993. *Genealogies of Religion: Discipline and Reasons of Power in Christianity and Islam*. Baltimore: Johns Hopkins University Press.
Campanini, Massimo. 2011. Alfarabi and the Foundation of Political Theology in Islam. In *Islam, the State, and Political Authority: Medieval Issues and Modern Concerns*, Middle East Today, ed. Asma Afsaruddin, 35–52. New York: Palgrave Macmillan US. https://doi.org/10.1057/9781137002020_3.
Hallaq, Wael B. January 1984. Caliphs, Jurists and the Saljuqs in the Political Thought of Juwaynī. *The Muslim World* 74 (1): 26–41. https://doi.org/10.1111/j.1478-1913.1984.tb03447.x.
———. 2014. *The Impossible State: Islam, Politics, and Modernity's Moral Predicament*. Paperback edition. New York: Columbia University Press.
Hamid, Eltigani. October 1, 2001. Al-Māwardī's Theory of State: Some Ignored Dimensions. *American Journal of Islam and Society* 18: 1–18. https://doi.org/10.35632/ajis.v18i4.1979.
Māwardī, ʿAlī Ibn-Muḥammad al-. 2000. *The Ordinances of Government: = Al-Aḥkām al-Sulṭāniyya w'al-Wilāyāt al-Dīniyya*. Edited by Wafaa Hassan Wahba. 1. paperback ed. Great Books of Islamic Civilization. Reading: Garnet.
Siddiqui, Sohaira. May 1, 2017. Power vs. Authority: Al-Juwaynī's Intervention in Pragmatic Political Thought. *Journal of Islamic Studies* 28 (2): 193–220. https://doi.org/10.1093/jis/etw057.

Ahmet Celik is a PhD candidate in the Department of Religion at Syracuse University. Primarily, his research interests include comparative political thought, Islamic political and legal theory, and early modern and modern political philosophy. His dissertation project sits at the intersection of religion, philosophy, and political theory, as it examines the concept of sovereignty in Islamic political thought. Dr. Ahmet Celik graduated from Marmara University Faculty of Theology, from where he also received his MA from the Islamic Law Department. He also received his Master of Philosophy and a Certificate of Advanced Study in Middle East Affairs from Syracuse University. He then went to Marmara University to obtain his PhD in Islamic political thought. Meanwhile, he was relocating to New York city as a visiting researcher at Columbia University for two years. Since 2017, he has been working and teaching at Syracuse University.

The Hateful Rhetoric Against Muslims and the Authority-Making of Islamic Identity

Etin Anwar

Introduction

The discursive narrative of 'violent Muslims' varies in its emergence, its usage, and its maintenance. I use the discursive narratives of 'violent Muslims' in two senses: (1) the American/European-dominant discourses of associating Islam with violence and (2) the Western political signification of Muslims as violent people. I make the correlation between the perception of Muslims as violent people and the mythic Western duality of the secular and the religious and attempt to situate this relationship within the contexts of the secularization project. Such a project defines Islam to fit into a genealogical model of religion that originates in the West. Historically, the Western discursive narratives of religion flourished within a series of periods from Late Antiquity, through the Middle Ages and early modern Europe,

---

This chapter was originally developed during my residency at the Center for Theological Inquiry, where I served as a Resident Fellow in the spring of 2019 and was completed with the support of the John R. & Florence B. Kinghorn Global Fellowship in 2023–2024.

E. Anwar (✉)
Department of Religious Studies, Hobart and William Smith Colleges, Geneva, NY, USA
e-mail: anwar@hws.edu

© The Author(s), under exclusive license to Springer Nature Switzerland AG 2024
M. Shafiq, T. Donlin-Smith (eds.), *Inclusion or Exclusion in the Sacred Texts and Human Contexts*, https://doi.org/10.1007/978-3-031-70180-1_13

to the modern state formation achieved following the Enlightenment, which resulted in the privatization of religion.[1] As Islam does not have a congruent history of religious institutionalization and privatization, it appears to resist a Western model of relegating religion to the private sphere.

The secularization project within Muslim contexts underlies the emergence of Islam with an increasing interest in political significance. The political use of Islam gains its significance in challenging the emerging authoritarian powers that undergird the state formation, especially during colonial and post-colonial periods. Radical groups within Muslim contexts elevate the role of Islam to a political position in the public sphere. This is where the second sense of the term 'violent Muslims' comes in. It refers to what is being projected and interpreted from acts of violence by those who identify themselves as Muslims and who find meaning in Islamic language to support their own ideological agendas within the local and global nexus. Acts of terror by radical Muslims feed the imagination of an American public that has already been consumed with prejudice against Muslims. Findings about US Muslims drawn from 2017 Pew Research Center show that American Muslims in the United States "perceive a lot of discrimination against their religious group, are leery of Trump, and think their fellow Americans do not see Islam as part of mainstream U.S. society."[2] The discrimination against Muslims largely stems from the ubiquity of Euro-American terms such as 'violent Muslims.' This narrative creates a societal bias that frames Muslims as violent people and concomitantly molds into the social imagery of Islam as a violent religion. In a broader context, individual biases toward Islam and Muslims wire self-authority among the public to perceive Islam or Muslims as being violent locally and globally.

I propose to locate the American 'discursive authority' of Muslims as violent by (1) finding out how certain narratives, such as the perception of violent Muslims, become a prominent mythic discourse that produces self-authority; (2) situating the narrative of violent Muslims within their own contexts; (3) offering an alternative discursive authority that resists the Western-prominent narrative of Muslims as violent people; and (4) advocating a new authoritative narrative of non-violent Muslims. I will discuss each point in a corresponding section.

---

[1] Armando Salvator, "Tradition and Modernity within Islamic Civilization and the West," in *Islam and modernity: key issues and debates*, eds. Muhammad Khalid Masud, Armando Salvatore, and Martin van Bruinessen (Edinburgh, Scotland: Edinburgh University Press, 2014. 2009), 14.

[2] Pew Research Center, U.S. Muslims Concerned About Their Place in Society, but Continue to Believe in the American Dream, July 26, 2017 (Washington DC.: Pew Research Center, 2017), 5.

Identifying the Violent Muslims as a Mythic-prominent Discourse

The American discursive narrative of violent Muslims achieves prominence and carries more authority in the post-September 11, 2001, era. This begs the question as to what mythic discourses contribute to the maintenance of the American portrayal of Muslims as violent people and nurture its hegemonic presence. There is also a question of why alternative narrative of Muslims as peace-loving individuals largely remains hidden from the public conversation. In this section, I will provide an overview of how the mythic discourses of violent Muslims allow for the labeling of Muslims as violent people and prevent non-stereotypical portrayal of Muslims to be known. I will address these questions by treating the American portrayal of violent Muslims as 'a mythical discursive authority.' I show the correlation between a hegemonic pattern of the American perception of Muslims as violent people and the myth of religion as transcultural and transhistorical. I will discuss in this section how the American perception of Muslims as violent people as a myth carries ideological 'discursive authority' in the contexts of mythic discourse, social imaginary, and the assumption of religion as prone to violence.

The scholarly myth of Muslims as violent coalesces with media empire escalating the machinery of Islamophobia. The discursive linkage between Islam and violence in this contemporary context stems from the September 11 attack and the political implication that comes with it. What follows afterward was strategical efforts to unilaterally categorize Islam as a violent religion. Some statements about Islam as a violent religion are quite shocking. Franklin Graham in his interview on NBC Nightly News on November 16, 2001, said that "[Islam] is a very evil and wicked religion." He is also known for saying that Islam is "intoleran[t] [to] those who follow other faiths."[3] In the following year on October 6, 2002, Jerry Falwell is known for characterizing the Prophet Muhammad as a 'terrorist' on CBS's '60 Minutes' segment. Even when there is a recognition for most Muslims as peaceful people, televangelist Pat Robertson characterizes Islam as a violent religion with a desire for world domination.[4] Noticeably, all these discursive narratives of Islam as evil and violent, as well as Muhammad as a terrorist, come from highly respected figures with a lot of political capital.

What is said by prominent pious leaders—about Islam as supporting violence and Muslims as enacting violent behaviors—carries authority and simultaneously

---

[3] Franklin Graham, *The Name* (Nashville: Thomas Nelson, 2002), 69.
[4] Mark Allman, *Who would Jesus kill?: War, peace, and the Christian tradition* (Winona, MN: Saint Mary's Press, 2008), 149.

molds into the trusting hearts and minds. Allport may be right in saying that "piety may thus a convenient mask for prejudices which intrinsically have nothing to do with religion."[5] Piety, indeed, coexists with prejudice. Prejudicial attitude often take root intrinsically in religious congregants' heart due to the religion's prescription of how to treat the other. For this reason, Batson and Stoks would consider the prejudicial narratives of Islam and Muhammad to fit into a model of extrinsic and intrinsic dimension, increased prejudice, and proscribed.[6] In other word, the more the religious followers cultivate the teaching that prescribes hate and prejudice toward the other, the more likely they internalize their belief as intrinsic to religion and view outsider to their faith as an external dimension of their life. When exercised, this religiously based ideological mindset could easily feed the discursive narratives of Islam as evil and Muslims as violent people.

The mythic discourses of Muslims as irrational, violent people reinforce the assumption of Islam as an irrational religion. The citation of a dialogue between erudite Byzantine emperor Manuel II Paleologus and an educated Persian about Christianity and Islam during year approximately 1391 by Pope Benedict XVI in his talk entitled "Faith, Reason and the University: Memories and Reflections," and delivered on September 12, 2006, at Aula Magna of the University of Regensburg is benevolent. As Pope Benedict XVI acknowledged in footnote 3 in the postscript to his talk, he intended to use this dialogue to show the relationship between faith and reason in Christianity. However, his benign intent did not fare well, especially among Muslim audiences. This dialogue is relevant to cite here as follows:[7]

> In the seventh conversation (διάλεξις - controversy) edited by Professor Khoury, the emperor touches on the theme of the holy war. The emperor must have known that surah 2, 256 reads: "There is no compulsion in religion". According to some of the experts, this is probably one of the suras of the early period, when Mohammed was still powerless and under threat. But naturally the emperor also knew the instructions, developed later and recorded in the Qur'an, concerning holy war. Without descending to details, such as the difference in treatment accorded to those who have the "Book" and the "infidels", he addresses his interlocutor with a startling brusqueness, a brusqueness that we find unacceptable, on the central question about the relationship

---

[5] Gordon W. Allport, *The Nature of Prejudice* (Cambridge: Massachusetts: Addison-Wesley Publishing Company, 1954), 447.

[6] C. Daniel Batson and E. L. Stocks, "Religion and Prejudice," in *On the nature of prejudice: fifty years after Allport*, ed. John F. Dovidio (Malden, MA: Blackwell, 2009), 419.

[7] Pope Benedict XVI, "Faith, Reason and the University: Memories and Reflections," Aula Magna of the University of Regensburg, Tuesday, 12 September 2006, 1–8. See http://www.catholic-ew.org.uk/Home/News/2006/2006-Offline/Full-Text-of-the-Pope-Benedict-XVI-s-Regensburg-Lecture (Assessed on May 7, 2019).

between religion and violence in general, saying: "Show me just what Mohammed brought that was new, and there you will find things only evil and inhuman, such as his command to spread by the sword the faith he preached."

As Pope Benedict XVI points out in footnote number 3 that the final quote has caused misunderstanding among Muslims. In his own word:[8]

> In the Muslim world, this quotation has unfortunately been taken as an expression of my personal position, thus arousing understandable indignation. I hope that the reader of my text can see immediately that this sentence does not express my personal view of the Qur'an, for which I have the respect due to the holy book of a great religion. In quoting the text of the Emperor Manuel II, I intended solely to draw out the essential relationship between faith and reason. On this point I am in agreement with Manuel II, but without endorsing his polemic.

While I respect the way Pope Benedict XVI distances himself from the above quote and his recognition of the Quran as "the holy book of a great religion," I find his explanation to the postscript of the talk is problematic.

If Pope Benedict's citation of the dialogue between Byzantine emperor Manuel II Paleologus and an educated Persian is framed in Lincoln's framework of scholarship as a myth with footnotes, his recollection reinforces the myth of Islam as a violent religion and, consequently, Muslims as violent people.[9] Lincoln evokes a rhetorical dialogue with his imaginary student saying "[i]sn't scholarship just another instance of ideology in narrative form? Don't scholars tell stories to recalibrate a pecking order, putting themselves, their favorite theories, and their favorite people on top?"[10] Pope Benedict chose to tell stories of Christianity as compatible with reason, and in the process, he indirectly associated Islam with lack of reason, violent conversion, and blind following of God's will. Thus, Muslims are incapable of dialogue. By recalling the authority of Byzantine emperor Manuel II Paleologus, the Pope warrants his audiences to infer a mythic discourse of Christianity as superior to Islam, especially on the issue of faith and reason relationship.

While Christianity has gained its reputation as a religion that accords with reason, it shared a violent past. Middleton shows how the book of Revelation offers a framework for martyrdom:[11]

---

[8] Ibid.

[9] Bruce Lincoln, *Theorizing Myth: Narrative, ideology, and scholarship* (Chicago: University of Chicago Press), 209.

[10] Ibid., 208.

[11] Paul Middleton, *Martyrdom: A guide for the perplexed* (London [etc.]: T & T Clark, 2011), 34.

Christians are called to be faithful to death (2.10); there are already martyrs under the altar (6.9); there is a vast crowd of martyrs (7.9–17, 14.1–5); two witnesses will be slain (11.1–14); the saints conquered the dragon by not loving their lives to death (12.10–11); the Beast slays faithful Christians (13.15); so that all who die in the Lord are blessed (14.13); those who have slain Christians are punished (16.4–6), the harlot is drunk with the blood of the saints and martyrs of Jesus (17.6); and those beheaded for Jesus will reign for 1,000 years (20.4).

Christianity as a religion grew out of the painful experience of suffering and persecution, as reflected in the New Testament, as well as the need to defend itself from the Jewish pressures that perceived Jesus' movement as heretic, the Roman persecution, and the pagan resentment of Christian beliefs and practices.[12] As early Christians expected their suffering as salvation for Jesus, they were familiar with the narrative of giving their lives for their faith.[13] While giving one's life for faith could be displayed in the most transformative manners, there was a time where it took forms of crusades, inquisitions, colonialism, enslavement, and wars.

While the debates over martyrdom in Christianity appear to revolve around its early development, this is not the case with Islam. Middletown correctly points out that the September 11 attacks on US soil by al-Qaida in 2001 shaped the ensuing debates of suicide bombing and its relationship with Islamic martyr tradition.[14] The masterminds of suicide bombing, like Osama Bin Laden and Ayman al-Zawahiri, invoke the Quranic verses and the historical precedence drawn from the Prophet's life to support the idea of giving life to God as a rewarding experience. Osama bin Laden, for instance, quotes among others, QS al-Baqarah, 2:193 and QS al-Anfal, 8:39 and 24 in his fatwa (ruling), to kill the American and their allies in order "to liberate the al-Aqsa Mosque [in Jerusalem] and the holy mosque [in Mecca] from infidel grip," in accordance with what Allah prescribes: "and fight all the pagans all together as they fight you all together [QS al-Baqarah 2:193]," and "fight them until there is no more tumult or oppression, and there prevail justice and faith in Allah [QS al-Anfal, 8:39]."[15] As suicide killing gains prominence among the followers of al-Qaida and its affiliates, especially in the ensuing War of Terror in many

---

[12] Ibid., 31 and 34.
[13] Ibid., 57.
[14] Paul Middleton, "'Unlock Paradise with your own Blood': Martyrdom and Salvation in Islam and Christianity," eds. Hannah Bacon, Wendy Dossett, and Steve Knowles in *Alternative Salvation: engaging the sacred and the secular* (London: Bloomsbury, 2017), 109–120.
[15] John Calvert, *Islamism: A Documentary and Reference Guide* (Westport: Greenwood Press, 2008), 227.

parts in the Muslim world ranging from Indonesia, Egypt, to Afghanistan, it becomes the hallmark of Islam as a violent religion and Muslims as violent people.

One of the underlying assumptions of how Islam comes to be perceived as a violent religion and Muslims as violent people pertains to the distinction of violence by the secular state and the followers of religion. Cavanagh argues that[16]

> [t]he argument that religion causes violence sanctions a dichotomy between, on the one hand, non-Western, especially Muslim, forms of culture, which—having not yet learned to privatize matters of faith—are absolutist, divisive, and irrational, and Western culture, on the other, which is modest in its claims to truth, unitive, and rational. This dichotomy, this clash-of-civilizations world view, in turn can be used to legitimate the use of violence against those with whom it is impossible to reason on our own terms. In short, their violence is fanatical and uncontrolled; our violence is controlled, reasonable, and often regrettably necessary to contain their violence.

The distinction of violence by the state and religious followers in the post-secular world echoes the sentiment of how Islam is perceived to offer a unison between religion and politics. While it is true that Islamist groups have framed Islam in terms of its political goal, this kind of understanding is not prominent. By calculations, there are only few states that have Islam serving as the foundations of the states, such as Saudi Arabia, Iran, Pakistan, and Afghanistan. Other than Saudi Arabia, these countries host elections as a mechanism to govern the states. Arguably, most post-colonial Muslim countries engage in some forms of electoral mechanism in deciding its governance.

Thus, it would appear that the problem with the majority Muslim countries is not so much about Islam as a religion that preaches for the unity of faith (*dīn*) and state (*dawla*), but the states' accountability in upholding justice for people living in their territories. The local grievances toward its government or those in control of power are also tied to the political and economic competition and military power at the global scale. To cast religion as the sole factor that shapes such violence due to its political potential is misleading. The same is true that it is difficult to pinpoint into secularism as the key to success in modern nation-states. Asad shows the difficulty for accounting secularism as "a doctrine of war and peace in the world is not that it is European (and therefore alien to the non-West) but that it is closely connected with the rise of a system of capitalist nation-states-mutually suspicious and grossly unequal in power and prosperity, each possessing a collective personality that is differently mediated and therefore differently guaranteed and threatened."[17]

---

[16] Cavanaugh, *The myth of religious violence*, 16–17.
[17] Talal Asad, *Formations of the Secular: Christianity, Islam, Modernity* (Redwood City: Stanford University Press, 2003), 7.

What remains to be seen is to situate the myth of violent Muslims within the contexts of War on Terror.

Situating the Prominent Narrative: Emergence, Repetition, and Materiality

It has been indicated how the contemporary discursive narrative of violent Muslims, especially in the United States, gains prominence through the politics of the War on Terror. Such a prominent discourse is cited, produced, and reproduced through a linkage between the said statement within the political constellation of the War on Terror and the power relation that shapes its significance and influence. In this section, I will discuss how the signification of Muslims as violent conveys three levels of relationships: (1) the analysis of the signifier and signified could lead to multiple meanings; (2) the repetitionality of the signifier and signified attests to the intended specific impact of a singular; and (3) the framing of the signifier and signified shapes the making of self-authority. This relationality shows how the meaning of Muslims as violent people has an impact on not only the signified but also on the way a singular self-authority is produced and maintained.

The analysis of the statement often lies on the relationship between the 'signifier' and the 'signified.' Such analysis is limiting in the sense that it leaves out the rarity—referring to what is not said behind such a statement. Barthes explains the 'signifier' to refer to "materials (sounds, objects, and images) and the 'signified' to "a mental representation of 'the thing'".[18] A sign makes the relationship between the 'signifier' and the 'signified' more coherent.[19] For example, 'violent Muslims' represents 'the signifier' for all Muslims who are conceptually 'signified' to symbolize 'the sign' of fear. While statements can be interpreted in terms of the 'signified,' 'signifier,' and signification, they also point to a plurality of meaning. Foucault indicates that "each discourse contains the power to say something other than what it says, and thus to embrace a plurality of meanings: plethora of the 'signified' in relation to a single 'signifier'."[20]

---

[18] Ronald Barthes, *Elements of Semiology* (NY: Hill and Wang, 1986, eleventh edition), 42 and 47.

[19] Ibid., 48.

[20] Michel Foucault, *The Archeology of Knowledge and the Discourse of Language*, trans. A. M. Sheridan Smith (New York: Panthean Books, 1972), 118.

Foucault, however, pushes for understanding a series of signs as constitutive of a statement. A series of signs becomes a statement on the condition that it concerns with "the relation of the signifier (signifiant) to the signified (signifie), of the name to what it designates; the relation of the sentence to its meaning; [and] the relation of the proposition to its referent (riferent)."[21] For example, I will give the statement that Muslims are snakes. This statement is grammatically correct and logical. At the same time, the statement in a Foucauldian sense is[22]

> linked rather to a 'referential' that is made up not of 'things', 'facts', 'realities', or 'beings', but of laws of possibility, rules of existence for the objects that are named, designated, or described within it, and for the relations that are affirmed or denied in it. The referential of the statement forms the place, the condition, the field of emergence, the authority to differentiate between individuals or objects, states of things and relations that are brought into play by the statement itself; it defines the possibilities of appearance and delimitation of that which gives meaning to the sentence, a value as truth to the proposition.

The statement that 'Muslims are snakes' has a plethora of meanings depending on the level at which such a statement operates. For example, I can interpret this statement of how Muslims (signifier) are like snakes (the signified) to denote their untrustworthy (referent) character. Connected to this, studies by Sides and Mogahed show how Americans look at Muslims less favorably in areas of trustworthiness and susceptibility to violence.[23] This characterization creates an imaginary threat (referent) that comes from the fear or imagery of Muslims as 'hidden terrorists.'

The statement that 'Muslims are snakes' is repeatable and can be invoked in every way possible. Such repetition stems from the social imagery among closed-minded buffered individuals who choose to enact the value of Muslims as violent. Foucault indicates that the statement as a repeatable materiality within different contexts and uses is "subjected to transferences or modifications, [and] is integrated into operations and strategies in which its identity is maintained or effaced."[24] The repeated materiality of 'Muslims as snakes' can be found in the citation of the Snake song to reinforce the image (signifier) and the concept (the signified) of Muslims as sleeper cell terrorists among Americans. This relationship between the image (signifier) and the concept (the signified) functions to reiterate how deep the fear of Muslims is (referent). During the 2016 presidential campaign, Candidate

---

[21] Ibid., 89.
[22] Ibid., 91.
[23] Sides and Mogahed, *Muslims in America Public Perceptions in the Trump Era*, 4–5.
[24] Foucault, *The Archeology of Knowledge and the Discourse of Language*, 105.

Trump invoked the Snake song to stir up the fear of Muslims as terrorists and violent people. Through the lyrics of the song, it can be inferred that Americans (or at least some of them) share the social imagery of Muslims as terrorists and that they should not be surprised if the latter engaged in violent terrorism"I saved you," cried that woman

> "And you've bit me even, why?
> And you know your bite is poisonous and now I'm gonna die"
> "Oh shut up, silly woman," said the reptile with a grin
> "You knew damn well I was a snake before you brought me in."
> Al Wilson, *The Snake*, 1968

The lyrics from the Snake were cited during the January 16, 2016, campaign and was again repeated on April 29, 2017, to mark the 100th day of the President Trump's presidency. The repeatable materiality of the Snake song serves to galvanize the fear of Muslims, especially refugees of Syrian origin, entering the United States. This statement that 'Muslims are snakes' assumes that all Muslim refugees admitted to the United States are susceptible to becoming potential terrorists. It goes without saying that the Muslim travel ban reiterates the link between prejudicial attitudes of Muslims as untrustworthy, like the snakes, and the support for policies that target Muslims.[25]

The immediate context for the perception of Muslims as violent and untrustworthy people in the United States is the September 11 attacks and the ensuing acts of terrorism (following the War on Terror) directed against US' interests or personnel, especially by al-Qaida and later ISIS. For almost two decades, Muslims in Muslim-majority contexts and Americans suffered the loss of human and material goods. For Muslims in the most affected areas, the suffering of the civilians was devastating as there was hardly any distinction between combatants and civilians. The September 11 attack took the lives of 2,977 people and caused physical causalities area of NYC, the side of the Pentagon, across the Potomac from Washington, DC, and outside Shanksville, Pennsylvania.[26]

In retrospect, the coalition states' violent responses to contain more violence have costed more human lives (3,557 NATO coalition soldiers in Afghanistan), the destruction of regional politics, especially the Middle East, and the creation of

---

[25] Sides and Mogahed, *Muslims in America Public Perceptions in the Trump Era*, 4–5.

[26] Jonathon Gatehouse, "War on Terror' by the numbers: What the response to 9/11 attack has cost so far," *CBC News*, Sep 11, 2018. Assessed on September 1, 2023, https://www.cbc.ca/news/thenational/national-today-newsletter-911-war-on-terror-india-growth-1.4814089.

ISIS. The breakdown of human cost of the seventeen years of War on Terror is as follows:[27]

> In Afghanistan, where the fighting started and hasn't stopped, 3,557 NATO coalition soldiers have been killed since 2001, including 158 Canadians. The death toll for the Afghan Army and police has been much higher — as estimated 25,000 between 2012 and 2016 alone… Last year, one former senior U.S. military commander estimated that ISIS had lost "between 60,000 and 70,000" soldiers in Iraq and Syria.
> Civilian deaths are likely even higher. One site that uses local news reports to track casualties puts the number of civilian deaths in Iraq at between 182,000 and 204,000 since 2003, including 2,500 people killed so far in 2018. In Afghanistan, the numbers are harder to come by. A 2016 report estimated that almost 31,500 civilians had died inside the country since 2001, and a further 22,000 had been killed in neighboring Pakistan.

These human costs do not calculate the amount of funding spent in the War on Terror, the destruction of built environment, the lost geographical heritage, and the moral and emotional abuses of tortures due to imprisonment in Iraq,[28] Afghanistan,[29] and Guantanamo Bay.[30] All these abuses feed the radical social imaginary of how to resist what they consider unjust treatment of Muslims. Simultaneously, the radical violent responses unfortunately have galvanized the "fear" that fuels the social imaginary of Muslims as violent people and Islam as a violent religion.

Within the realm of the American social imaginary, the myth of Muslims as violent people has long gained ground following the September 11 attacks and has been immortalized through the self-authorization of prejudice and the state's policies. Former President Bush set the tone of how the September 11 attacks signified the war between good and evil. He spoke to Americans at the White House after a weekend war council meeting with senior aides at Camp David describing the September 11 attacks: "[t]his is a new kind of evil, …and we understand, and the American people are beginning to understand, this crusade, this war on terrorism, is going to take a while, and the American people must be patient…We will rid the

---

[27] Ibid.

[28] CNN Library, "Iraq Prison Abuse Scandal Fast Facts," CNN, updated 2:58 PM ET, Mon March 4, 2019, assessed on September 1, 2023, https://www.cnn.com/2013/10/30/world/meast/iraq-prison-abuse-scandal-fast-facts/index.html

[29] Sarah Left and agencies, "US abuse of Afghan prisoners 'widespread'", *The Guardian*, May 20, 2005, assessed on September 1, 2023, https://www.theguardian.com/world/2005/may/20/afghanistan.usa

[30] Matt Apuzzo, Sheri Fink and James Risen, "How U.S. Torture Left a Legacy of Damaged Minds," New York Times, October 8, 2016), assessed on September 1, 2023, https://www.nytimes.com/2016/10/09/world/cia-torture-guantanamo-bay.html

world of the evil-doers."[31] President Bush's statements established the linkage between the September 11 attack and the deployment of a crusade, in order to sow fear among Americans.

The repeatable materiality of the term 'crusades' in response to the September 11 attack became more apparent as the War on Terror ensued. President Bush solidified his stance on the US's War on Terror as a crusade using a providential justification. He perceived his presidency as enacting God's divine plan as he was called to fight evil. The religious language of Providence was invoked to show how wars—in Afghanistan and Iraq—were an act of God in world affairs, calling for the United States to lead a liberating crusade in the Middle East: "this call of history has come to the right country."[32] The invocation of the crusades as a rhetorical device to support the wars in Iraq and Afghanistan is unsettling. The history of two hundred years and more of crusades is recalled and used to reiterate the social imaginary of who constitutes the enemy. At the same time, it is repeated to invoke fear. The crusades' narratives serve as the referent to reinforce the relationship between the War on Terror (the signifier) and the wars against evil (the signified). The conditions for the War on Terror are collapsed and then equated with the settings in which Pope Urban II delivered his speech at the Council of Clermont in 1095 asking the Christian West to aid the Byzantine Empire against the Turks in the Holy Land.[33] As the crusades spanned over two hundred years and involved a plethora of political systems (Arab, Mongol, and Persian), the rhetoric of crusades was a broad generalization of the War on Terror as a war directed against Muslims from all over the world. While the language of the War on Terror was amended as a war against radical Muslims and any countries that sponsored terrorism, the impact on the image of Muslims as violent people has not faded away. If anything, the killing of Muslims in the al-Noor and Linwood mosques in Christchurch, New Zealand, is an indicator of how the Western concept of Muslim as violent is ideological.[34]

---

[31] Todd Purdum, "After the attacks: The White House; Bush Warns of a Wrathful, Shadowy and Inventive War," accessed on September 1, 2023, https://www.nytimes.com/2001/09/17/us/after-attacks-white-house-bush-warns-wrathful-shadowy-inventive-war.html

[32] Jackson Lears, "How a War Became a Crusade," accessed on September 1, 2023, https://www.nytimes.com/2003/03/11/opinion/how-a-war-became-a-crusade.html

[33] Jo Ann Hoeppner Moran Cruz, "Popular Attitudes Towards Islam in Medieval Europe," in *Western Views of Islam in Medieval and Early Europe: Perceptions of Others*, eds. David R. Blanks and Michael Frassetto (New York: St. Martin's Press, 1999), 62.

[34] Daniel Victor, "In Christchurch, Signs Point to a Gunman Steeped in Internet Trolling," accessed on March 15, 2019, https://www.nytimes.com/2019/03/15/world/asia/new-zealand-gunman-christchurch.html?module=inline

When the ideological framework of Muslims as violent people shapes behaviors and policies, it is concerning. The framing of Muslims to signify 'violence' makes Muslims living in the United States subjected to scrutiny and discrimination. Muslims appear to represent the archenemy of the good that the United States promotes. While the United States prides itself as the land of the free and the vanguard of democracy, it fails to warrant Muslims the most basic promise of liberty and tolerance. Asad traces the historical pattern of American nationalism "where internal difference, especially, when it is identified as "foreign," becomes the focus of intolerance from the end of the eighteenth century—that is from the foundation of the republic—to the present" to "the ideology of "good" in opposition to its "evil" enemies at home and abroad."[35] As Muslims are casted in the language of the "evil" enemy, it is important to defy such narrative and find an alternative narrative drawn from Islamic tradition.

Finding a Constructive Narrative that Provides an Alternative Discursive Authority

One key theme that emerges from the linkage between the view of "violent Muslims" and the fear of Islam is the different way the West and Muslims engage with Islam. The relationship between Islam and the West is cast in terms of a conflicting interest of whether or not Islam is compatible with the West and whether Muslim can be a good citizen within a liberal democratic context. These kinds of questions are cast in terms of clash of civilization and compatibility. Keys to this debate are the hegemonic narrative of the relationship between Islam and the state based on the secular and religious paradigm and the way Muslims value what they consider Islamic tradition.

The Euro-American paradigm looks at Islam using the religious and the secular divide and promotes the discursive narrative of Islam as incompatible with the West. Rodríguez shows how the Western mischaracterization of Islam as premodern and barbaric, failing to secularize and go through the modernization process like Christianity, and the reinforcement of such images by politically oriented militant Muslims in the Middle East, South Asia, and Southeast Asia shed a negative light on Islam and Muslims.[36] Although the West applies a misconstrued image

---

[35] Asad, Asad, *Formations of the Secular: Christianity, Islam, Modernity*, 7.
[36] Rubén Rosario Rodríguez, *Christian Martyrdom and Political Violence: a comparative theology with Judaism and Islam* (Cambridge, United Kingdom Cambridge University Press, 2017), 126–127.

of violent agency to all Muslims, this portrayal does not always have a corresponding reality. Specifically, the United States' foreign policies hardly make any connection between their military actions directed against radical Muslims and the way they have reacted to them.

The Western narratives of Islam as the cause of violence and Muslim story of defending religion get exacerbated by the violent exchanges between foreign military occupying certain Muslim countries and extremist Muslims. Rodríguez argues that the Western characterization of Islam as a violent intolerant religion due to the actions of radicalized individuals behaving in the name of political Islam runs parallel to a certain degree with Muslims' perception of Christianity as an imperialist religion "continuing to fight the medieval Crusades by equating Christian beliefs and US policy."[37] Here, Rodríguez suggests equating political Islam with "the theologies" that support US and Israeli policies in the Middle East and at the same time to recognize that jihadism does not represent all types of Islam and that the two aforementioned secular governments do not represent Christianity and Judaism.[38] By constructing both narratives of the United States and Islam in their own terms and contexts, this process allows for a new concept that does not necessarily characterize Muslims as violent to emerge.

While there is no denial of intended harm posed by radical Muslim militants for whom they consider the enemy, the category of militancy and the suspicion that comes with it cannot be generalized to all Muslims. Muslim Americans are just like Americans, in general, in that they are concerned with Islamic violence and being labeled as violent people. The 2017 Pew Research Center shows that:[39]

> Overall, eight-in-ten Muslims (82%) say they are either very concerned (66%) or somewhat concerned (16%) about extremism in the name of Islam around the world. This is similar to the percentage of the U.S. general public that shares these concerns (83%), although Muslims are more likely than U.S. adults overall to say they are very concerned about extremism in the name of Islam around the world (66% vs. 49%).

While the violence performed by Muslims has some parallels to violent realities in the majority and minority contexts, the Western perception of it as an ideological mechanism to represent all Muslims constitutes as a moral issue. The task at hand is to locate the non-stereotypical portrayal of Muslims within the Islamic tradition.

---

[37] Ibid., 163.
[38] Ibid.
[39] Pew Research Center, *U.S. Muslims Concerned About Their Place in Society, but Continue to Believe in the American Dream, July 26, 2017* (Washington DC.: Pew Research Center, 2017), 9.

The Islamic tradition carries institutional significance within Muslims' religious beliefs, practices, and authorities. This institution has no parallel weight within contemporary Western societies. By comparison, the Islamic tradition plays a role as important as the modern concept of "society" does in the Western sense. Authority within the Western discourse stems from what society deems important. Zemmin considers "society as the most constitutive concept of modernity"… that is associated with rationality and individualism.[40] This type of societal authority undergirds the development of modern democracy where society decides what is best within the nation-state as well as what matters individually. Any society also creates its values and functions drawn from the regulatory bodies that govern the relationship between the private and the public, the secular and the religious, and the individual and the people. While the West perceives social relations as the origin of religiosity and culture, it does not share a similar approach with Islam.

Authority in Islam is drawn from the Islamic tradition. Muslims derive their self-authorities from what Islamic tradition describes and prescribes. For this reason, understanding Muslims should take into consideration the study of Islam from the perspective of Islamic tradition. Asad argues that the study of Islam, including the anthropology of Islam, should focus on Islam as a discursive tradition. Treating Islam in terms of an Islamic discursive tradition simply means "a tradition of Muslim discourse that addresses itself to conceptions of the Islamic past and future, with reference to a particular practice in the present."[41] In this sense, any attempts to propose an alternative narrative to the statement of Muslims as violent requires scholars and lay individuals to contextualize such a statement within the conditional contexts of their emergence and their enunciative function in both Western politics and the Islamic tradition.

The Islamic tradition plays a significant role for Muslims. What constitutes Islamic tradition includes the legacy of the Prophet Muhammad as written in the Quran and Hadith as well as a plethora of Muslims' interpretation and practices as expressed throughout centuries and cultures. Keys to understanding the legacy of the Prophet Muhammad are shown in how Islam is interpreted and how interpretation is carried out through practices. Within the multitude of Islamic traditions, some ideas and practices become hegemonic as well. For instance, Sunni and Shia become the only dominant groups known as a historical response to the political

---

[40] Florian Zemmin, *Modernity in Islamic tradition the concept of 'society' in the journal al-Manar* (Cairo, 1898–1940) (Berlin: De Gruyter 2018), 44 and 53.

[41] Talal Asad, "The Idea of an anthropology of Islam," eds., John A Hall and Ian Charles Jarvie in *The social philosophy of Ernest Gellner* (Amsterdam; Atlanta, GA: Rodopi, 1996), 398.

succession to the Prophet. There are some similarities between Sunni and Shia. Both believe in God, the Prophet, the Quran, and the measuring out. However, Sunni and Shia differ in the order of political succession. Sunni Islam believes that Abu Bakr (632–634), Umar ibn Khattab (634–644), Utsman bin Affan (644–654), and Ali bin Abi Thalib (654–661) were the rightly guided successors (caliphs) to the Prophet Muhammad, whereas the Shia Islam makes the case for Ali bin Abi Thalib as the only legitimate successor followed by a succession by imams. Both Sunni and Shia Islam developed the caliphate and imamate institutions, respectively, and gained followers depending on the regime of powers where resided. The Sunni and Shia's political institution in the post-caliphate takes form in the sultanate model where the succession of political power is inherited through bloodline. As the term 'caliphate' is often used as an umbrella term to describe and justify 'Islamic political model,' it becomes synonymous with the ideal form of politics in Islamic tradition. Within the social imaginary of the caliphate institution as an ideal form of Islamic politics and ethics, the Islamic tradition is constituted, reproduced, and maintained.

The multiplicity of Islamic tradition gives birth to various traditions, including the legal schools. Various legal schools dominate some parts of Muslim countries and less so in others. The Shafi'ite school, founded by Muhammad Idris bin Shafi'i (d. 819), is common in Southeast Asia, Lower Egypt, East Africa, and Southern Arabia, whereas the Hanafi School, founded by Abu Hanifa, (d. 767), is prevalent in Afghanistan, Egypt, India, and Turkey. Similarly, the Maliki School, founded by Malik bin Anas (d. 795), is widespread in North Africa and Upper Egypt, and the Hanbali School, founded by Ahmad Hambali (d. 855), is common in Saudi Arabia. The majority of the Shi'ite law users live in Iran. The legalistic mode of thinking and doing very much shapes how Muslims express Islamic tradition and the extent to which Muslims are able to accept and reject them. The dominant narrative of Islam in legal terms is problematic as it emphasizes selected parts of historical Islam, totalizes Islam as a way of life through the adoption of sharia, neglects the significance of other areas of Islamic scholarship, and prioritizes *fiqh* (Islamic jurisprudence) as the centerpiece of Islam.[42]

At the heart of the political and legal debates is the question of authority. The Islamic tradition provides a wide range of point of reference that provides the basis for the orthodoxical framework of what is Islamic and non-Islamic. Arguably, Islam as discursive tradition has come to mean prescription where "Islam is ori-

---

[42] Shahab Ahmed, *What Is Islam: The Importance of Being Islamic* (Princeton and Oxford: Princeton University Press, 2016), 117, 120, 122, and 123.

ented towards the prescription of correctness."[43] The quest for correctness becomes hegemonic as the desire for establishing orthodoxy is intertwined with the possession of the social authority. In Ahmed words, "...orthodoxy is any truth-claim that Muslims in a given time and place institute, regulate, and require through a process of exercise of power as being authoritatively correct—thus as not welcoming or accommodative of contradictory claim, which are duly condemned, excluded, undermined, and replaced."[44] As the production of authority coincides with the power to initializes, institutionalizes, and maintains it, it both prescribes and restricts the truth.[45] Some Islamic traditions become hegemonic, others are unsaid, buried, and forgotten.

As religious interpretation carries a plethora of authority, the truth of it depends on what individuals perceive to be meaningful. In producing meaning,[46]

> ...Islam becomes idiom...[and] a shared language by and in which people express themselves so as to communicate meaningfully in all their variety...Islam is... both means and meaning. Islam is thus located in the nexus, the relationship, the field and the process of engagement with and between the source of meaning, the mode of production of meaning from the source and the end product of meaning.

The individual process of making meaning is depended on the source of meaning (i.e., Islamic tradition), the method by which the meaning is produced, and the outcome of the deliberative process. This cyclical process does not hinge on the orthodoxical framework but on what Ahmed calls 'explorative authority,' which allows for the expansion of meaning.[47] Acting authoritatively would mean displaying self-engagement with the Divine, carrying existential awareness, and embodying self-knowledge, self-realizing, and self-truth making.[48]

The explorative authority approach in some ways answers the concerns issued by Asad. The [Euro-American] prominent discourse on "Islamic terrorism" [or Islamic violence] rests on the contradictory position between text and reader: on the one hand, the religious text is read literally rendering readers to be passive; on the other hand, the religious readers actively interpret contextually making such texts to be passive.[49] By attributing passivity to text and reader, respectively, it

---

[43] Ibid., 272.
[44] Ibid, 273.
[45] Ibid.
[46] Ibid., 323.
[47] Ibid., 282–289.
[48] Ibid, 330, 332, 329, 338, and 345.
[49] Asad, Asad, *Formations of the Secular: Christianity, Islam, Modernity*, 11.

makes the text accountable for violence and readers susceptible to a singular [textual] reading. While this kind of reading is monolithic, it caters the need for individuals and group to render the responsibility of violence to the texts where the violent individuals passively accept such text as the only authoritative source that commands violent acts. Such reading may constitute "a correct reading of the Quran" if orthodoxy (a correct doctrine) is defined based on the only correct prescription and prohibition. This interpretative approach is common to Muslims who read the Quran and the hadith textually rather than contextually. A textual reading of Islamic sources yields a fixed interpretation that caters the need for correct doctrines and practices and for an unchanging authority. This presumptive attitude is common to insiders and outsiders of Islam who look for the truth in the Quran and believe what they read literally. Quite differently, the explorative authority mirrors engagement with texts, contexts, and encounters within and beyond the Islamic settings. In this manner, a new discursive authority is constantly reproduced and maintained within the constellation of power and knowledge.

Advocating a New Authoritative Narrative of Non-violent Muslims

Explorative authority is best expressed in statements. Analyzing concepts and images within the conditions of their emergence allows for the making of statements about Islam and Muslims in a meaningful manner. I borrow from Foucault's archeology the importance of describing statements according to the conditions of their emergence, their enunciative existence, their rarity, and their exclusion. Islam claims to emerge as the continuation of the Judeo and Christian traditions, which eventually underlies the foundation of the Western civilization. The first millennial and half of encounters between Islam, Judaism, and Christianity resulted in civilizational exchanges, whereas the last century has been marked with competing interest between secularization and Islamization.

The United States of America provides a rich tapestry of Islamic expressions and practices. This type of Islam mirrors the plurality of Muslim cultures within the Islamic tradition. The pluralistic expression of Islam makes the particularity of American Islam unique and culturally specific. The particularity of American Islam here refers to a specific version of Islam as practiced by individuals or a particular group in a particular setting, whereas the universality of the Islamic tradition points

Table 13.1 Total percentage of ethnic background in mosque attendances

Ethnic group	2000	2011
South Asian	33%	33%
Arab	25%	27%
African American	30%	24%
African (sub-Saharan)	3%	9%
European (Bosnian, etc.)	2%	2%
Iranian	1%	2%
White American	2%	1%
Caribbean	1%	1%
Southeast Asian	1%	1%
Latino	1%	1%
Turkish	1%	1%

to the importance of Islam as a religious marker. The ethnic particularity of Islam can be seen in diversity of Muslims as described in Table 13.1.[50]

What does a diverse ethnic background of mosque's attendees mean? There is a wide spectrum of Muslims across America. The large number of African Americans shows that Islam is not only limited to immigrants but is also inclusive of American-born citizens. Further, according to Pew Research Center, there are about 3.45 million Muslims living in the United States, with 58% of them born outside the United States.[51] Overall, American Muslims make up approximately 1.1% of the US population. As Muslim Americans are largely immigrants, they embrace values that are meaningful within the contexts of their past life and appropriate them within the bounds of the US settings.

While Muslims carry the banner of Islam as a transnational marker beyond the boundaries of nationalities, ethnicities, and cultures, they appeal to various forms of authority that Islam offers. Muslims derive their agency from statements that are described and prescribed in the Qur'an, the hadith—the written collection of the Prophet Muhammad's sayings, deeds, and wishes—and the interpretation of them that are considered "correct doctrine (orthodoxy)." As indicated earlier, the search for correct practice creates a discursive narrative of Islam that is "oriented towards

---

[50] Ihsan Bagby, "The Mosque and the American Public Square," in *Muslims' Place in the Public Square: Hope, Fear and Aspirations*, Zahid H. Bukhari, Sulayman S. Nyang, Mumtaz Ahmad, and John L. Esposito (Walnut Creek, Lanham: Altamira Press, 2004), 326.

[51] Pew Research Center, *U.S. Muslims Concerned About Their Place in Society, but Continue to Believe in the American Dream, July 26, 2017* (Washington DC.: Pew Research Center, 2017), 22.

the prescription of correctness."[52] Watt argues that the word "orthodox" is out of context in Islam as there is no equivalent institutions as in Christianity.[53] Likewise, Ahmed reiterates how the concept of orthodoxy does not hold up due to variations in Muslims' practices of Islam.[54] As the concept of correct doctrine is misleading, Dabashi suggests to look for the underlying forces that help create authority in Islam. He is particularly interested in the interplay between "two modes of authority—traditional Arab and charismatic Muhammadan,"[55] whose confrontation and legacy provide continuity from pre- to post-Muhammadan periods as they point to a common repertoire of cultural traits for Muslims to cherish and invoke. It is within this underlying force that Muslims continue to produce a new discursive narrative of Islam and Muslims within their own settings. This effort constitutes the explorative authority that is inclusive of text, context, and meaning.

There is indeed an opportunity to understand Islam in its own term. Ahmed suggests reading Islam as a hermeneutical engagement. The term 'hermeneutical' draws "attention to truth and meaning, to the interactions and process of interpretation and understanding, to the identity of the sources of meaning interacted with, to the methods employed in the process of truth making and meaning-making."[56] As for engagement, it deals with "the role of human actor in the process of truth and meaning-making."[57] Thus, hermeneutical engagement reflects a process of bringing "one's self into the process of truth-making and meaning-making from a source."[58] What constitutes to be Islamic results from "the *hermeneutical engagement with Pre-Text, Text, and Con-Text of revelation to Muhammad*" that gives birth to Islam as a multi-dimensional phenomenon.[59] This engagement is not coherent, full of contradiction, conflicting view of prescription and prohibition, and multi-dimensional. Despite of all these, the self-as-the-agent-of making meaning creates coherence and makes their understanding meaningful within their own contexts. For this reason, any Muslim can make a claim about Islam, but such an identification only belongs to the follower of Islam. Outsiders to the faith of Islam

---

[52] Ahmed, *What Is Islam: The Importance of Being Islamic*, 272.

[53] W. Montgomery Watt, *The Formative Period of Islamic Thought* (Edinburgh: Edinburgh University Press, 1973), 6.

[54] Ahmed, *What Is Islam: The Importance of Being Islamic*, 277.

[55] Hamid Dabashi, *Authority in Islam: From the Rise of Mohammad to the Establishment of the Umayyads* (New Brunswick, New Jersey: Transaction Publishers, 1989), 16 and 19.

[56] Ahmed, *What Is Islam: The Importance of Being Islamic*, 345.

[57] Ibid.

[58] Ibid.

[59] Ibid, 363.

have no rights to define Islam and Muslims, especially when the definitions of Islam as a violent religion and Muslims as violent people are politically motivated. What makes Islam Islamic is the way the individuals *make* it authoritative within the boundary of Islamic tradition and their encounters with their own contexts.

Conclusion

This chapter discusses how the indirect outcomes of Western encounters with Islam were marred by political exchange and violence. It attempts to understand how the hateful rhetoric against Islam and Muslims as violent within Western contexts offers a plethora of meanings: (1) Islam is seen as homogeneous and transhistorical, and (2) Muslims are generalized as similar across cultures. The problem is that attributing the homogeneity of Islam denies all variations within the Islamic tradition. Similarly, putting all Muslims within a category of violent people defies the reality that Muslims live in every part of the world and most of these Muslims are peaceful individuals.

The chapter brings into the conversation the need for Muslims to examine the statement of that Muslims are violent people by locating its emergence and claiming a position that is not hegemonic yet meaningful personally and communally. The process of claiming a position in the Islamic tradition involves the mechanism called *Ijtihād*—referring traditionally to a process of obtaining juristic opinion (*fatwā*) by individual jurists on issues that are not necessarily addressed in detail in the Qur'an and the prophetic traditions.[60] While *Ijtihād* as a method for deliberation dominates the legal area to the extent that it is open only to the most qualified and knowledgeable Muslims, it is also applicable to non-judicial issues.

I appeal to the non-judicial use of *Ijtihād* as a mechanism to promote the discursive process that is personalized in accordance with the elevation of human agency as well as honoring all forms of thinking and deliberation within the Islamic tradition(s). This process can lead into the production of an explorative authority—where individuals attempt to identity the problem, situate it within the constellation of its emergence and maintenance, and produce a narrative that is meaningful. With the application of the non-judicial use of *Ijtihād*, Muslims can make use of their explorative authority and, in the process, address the American myth of Muslims as violent people.

---

[60] See various definition and historical contexts in Muhammad Khalid Masud, *Shatibi's Philosophy of Islamic Law* (Islambad, Pakistan: Islamic Research Institute, 1995), 226–227.

This non-judicial use of *Ijtihād* intersects with the feminist call for the personal as political. While the process of this *Ijtihād* is personal, it intersects with feminist agency. This intersection could facilitate the emergence of ethical agents whose religiosity is profoundly rooted in Islamic tradition and whose social orientation is deeply grounded in their contexts. This *Ijtihādi*-feminist approach is going to be useful in addressing the perception of Muslims as violent people across Euro-American cultures and beyond. The experience of being grouped with people who did engage in violence is personal, yet this kind of treatment calls for a political response. Our political response is grounded in the need to talk about Islam in Islamic terminology, not in a Western paradigm. If each Muslim speaks about Islam, including the issue of violent Muslims, authoritatively, the charge that Muslims are not loud enough in condemning terrorism and violence is expected to gradually fade.

References

Ahmed, Shahab. 2016. *What is Islam: The Importance of Being Islamic*. Princeton and Oxford: Princeton University Press.

Allman, Mark. 2008. *Who Would Jesus Kill?: War, Peace, and the Christian Tradition*. Winona, MN: Saint Mary's Press.

Allport, Gordon W. 1954. *The Nature of Prejudice Cambridge*. Massachusetts: Addison-Wesley Publishing Company.

Apuzzo, Matt, Sheri Fink, and James Risen. 2016. How U.S. Torture Left a Legacy of Damaged Minds. *New York Times*, October 8. Accessed September 1, 2023. https://www.nytimes.com/2016/10/09/world/cia-torture-guantanamo-bay.html.

Asad, Talal. 1996. The Idea of an Anthropology of Islam. In *The Social Philosophy of Ernest Gellner*, ed. John A. Hall and Ian Charles Jarvie, 381–406. Amsterdam; Atlanta, GA: Rodopi.

———. 2003. *Formations of the Secular: Christianity, Islam, Modernity*. Redwood City: Stanford University Press.

Bagby, Ihsan. 2004. The Mosque and the American Public Square. In *Muslims' Place in the Public Square: Hope, Fear and Aspirations*, ed. Zahid H. Bukhari, Sulayman S. Nyang, Mumtaz Ahmad, and John L. Esposito, 323–346. Walnut Creek, Lanham: Altamira Press.

Barthes, Ronald. 1986. *Elements of Semiology*. 11th ed. NY: Hill and Wang.

Batson, C. Daniel, and E.L. Stocks. 2009. Religion and Prejudice. In *On the Nature of Prejudice: Fifty Years after Allport*, ed. John F. Dovidio, 413–427. Malden, MA: Blackwell.

Calvert, John. 2008. *Islamism: A Documentary and Reference Guide*. Westport: Greenwood Press.

Cavanaugh, William T. 2009. *The myth of Religious Violence*. New York: Oxford University Press.

13 The Hateful Rhetoric Against Muslims and the Authority-Making of Islamic... 223

CNN Library. 2019. Iraq Prison Abuse Scandal Fast Facts. CNN, updated 2:58 PM ET, Mon March 4. Accessed September 1, 2023. https://www.cnn.com/2013/10/30/world/meast/iraq-prison-abuse-scandal-fast-facts/index.html.

Cruz, Jo Ann, and Hoeppner Moran. 1999. Popular Attitudes Towards Islam in Medieval Europe. In *Western Views of Islam in Medieval and Early Europe: Perceptions of Others*, ed. David R. Blanks and Michael Frasetto, 55–81. New York: St. Martin's Press.

Dabashi, Hamid. 1989. *Authority in Islam: From the Rise of Mohammad to the Establishment of the Umayyads*. New Brunswick, New Jersey: Transaction Publishers.

Euben, Roxanne Leslie. 1999. *Enemy in the Mirror: Islamic Fundamentalism and the Limits of Modern Rationalism: a Work of Comparative Political Theory*. Princeton: Princeton University Press.

Foucault, Michel. 1972. *The Archeology of Knowledge and the Discourse of Language*. Translated by A. M. Sheridan Smith. New York: Panthean Books.

Gatehouse, Jonathon. 2018. War on Terror' by the Numbers: What the Response to 9/11 Attack has Cost So Far. *CBC News*, September 11. Accessed September 1, 2023. https://www.cbc.ca/news/thenational/national-today-newsletter-911-war-on-terror-india-growth-1.4814089.

Graham, Franklin. 2002. *The Name*. Nashville: Thomas Nelson.

Jackson Lears. 2003. How a War Became a Crusade. *New York Times*. March 11. Accessed September 1, 2023. https://www.nytimes.com/2003/03/11/opinion/how-a-war-became-a-crusade.html.

Left, Sarah and Agencies. 2005. US Abuse of Afghan Prisoners 'Widespread'. *The Guardian*, May 20. Accessed May 7, 2019. https://www.theguardian.com/world/2005/may/20/afghanistan.usa.

Lincoln, Bruce. 2007. *Theorizing Myth: Narrative, Ideology, and Scholarship*. Chicago: University of Chicago Press.

Masud, Muhammad Khalid. 1995. *Shatibi's Philosophy of Islamic Law*. Islambad, Pakistan: Islamic Research Institute.

Middleton, Paul. 2011. *Martyrdom: a Guide for the Perplexed*. London [etc.]: T & T Clark.

———. 2017. 'Unlock Paradise With Your Own Blood': Martyrdom and Salvation in Islam and Christianity. In *Alternative Salvation: Engaging the Sacred and the Secular*, ed. Hannah Bacon, Wendy Dossett, and Steve Knowles, 109–120. London: Bloomsbury.

Pew Research Center. 2017. *U.S. Muslims Concerned About Their Place in Society, but Continue to Believe in the American Dream, July 26, 2017*. Washington DC.: Pew Research Center.

Pope Benedict XVI. 2006. Faith, Reason and the University: Memories and Reflections. Aula Magna of the University of Regensburg, Tuesday, September 12, 1–8. Accessed May 7, 2019. http://www.catholic-ew.org.uk/Home/News/2006/2006-Offline/Full-Text-of-the-Pope-Benedict-XVI-s-Regensburg-Lecture.

Purdum, Todd. 2001. After the Attacks: The White House; Bush Warns of a Wrathful, Shadowy and Inventive War. *New York Times*, September 17. Accessed March 7, 2019. https://www.nytimes.com/2001/09/17/us/after-attacks-white-house-bush-warns-wrathful-shadowy-inventive-war.html.

Rodríguez, Rubén Rosario. 2017. *Christian Martyrdom and Political Violence: a Comparative Theology with Judaism and Islam*. Cambridge: United Kingdom Cambridge University Press.

Salvator, Armando. 2014. Tradition and Modernity within Islamic Civilization and the West. In *Islam and Modernity: Key Issues and Debates*, ed. Muhammad Khalid Masud, Armando Salvatore, and Martin van Bruinessen, 1–35. Edinburgh, Scotland: Edinburgh University Press, 2009.

Sides, John, and Dalia Mogahed. June 2018. *Muslims in America Public Perceptions in the Trump Era*. Washington DC.: A Research Report from the Democracy Fund Voter Study Group.

Victor, Daniel. 2019. In Christchurch, Signs Point to a Gunman Steeped in Internet Trolling. *New York Times*, March 15. Accessed March 15, 2019. https://www.nytimes.com/2019/03/15/world/asia/new-zealand-gunman-christchurch.html?module=inline.

Watt, W. Montgomery. 1973. *The Formative Period of Islamic Thought*. Edinburgh: Edinburgh University Press.

Etin Anwar is Professor of Religious Studies at Hobart and William Smith Colleges, Geneva, NY, and serves as the Chair of the Department for the fall of 2024. She is a passionate teacher and an emerging artist. She teaches classes on Islam as it relates to gender, visual culture, environment, and comparative ethics. She is a published author of *A Genealogy of Islamic Feminism: Pattern and Change in Indonesia* (Routledge, 2018) and *Gender and Self in Islam* (Routledge, 2006). Both texts had been translated and published in Bahasa Indonesia by Mizan Publishing House as *Feminisme Islam: Geneologi, Tantangan, dan Prospek* (2021) and *Jati Diri Perempuan dalam Islam* (2017). She is also currently doing research on AI art in Islam, and her work can be found at https://encollaborate.io

Religious Identity in a Pluralistic Age: The Paradox of Being Simultaneously Rooted and Open

Mark King

> *Behold who you are, become what you receive.*
>
> St. Augustine
>
> *The Christian of the future will be a mystic, or he will not exist at all.*
>
> Karl Rahner

Introduction

The challenges of religious pluralism and postmodernist thought are forcing many theologians and religious educators to grapple with the question of how to remain rooted yet open: rooted in the practices and beliefs of their tradition, yet open to the wisdom and truth of others. Such an educational task presents a number of theological and educational challenges, especially for Roman Catholics. This can further be understood in terms of identity. This challenge of identity in a particular religious tradition, and how to navigate similarity and difference in a complex, pluralistic world, inevitably involves developing an academic language that engages both religious and the educational forms of learning. This challenge of iden-

---

M. King (✉)
Psychology of Faith and Church History, Maria Regina High School, Hartsdale, NY, USA
e-mail: MKing@mariaregina.org

© The Author(s), under exclusive license to Springer Nature Switzerland AG 2024
M. Shafiq, T. Donlin-Smith (eds.), *Inclusion or Exclusion in the Sacred Texts and Human Contexts*, https://doi.org/10.1007/978-3-031-70180-1_14

tity is further understood as a paradox of self and other. This paradox points to arguably the central Christian message of Jesus of Nazareth: the more one recognizes the other in oneself, and one's self in the other, the more authentic one's self becomes.

A Problematic Cultural Context

Roger Haight (2022) argues that theology is inevitably linked to and shaped by culture: in effect, culture must be taken seriously. He notes remarkable changes to contemporary Western culture over the last three decades that have impacted both secular and church culture. These shifts, variously labeled postmodern and pluralistic, shape how faith practitioners understand themselves and their relationship to others. He further notes how secularization meets religion and religious belief at a number of intersections. The place it most impacts, however, is in one's religious imagination. Our contemporary secular world, with its acute rationalist and materialist bent, powerfully influences belief by conditioning practitioners' imagination to conform to present-day reality (Haight, 9). Haight further notes a growing diversity of lifestyles and worldviews that cannot help but lead to metaphysical skepticism concerning some, or all, of one's tradition (Haight, 11). Such a cultural mindset calls for more dialogical forms of education.

Dennis Gunn (2020) proposes an educational philosophy that takes seriously such a cultural context and outlines a dialogical form of teaching grounded in the work of the Canadian Jesuit Bernard Lonergan. He calls for educating toward an authentic cosmopolitanism, or cosmopolis: a basic worldview that does not impose any universal, totalizing metanarrative on the participants. It affirms the value of honoring the particularity of one's cultural, religious, and intellectual traditions, while simultaneously remaining open to the other through intentional, conscious dialogue (Gunn, 4–5).

Gunn uses the Tower of Babel story (GN 11: 1–9) as a metaphor for better understanding the nature of our contemporary society and the unique challenges it poses. In short, we are "living in the midst of babel," referring to our increasingly polarized, divided society, marked by algorithm-driven news and social media that prioritize extremist views that tend to demonize and dehumanize the "other" through crafted fear-generating memes and infotainment factoids passing as news. This has spilled over to our politics and national discourse, driven by the desire for more clicks: therefore more money.

14 Religious Identity in a Pluralistic Age: The Paradox of Being Simultaneously...

Gunn continues that if this is the case, then overcoming babel is a key educational challenge for today's educators, whether public or parochial. At the core of teaching for cosmopolis is the call and challenge of conversation across differences. As such, pluralism (and the other) is not seen as a threat but as an essential aspect to such teaching and learning centered on the cultivation and nurturing of such crucial conversations (Gunn, 7).

The issue of self and other, and what our sacred texts have to say about their relationship, points to what Paul Knitter referred to as the "problem and promise" of religious pluralism: a problem in the other inevitably represents a threat, rejection, or relativization of your faith tradition and its metanarrative; a promise in that the other holds the potential for new perspective and deepening of one's own faith understanding. In terms of crafting and nurturing identity, it is assumed to aid both individuals and groups in finding a place to stand: morally, religiously, and culturally. In her recent keynote address at the Hickey Center symposium for Interfaith Studies and Dialogue: Sacred Text & Human Context, Diana Eck suggested the categories of inclusion and exclusion were no longer adequate guides to fostering a pluralist ethic.[1] This author agrees, arguing that the self and other—particularly those within the Roman Catholic tradition—must strive to meet at a deeper, more mystical level where the boundaries of the two blur and intermingle.

The term "paradox" refers to the educational goals that on the surface may appear to conflict, even oppose each other, yet together point to a deeper truth or reality. Crafting a religious identity appropriate and responsive to our pluralistic, postmodern world requires an identity that is by necessity, relational, fluid and conditional, and includes aspects of the other. Mary Boys (2000) refers to this as educating for paradox; the challenging and uniquely adult capacity to hold contrasting truths in creative tension with one another.

For Roman Catholics, it is proposed that a rediscovery and refashioning of the mystical, contemplative traditions, specifically the apophatic, dark mystic tradition, is essential to meeting this religious and educational challenge of reconciling self and other in a way that is both faithful to the best of the Catholic tradition, while also leaving a creative space within one's identity for the other. It is argued later that it is in the quiet, still center of contemplative silence that the self and other most authentically meet. The term "paradox" further centers on an existential awareness that the more open and connected we are, the more authentically we

---

[1] Diana Eck, PhD, Harvard University. 'Beyond Inclusion or Exclusion: The Case for a Pluralist Ethic. Keynote address given May 23, 2023, Nazareth College's Hickey Center for Interfaith Studies and Dialogue; Sacred Text & Human Contexts 7th International Symposium.

become our true self. This deeper, non-dualistic space within is also where the Divine is encountered. This paradoxical truth is nothing more than what Jesus of Nazareth preached in his usual poetic simplicity: "I was hungry and you gave me food; thirsty, and you gave me drink" (MT 25:35).

Educating toward a rooted yet open religious identity is presented as a responsible and effective response to our religiously pluralistic world. These two contrasting calls can be understood as intrinsically related and not antagonistic toward each other. Kieran Scott (2005) explains this challenge in terms of continuity and change; maintaining meaningful, essential connection with the past, while being open and responsive to the intellectual and cultural trends of contemporary society. Boys "educating for paradox" also points to the theological and spiritual challenges related to this postmodern understanding of identity as essentially relational and fluid, and takes seriously the place of the other in crafting one's own worldview.

What is the Apophatic Tradition?

Read from a mystical, contemplative perspective, Christian scripture is shown to contain three characteristics key to rooting any proposed Catholic identity in orthodox belief and tradition, while simultaneously allowing for a creative space for the other: (1) non-dualistic conceptions of God and other; (2) holding paradoxical truths in creative tension; and (3) negation and the limits of language when discussing the nature of the divine.

Reading sacred scripture in a contemplative, meditative way is one possible practice that is old and just as authentic as the medieval Scholastic tradition. Long neglected, the monastic practices of this silent prayer have led practitioners beyond a rational, intellectual acceptance of divinely inspired truths, to a deeper, intuitive, more-than-rational understanding of God's ongoing revelation in the present moment.

While the contemplative tradition has long been marginalized and, until recently, limited to the monastic religious orders, this marginalization of a much-needed wisdom tradition was further aided by a pervasive spirit of rationalism and scientism that emerged during the modern era, and continues to hold sway over much of the West's intellectual and cultural mindset. The rise of Enlightenment Europe led to a general cultural and intellectual mindset that esteemed concepts, ideas, and images as the surest way to know and understand the divine. This modern mindset tended to view the silent darkness of the mystical tradition with suspicion and/or contempt. This overall intellectual climate also affected the Church and its

14 Religious Identity in a Pluralistic Age: The Paradox of Being Simultaneously...

approach to theological discourse. Largely in response to modernism's general and severe critique of religion that assessed the Catholic tradition and its revealed truth claims as little more than paganistic superstition, the Church was inevitably led to reassert the cognitive acceptance of doctrine and dogma as the most desirable path to salvation for its lay faithful.

A quick overview of what the apophatic mystical tradition is and its place in Christian history is instructive and places the subject in further context. The apophatic tradition goes back to the earliest Christian communities and has remained an authentic, orthodox tradition within the Catholic Church. Concerning the development of an adequate religious and educational language, it holds helpful insights and wisdom into how to better appreciate the limitations of language, ideas, and images whenever speaking or understanding the divine.

William Johnston (2003) notes that when Christianity came into contact with Greek philosophy, particularly Neo-Platonism, something new was born: the apophatic school of dark mysticism. This ancient tradition is best articulated in the writings of Gregory of Nyssa and pseudo-Dionysius. A number of foundational themes to the apophatic tradition are found in Gregory's writings. His role in the formulation of the doctrine of the Trinity (a fundamentally non-dualistic image of God), at the Council of Nicaea gives him an unquestioned authoritative voice. This core Christian doctrine with its fundamentally relational and paradoxical view of God has further relevance to our proposed postmodern model of identity.

This apophatic mystical tradition is contrasted with the more culturally dominant dualistic forms of thinking, or "dualisms," long definitive of Western philosophy and culture. Dualistic thinking is the very strong, almost unavoidable human tendency to break everything down into either/or, good/bad, right/wrong categories, and thinking. This way of seeing and understanding the world, our selves, and others, powerfully shapes our belief systems, morality, overall worldview, and ultimately, our actions.

Such dualisms further tend to divide everything into polar opposites, with one aspect of the binary held up as superior and more important. From the beginning of the Christian era this dualistic mentality tended to value the spirit, the soul, heaven, rationalism, and the male, while simultaneously devaluing the body, nature, earth, emotion and intuition, as well as the female.

Both a Jesuit priest and Roshi Zen master, Johnston notes the characteristics of an emerging contemporary mystical movement in the West. This revival of the mystical-contemplative Christian tradition is marked by its lay-centeredness; its use of psychological language, and its emphasis on posture and breathing to achieve a calm, meditative state similar to that experienced by the great Christian mystics of the past. Similar to yet distinct from this largely lost and forgotten

Christian tradition, this emerging movement cultivates a greater appreciation of, among other things, non-dualistic images of God and Christ, the reality of the Incarnation and the Holy Spirit in the present moment, and the divine mystery both within one's self and without: where the other is encountered.

Generally not considered within the apophatic tradition, Augustine's place in the development of the Latin Church is unparalleled and his writings so wide-ranging that the premiere Latin Father had much to say on the apophatic tradition to the point of being called the Father of Western Christian mysticism. Bernard McGuinn notes how Augustine first and most significantly grounds the chance for all Christian's to experience a deep and transforming awareness of God not so much in some individual mystical journey toward a questionable and suspect "union" with God, but through full and active participation in the corporate life of the church community (McGinn and McGinn 2003, 154). This is reflected in Augustine's classic work, *City of God,* where he notes: "No one should be so contemplative that he does not think of his neighbor's needs; no one so active that he does not seek the contemplation of God" (McGinn, 158).

Augustine's overall conception of language illustrates the themes of negation and maintaining "opposites-in-tension." He warned how we should always be mindful to balance what can and cannot be said about God and being aware of the profound limits' language has in describing ultimate reality. For Augustine, the incomprehensibility of God is a basic principle that guides all interpretation of language about God. He warns that one cannot talk about God since God is, in the end, mystery and unknowable. Augustine developed a dialectic between the said and unsaid about God that ultimately leads to paradox; a paradox Augustine suggests we pass over in silence (Lefebure 1993, 118).

Following his spiritual mentor Paul, Augustine claims the cosmic Christ is found in the depths of the human person and is quite beyond any words, even words of doctrine. Yet Augustine's responsibilities as bishop and his public demands to both write and speak about the meaning and reality of God to his parishioners, forced him to balance these contradictory aspects as best as possible (Lefebure, 120). Illustrating his approach to language, as well as his non-dualistic understanding of the self, Augustine—when dispensing the Eucharist—was fond of saying,

> Behold who you are, become what you receive. (Lefebure, 120)

More than any other patristic author, pseudo-Dionysius (fifth century) used language to subvert the claims of language. He had a well-developed sense of viewing words and ideas as limited tools that imperfectly point the way to the inexplicable, paradoxical core of our being. His most common metaphors used were that of darkness, cloud, and, in the end, silence. This language and method helped reinforce the apophatic ideal that God can be attained only through unknowing (McGinn, 185).

To resist and counteract such misleading, even negative dualistic thinking, it is proposed that identifying and meditating on particular scriptural passages that illustrate non-dualistic images of Christ and self, paradoxical truths-in-tension, and language as negation is a valid religious and educational practice to deepen one's spirituality and more authentically encounter the other. The Pauline Letters, the Synoptic Gospels, and the fourth gospel of John are cited below to illustrate these three key features.

Scripture Read as Koan

This author's doctoral dissertation explored how Zen Buddhism's meditative practices parallel many of the contemplative and mystical practices of the ancient church, offering devout Christians a particular way to read scripture in a meditative, contemplative way. One tool used by Zen practitioners is the koan; a kind of paradoxical riddle that has no logical solution through the mind but is designed to push the practitioner beyond his or her rational, dualistic thinking to a non-dualistic awareness of the unity and oneness of all. This is the state of satori, where the dualistic either/or, I/Thou, self/other dichotomy is broken down. Scholars have further noted how Jesus of Nazareth—the first and greatest Christian mystic—likely experienced a similar non-dualistic mystical awareness, leading him eventually to claim he and the Father were one.

Kenneth Leong (2001) argues that numerous examples of koan-like situations are present within scripture. The greatest Christian koan is that of Jesus the Christ, the Divine God come down from heaven and crucified on the cross. At first glance such an image seems nonsensical, but in fact points to the heart of the Christian story of death and resurrection to new life. Johnston further notes that it is completely acceptable to read scripture as koan since the authors of the gospels were themselves koan-makers who primarily viewed scripture from a mystical perspective. A deeper reading of scripture is therefore achieved not so much through the intellect but through the heart and contemplative practice.

Reading scripture as koan also holds the potential for Christians to gain deeper insight into the nature of Jesus the Christ as an icon for a refashioned Christian Catholic identity. The Son of Man koan is grounded in the Story of Nicodemus the Pharisee found in John 3:1–15, as well as Luke 22:66. Here is an example of both non-dualistic images of Christ and self, as well as opposites in creative tension. The

Son of Man appears in numerous parts of the Hebrew and Christian Bibles and points to both a prophetic, messiah-like figure, as well as any person born of woman. This koan further highlights the ambiguous manner in which Jesus is portrayed in these gospel stories. While so many Christian apologists have focused on defending the divinity of Christ, many seem to overlook the fact that Jesus appears at times to deny any exclusive claim to the title "Son of God." The Gospel of Mark refers to this as the "Messianic Secret," where Jesus repeatedly urges people not to refer to him as messiah as he knew most would misunderstand his identity. Whenever asked if he is the Son of God, he is evasive and begins to talk of the Son of Man. In John 10:34–36, while being interrogated by the Pharisees, Jesus questions back and asks why they would be offended at such a claim. He quotes Psalms, which says, "You are gods, sons of the Most-High, all of you. Yet you shall die like men, and fall like any prince" (Psalms, 82:6–7).

The intention here is to resist the traditional understanding so many have that Christ is separate and apart from us, and that the divine life present in Jesus is not present in each of us, including the other. The Son of Man koan further points to the non-dualistic nature of all people's relationship to God. For Christians this relationship is most fully represented through the person of Jesus of Nazareth who fully realized the ever-living Christ. Christian mystics describe this as the Beatific Vision where the traditional I/Thou relationship of believer and God is replaced by the realization of the Christ Within.

It has been noted by numerous scholars that both the gospel writers and Paul viewed scripture through the psychedelic eyes of the mystic. Such mystical readings naturally lead to non-dualistic images of Christ and God; the clearest example from Paul being Galatians 2:19–20: "I have been crucified with Christ, yet I live, no longer I, but Christ (living) in me."

The doctrine of the Incarnation is also best understood as a non-dualistic, even paradoxical image of God, and refers to the core Christian belief that the Divine dwelt in human flesh in the person of Jesus Christ. What constitutes the Body of Christ today further has an ambiguous, therefore instructional meaning. Scripture uses the expression "Body of Christ" to refer to three distinct things: (1) the physical body of Jesus of Nazareth; (2) the Eucharist, which also represents the physical presence of God among the assembled believers; and (3) the actual body of believers that become a physical presence of the Body of Christ. As Catholics, it is completely orthodox to say that, collectively, we are the Body of Christ. This has profound implications for Catholic spirituality, reminding us that the Word of God did not just become flesh and leave; it became flesh and remains with us today. For Rolheiser, this fact is not simply theology or dogma, but represents the core of Christian spirituality (Rolheiser 1999, 79).

Religious Education as Paradox: Being Rooted and Open

Consistent with being simultaneously rooted to one's faith tradition yet open to others, Gabriel Moran long articulated religious education as consisting of two contrasting aims: (1) to educate practitioners within a particular religious way of life (catechesis for Roman Catholics, Christian, Muslim, and Jewish education for other traditions) and (2) to educate on the nature of religion itself, which inevitably involves understanding one's faith tradition in the context of our religiously pluralistic world. Boys expresses this dual call in terms of educating toward paradox, while Scott frames it in terms of continuity and change. His answer to this practical theological challenge is a tripartite framework for religious education, comprising catechetical, prophetic, and wisdom forms of teaching and learning, which allows for both rootedness and openness.

Scott applies Brueggemann's view of the Hebrew canons of Torah, Prophets, and Writings to provide a helpful framework for a pluralistic form of religious education. Each part of the canon served a different function and offered different forms of knowledge (Scott, 83–84).

A rediscovery and refashioning of the apophatic mystic tradition are presented as essential to better reconciling self and other, and is consistent with Mary Boys' catechetical form of "educating for paradox." Here, religious educators seek to cultivate clear and distinct commitments rooted in the traditions past. However, given the reality of our religiously pluralistic world, acknowledging the inherent mystery at the heart of all religious traditions is more essential than ever. As such, in a mature faith identity, all expressions of the religious tradition need a degree of ambiguity, given the acknowledgment and appreciation of the inevitable mystery at the core of all religious traditions, and religious experience.

In terms of identity formation, educating for cosmopolis must—by necessity—examine the effects interreligious dialogue has on the efforts of a faith community to form and maintain its religious identity, both collectively and individually. For Roman Catholics, a catechetical nurturing of identity and educating for pluralism can—on the surface—appear to be in conflict, yet do not have to be. Catechetical forms of religious education with a more explicit mystical dimension can both honor particular doctrines, traditions, and rituals within the church, while simultaneously not opposing the values of pluralism (Veverka 2004, 47).

A prophetic form of religious education is education against the finalizing and limiting of life's meaning. As Brueggemann and Scott note, prophetic forms of education have two basic movements: criticism, and energizing. There is a constant reminder to those who teach and those who strive to deepen their personal faith that no-thing is God, no final perspective can be drawn, and no doctrine, no ritual, is to be taken as a complete representation of the divine will. Here, the educational task is to prevent the creation of further idols (Scott 2005, 88). As shown above, Roman Catholics and Christians are sometimes susceptible to an odd form of idolatry when they literalize and absolutize words of scripture. Even the person or image of Jesus can become idolatrous, where he is less listened to than worshipped. Here, the figure of Jesus Christ becomes less the Christ of faith and more a projected image of one's own hopes and fears.

For both Scott and Brueggemann, the second movement for prophetic forms of religious education is to energize, reminding all practitioners that to end in criticism is not acceptable. The criticism must lead somewhere better—to a better, but yet unseen Promised Land.

Much of Boys' work has focused on Christian-Jewish dialogue. Her call to educate for paradox is effectively illustrated by John's "man born blind," as well as providing helpful insight into the theme of negation, or unknowing (Boys, 24). To review John 9, Jesus encounters an anonymous man born blind. Jesus spits into some mud and rubs it into the man's eyes and tells him to go wash it out in the pool of Siloam. Neighbors eventually see him and ask how his eyes were opened. He explains how Jesus healed him. They bring him to the Pharisees. Since it was the Sabbath, the Pharisees reason he cannot be from God, for he does not observe the Sabbath. The Pharisees demand that the cured man give glory to God since they knew the man Jesus to be a sinner. The man has no idea whether Jesus is a sinner or not; he only knows that he was blind and now sees. Described as no religious genius, the man is puzzled the Pharisees keep asking about Jesus. Jesus eventually hears this and goes to find the man. Jesus asks whether or not he believes in the Son of Man.

The man asks back who this Son of Man might be so he can offer worship and thanks. Jesus answers it is he who is now speaking. Jesus continues, "I came into this world for judgment so that those who do see may become blind." Some of the Pharisees nearby overhear this and say "Surely, we are not blind, are we?" Jesus' answer: "If you were blind, you would not have sinned. But now that you say 'We see', your sin remains" (John 9:1–41).

According to Boys, her reflection on John came during a Jewish-Christian retreat during Lent, lending a new poignancy and perspective, as this story can also be perceived as explicitly anti-Semitic. During her homily, Boys identifies two groups of characters. The first is the blind man who is portrayed growing in religious awareness and maturity due to his ability to accept new knowledge, grow in faith, and recognize Jesus as God's revelation (Boys, 26). In fact, it is because of his blindness (aka, his "unknowing") that he is able to see this new truth.

The second group is made up of both the neighbors and the Pharisees. The neighbors are "busybodies" with sight but no insight. According to John, it is both the neighbors and the Pharisees who are blind and who represent the established religious authority concerned primarily with orthodoxy and correct, visible observances. Both represent those so convinced of their own righteousness that they remain blind to the new truth. Hinting at an underlying paradox here, Boys continues,

> Lent... is a season for acknowledging that we have the neighbor in us, that we, too, may operate from such limited horizons that we are unable to recognize God's revelation, which often comes from surprising sources. (Boys, 26)

This prophetic form of religious education is always in search of corrupting and limiting "idols" often disguised as devout, orthodox belief and practice, of which Catholics and Christians are far from immune.

The third aspect of religious education—the cultivation of wisdom—is best described as neither proclamation and formation nor criticism of tradition but as a discernment of our common human experience (Scott, 89). Scott notes this form of religious education is comparatively underdeveloped in the Roman Catholic tradition (Scott, 93).

Patterned after the Hebrew sage, the religious educator is here called to cultivate a different form of knowing. Such knowing is best described as a wisdom that honors not knowing; that respects the mystery present at the center of everyday life, and lies at the center of each of us (Scott, 90). As Judaism's wisdom literature highlights, it is the pedagogical task of the sage to teach receptivity to the ordinary world, to hear the divine voice of mystery in one's everyday experience (Scott, 90). Scott concludes with how the final word of the sage is never critique but wonder: in the end, wonder at the holy interconnectedness of all things.

Another key characteristic of wisdom forms of teaching and learning is resistance to certainty. Here the sage resists quick, readymade answers and sweeping universal truths. One is reminded of Jesus' assertion that those striving for the Kingdom of God must retain the faith, wonder, and openness of a child. As such, the teaching of the sage is always provisional; contingent on the immediate present experience. Scott concludes that envisioning the religious educator as sage, a distinct postmodern educational approach emerges honoring a particularity, ambiguity, and a pluralism of perspectives (Scott, 93).

Gabriel Moran had a fundamentally mystical, intuitive conception of teaching that parallels and compliments the above-mentioned teachings found in the Christian mystical tradition. Moran (1997) presents a broader, deeper meaning of the verb to teach that resists traditional modern understandings. The modern assumptions surrounding teaching tends to reduce this inherently mysterious and unpredictable human activity to a classroom activity consisting primarily of giving rational explanations. In contrast, Moran describes teaching in terms of showing how. At its most expansive and profound meaning, teaching becomes showing others how to live and die more meaningfully (Moran 1997, 38).

Paralleling a Christian mystical approach, Moran asserts that religious language is inherently paradoxical and limited. He suggests the best example of this paradoxical aspect is illustrated in the term "unique revelation," hinting at the commonly used terms to set Jesus the Christ above and beyond any meaningful comparison to other potential sources of divine revelation (Moran 2002, 162).

Regarding religious pluralism and the religious other, Moran's theory of uniqueness offers a new perspective on the central, yet often problematic place of Jesus the Christ when placed in the context of the interreligious. Key to unpacking the meaning of Jesus Christ as the unique and fullest example of revelation for Christians is distinguishing the meanings of the terms Jesus, Christ, and unique.

Moran (1992) looks at Jesus the Christ through an articulation of exclusive and inclusive meanings of unique, the intention being at least the partial reconciliation of the inevitable conflicts arising from introducing the non-negotiable Christian belief of Christ as the fullest and unique universal savior of all humanity. In short, Jesu bar joseph—Jesus' proper name—provides an exclusively unique revelation in that he was a unique individual living in first-century Palestine. The term "Christ," from the Greek Christos, a translation of the Jewish term "messiah," came to have a fundamentally different meaning than messiah: specifically, Christ becomes the second person of the Trinity and universal savior of all humanity. This divine revelation is best understood as inclusively unique in that it includes all other unique revelations, as expressed by Paul and Augustine. It is also instructive regarding our proposed religious identity and how it might honor both the faithful self and the other.

A Christian use of the word unique reflects one of the main ways people deal with an inherent, "paradoxical relation of sameness and difference" (Moran 1992, 5). In more postmodern language, this means everyone and everything from people, religions, and truth, need to be defined in relation to everything else (Moran 1992, 5).[2]

---

[2] According to Moran, the word "unique" has two distinct, almost opposite meanings that give it a paradoxical quality (Moran 1992, 11). These contrasting meanings can be labeled "exclusive" and "inclusive." An exclusive meaning of unique can be represented by the sequence: 1, 1, 1, 3, 1. In this set, the number 1 is not unique, whereas 3 is. There can also be degrees of uniqueness. In the sequence 1, 1, 3, A, 1, 1, the letter A is even more exclusively

14 Religious Identity in a Pluralistic Age: The Paradox of Being Simultaneously...

Moran (1992) further notes how believing in a revealing God is a simple-enough idea that expresses the relation between divine activity and human response. This has traditionally been described in terms of faith and revelation; and while the two have throughout Christian history been understood as two separable things, Moran argues they are actually two parts of one ongoing process or reality if revelation is to be understood as an ongoing present experience. He continues that each are at the heart of Christian theology, church authority, and Christian instruction (Moran 1992, 3). He says it best here:

> The choice is a simple one. Either faith is a thing directed to something in the past called revelation, or faith is an act directed towards what is revelatory in the present. In the first case faith is imagined as a cognitive question: that is, its concern is with assent to divine truths. In the second case, faith engages the whole person and is concerned with today's life. The first version of faith, as I have described it, no longer has many defenders. (Moran 1992, 3)

Scripture read contemplatively ultimately leads one into a non-dualistic awareness of Christ Jesus as infusing one's own being, and the being of the other. This too has its own challenges and caveats when linked to interreligious and interfaith dialogue. Rahner's creative label of "anonymous-Christians" was taken by some as offensive to practitioners of other faiths. A contemplative way of reading scripture is key to this educational and theological challenge of being rooted and open. Directed practices such as contemplative, silent prayer increase the possibility of developing a mystical consciousness that allows for a creative—even instructional—space for the religious other. As the Catholic theologian Kark Rahner famously said, in the coming centuries, Christians need to become mystics if they are to survive at all as a faith community.

---

unique in that it is not even a number. The point, according to Moran, is that nothing is simply and totally unique. In theory, one could continue moving toward ever-greater degrees of uniqueness until one reaches what Moran refers to as "splendid isolation," where a particular thing cannot be compared to anything else (Moran 1992, 19).

An inclusive meaning of uniqueness can be represented by the sequence: a, ab, abc, abcd, where the fourth set is unique from the previous three. Each successive set after "a" is more inclusively unique than the previous. It is significant to note that the fourth set "abcd" cannot be considered simply unique since the logic of the sequence suggests the possibility of more unique sets (Moran 1992, 20).

Final Thoughts

This is an ambitious chapter examining the educational and theological challenges related to forming a dialogical, pluralistic form of religious education that allows both communities and individuals to be simultaneously rooted in the best of their tradition, yet open to the wisdom of the religious other.

A number of significant related issues were barely touched on and are in need of further study. Our increasingly divided and polarized society continues to struggle with a number of existential challenges and issues; increasing wealth polarization, climate change, increasing immigration and refugee crises, rising authoritarianism, dwindling resources, all are pushing our democratic institutions to their breaking point. The extreme concentration of corporate and personal wealth takes further forms in the destructive and manipulative influence of our concentrated, corporate news and social media finely tuned to reward extremist, inflammatory sound bites that increasingly demonize an ever-present, threatening other, all of which tries to pass as news.

People of faith are further reminded that the demonization and dehumanization of the other continues in many of our faith traditions and further understood as faithful belief and practice. To resist this still present tendency, more dialogical forms of religious education—coupled with a healthy, even essential awareness of the inherent divine mystery present at the center of our collective religious and spiritual traditions—are needed more than ever.

A further aim was to demonstrate how the apophatic Christian tradition has a much-needed and relevant wisdom in need of rediscovery and refashioning that has the potential to heal our divided and increasingly dysfunctional society. It is proposed that our three themes of (1) non-dualistic images of Christ, God, and self; (2) paradoxical truths held in creative tension; and (3) language as negation provide a framework to read scripture in a contemplative, meditative, and educational way, thus allowing for a more intuitive, mystical, and intimate encounter with both the other and the divine. These lenses so prevalent within this tradition are instructive in forming a more effective academic language that aims to articulate the inherent paradox at the heart of being rooted and open. Such educational and spiritual practices ultimately lead to a creative space for the other within one's sense of self. To do so is also to educate for cosmopolis.

Whether or not our Christian and Catholic churches have the spiritual energy and persuasion to attract those searching for a meaningful faith identity remains to be seen.

References

Boys, Mary C. 2000. *Has God only one Blessing? Judaism as a Source of Christian Self Understanding.* New York, Mahwah, N.J.: Paulist Press.

Brueggemann, Walter. 2001. *The Prophetic Imagination.* 2nd ed. Minneapolis, MN: Augsburg Fortress.

Gunn, Dennis. 2020. *Educating for Civic Dialogue in an Age of Uncivil Discourse.* New York, NY: Routledge, Taylor and Francis Group.

Haight, Roger. 2022. *The Nature of Theology: Challenges, Frameworks, Basic Beliefs.* Maryknoll, NY: Orbis Books.

Johnston, William. 2003. *Letters to Friends: Meditations in Daily Life.* New York: Fordham Press.

Lefebure, Leo D. 1993. *The Buddha & the Christ: Explorations in Buddhist and Christian Dialogue.* Maryknoll, N.Y.: Orbis Books.

Leong, Kenneth S. 2001. *The Zen Teachings of Jesus.* New York: Crossroads, 1995.

McGinn, Bernard, and Patricia Ferris McGinn. 2003. *Early Christian Mystics: The divine vision of the spiritual masters.* New York: The Crossroad Publishing Company.

Moran, Gabriel. 1992. *Uniqueness: Problem or paradox in Jewish and Christian traditions.* Maryknoll, N.Y.: Orbis Books.

———. 1997. *Showing How: The Act of Teaching.* Valley Forge, PA: Trinity Press International.

———. 2002. *Both Sides: The Story of Revelation.* New York, Mahwah, N.J.: Paulist Press.

Rolheiser, Ronald. 1999. *The Holy Longing: The Search for a Christian Spirituality.* New York, London, Toronto, Sydney, Auckland: Doubleday.

Scott, Kieran. 2005. Continuity and Change in Religious Education: Building on the Past, Re-imagining the Future. In *Emerging Issues in Religious Education in Ireland,* ed. Oliver Brennan, 79–98. Dublin: Veritas.

Veverka, Fayette B. 2004. Practicing Faith: Negotiating Identity and Difference in a Religiously Pluralistic World. *Religious Education Journal* 99 (1): 38–55.

Mark King has spent thirty years teaching theology, comparative religion, philosophy, psychology, and history to a variety of graduate, undergraduate, and secondary education students. He is a published author, has mentored master's theses, and sat on doctoral committees. He received his PhD in Religion and Education from Fordham University's Graduate School of Religion and Education, Rosehill Campus. He presently teaches Psychology of Faith and Church History at Maria Regina High School in Hartsdale, NY.

Concluding Remarks

Muhammad Shafiq

This issue of inclusion or exclusion, the self and the other, has deeply impacted me during my entire career. I have lived a story of transformation away from a narrow, conservative, and self-centered interpretation of the sacred texts to a more deeply pluralistic view. I have done so under the influence of the two cultures by which my life has been shaped—the culture of Pakistan, the land of my birth, and the culture of my adopted country, the United States. The in-depth study of the world religion and of Islam has played a key role in this transformation along with my graduate studies at Temple University. But the real story is about my commitment to interfaith dialogue, to promote inclusivity and respectful coexistence for all.

Exclusive thinking is natural as people like to believe that they are special and unique. The same is true of all faiths, ethnicities, and even races believing that their faith, race, or ethnicity is special. This is what keeps them loving and appreciating their faith or origin. Similarly, faith communities are internally divided over belief and practice, with orthodox, conservative, and reform movements and further subdivisions within each. There are many denominations among Protestant Christians, and similarly, the Catholics, Muslims, Hindus, Buddhists, and others are also di-

---

M. Shafiq (✉)
Hickey Center & IIIT Chair for Interfaith Studies and Dialogue,
Nazareth University, Rochester, NY, USA
e-mail: mshafiq5@naz.edu

© The Author(s), under exclusive license to Springer Nature Switzerland AG 2024
M. Shafiq, T. Donlin-Smith (eds.), *Inclusion or Exclusion in the Sacred Texts and Human Contexts*, https://doi.org/10.1007/978-3-031-70180-1

vided within. Once there was a Catholic-Muslim dialogue and, in the Q&A session, a Catholic speaker was asked about who will enter heaven. The speaker replied that when other Christians, Muslims, and Jews arrived at the gate of heaven, the Catholics had taken the key spaces.[1] The Vatican II document, Nostra Aetate, recognizes Judaism and Islam as monotheistic faiths and Protestant Christins as fellow Christians, but at the same time professes the Roman Catholic faith as the true and right one. There is nothing wrong with commitment to a particular faith if there is respect for other faiths and people of other faiths. Faith should not involve condemning other faiths and people, spreading hatred, or disrupting peaceful coexistence.

Human life is sacred. God created people in 'His' image in Abrahamic faiths. As the Qur'an says, the *Ruh* (soul) of people is the *Ruh* (Soul) of God.[2] It is a commandment to protect human life. Killing an innocent one is like killing the whole of humanity and saving one is like saving the whole of humanity.[3] But some very conservative people not only curse people of other faiths, using evil words, but even do not hesitate from violence against humanity. In terms of their anger to Islam, even some well-known religious conservatives in America call Islam an evil religion. Some do not hesitate to call Allah "evil" without understanding that the Arabic Bible uses the word Allah for God.[4] The Qur'an prohibits strictly abusive and hateful language against other religions and people of other religions. The Qur'an asks the believers to address followers of other religions with respect but there are some Muslims using hateful language violating the very basic principle of their own religion.[5] This exclusive attitude toward religious beliefs at the cost of human dignity has contributed to an explosive tribal nationalism around the world

---

[1] The writer was present in the seminar when the discussion took place.

[2] Qur'an, 32:9, "and then He forms him in accordance with what he is meant to be, and breathes into him of His spirit: and [thus, O men,] He endows you with hearing, and sight, and feelings as well as minds: [yet] how seldom are you grateful."

[3] Qur'an, 5:32.

[4] Read the article in the New York Times: https://www.nytimes.com/2003/05/27/us/seeing-islam-as-evil-faith-evangelicals-seek-converts.html.

[5] Qur'an, 6:108 says: "But do not revile those [beings] whom they invoke instead of God, lest they revile God out of spite, and in ignorance: for, goodly indeed have We made their own doings appear unto every community In time, [however,] unto their Sustainer they must return: and then He will make them [truly] understand all that they were doing".

The Qur'an in verse 16:125, admonish Muslims: "CALL THOU (all mankind) unto thy Sustainer's path with wisdom and goodly exhortation, and argue with them in the most kindly manner- for, behold, thy Sustainer knows best as to who strays from His path, and best knows He as to who are the right-guided.

Concluding Remarks

in the twenty-first century. To place religion above people runs contrary to the very foundation of religions' 'golden rule' to treat others as you would treat yourself or love your neighbor as you would love yourself.

In some parts of the world, some religious conservatives may become aggressive even violent, if their arguments are refuted. Conservatives here in the United States may not get violent but would use hateful rhetoric in their sermons or speeches. This hateful rhetoric, especially among those of the Abrahamic faiths, is breeding antisemitism and Islamophobia in America and elsewhere.

It is true that sacred texts have some verses that could be interpreted both exclusively and inclusively. This volume thoroughly discusses the misleading verses and words in the sacred texts. Saundra S. Epstein discusses the word Mitzvot (dictated actions), who are exempt and who are forbidden, and how these categorical groupings have been misunderstood in the Jewish historical journey. Conservative Christians have exclusive claims referring to the New Testament words: "I am the door" through whom one will be saved (John 10:9), or "I am the way and the truth and the life (John 14:6) through whom one comes to the 'Father.'" Abdul Aziz's (May his soul rest in peace) chapter refers to the misuse of Al Wala' and wa al Bara' (the principle of loyalty and disloyalty) by the Wahabi theology and later used by some other conservative Islamic and extremist groups.

Similarly, like Abrahamic faiths, Mathew Foust's chapter demonstrates exclusive attitudes and actions exhibited by Confucius as he was portrayed in the Analects. The same goes for the Lotus Sutra according to Thomson's chapter on Buddhism: It could stand for inclusive, universal salvation in the Buddhist tradition, but at the same time, devotees have interpreted it exclusively resulting in violent conflicts. The same is true of Hinduism: although it has a pluralistic foundation, today the 'Hindutva' movement is violently suppressing minority ethnic and religious groups.

Another problem with exclusivity is the intersection of faith and race, thus dividing humanity and faiths into racial categories. 'The other' in religion was not only the other faith but also a racial category to demonize the other as 'savage' and uncivilized. The intersection of race and religion then leads to the perception of inferior biological traits and the other is labeled as intellectually inferior, lazy, barbaric, and violent. The traces of this intersection can be found, for example, in the Laws of Manu in Hinduism in justification of the caste system and even in the Bible dividing humanity into chosen and gentile or Isaac verses Ishmael. Such toxic combinations of race and faith in American Protestantism contributed to the subjugation of Native Americans and the enslavement of Africans. The same process is at work in the treatment of Asian Americans, Latinx-Hispanic Americans, and Muslims today in America.

Religions have universal foundational principles of healing, reconciliation, and peaceful coexistence which should empower us with the spiritual awareness to be responsible citizens of the mother earth. Human life is sacred in all religions. Conflicts are natural and religions alone are not responsible for why we cannot get along. Economic, political, and other factors play a key role in creating these conflicts. However, religious and interfaith leaders must stand together to seek peaceful resolution to conflicts to protect humanity and the natural environment. If the creation and the very presence of people on earth represent the image of the 'Sacred' on earth, and if the 'Sacred' is a universal sacred being transcending race and sex, then dividing and dehumanizing 'His' people must stop. Interfaith leaders must promote interfaith and intra-faith dialogue to protect the dignity of people. They should engage wholeheartedly in social justice dialogue in service of humanity.

Index

A
Abraham, 146
Abrahamic Promise, 47
Agapic love, 93, 106
Ahd, 60
Ahl al-hadīth, 114
Ahl al-Ra'y, 114
Ahl at-tawḥīd, 170
"Al-iḫwān" ("the brothers") movement, 172, 175, 178
Al-Qaida, 206, 210
Ambiguity, 124
American/European dominant discourses, 201
Analects, 75–87
Ansar, 65, 68
Apocalyptic ultimacy, 46
Apophatic mystical tradition, 229
Arab League in 1945, 179
Ash'arite school, 113
Ashkenazic Jews, 15
Asurim, 3
Augustine of Hippo, 108
Awliyā' Allāh, 118

B
Bais Yaakov, 8
Barbarian, 77–81, 86
Beatific Vision, 232
Believer, 147–150
Belonging, 160, 161, 163
Be'Tzelem Elokim, 5
Black Freedom Movement, 99, 106
Braille Institute, 19
British Empire, 102–104
Brothers, 169, 172, 174, 180
Buddha Padmaprabha, 33
Burhān, 187, 188
Bus Boycott, 96, 97, 103, 106
Bush, George W., 211, 212

C
Caliphate, 216
Canaan, 157
Caṇḍālas, 31
Catechetical, 233
Chi, 78
Christianity, 125

Christ Within, 232
Chrystal Nacht, 48
Citizens of Heaven, 156, 161–164
Co-existence, 59–62, 66, 67, 71, 72
Collegia, 160, 161
Colonialism, 94, 98–100, 106
Confucian exclusivism, 75–87
Confucius, 75–87
Consanguinitism, 77
Cosmopolitanism, 226
Courtiers, 140, 141
Culturalism, 77–81, 83, 86, 87

D
Dāif, 117
Daʿīf, 115, 117
Dao, 79, 80
Dark mysticism, 229
Dawla, 207
Deus Migrator, 164
Dexter Avenue Baptist Church, 94, 96, 98, 101, 103, 105
Dhāraṇīs, 34
Di, 78, 79
Dialogical forms of education, 226
Dialogue, 129–133
Dīn, 207
Discursive narrative, 201, 203, 204, 208, 213, 219, 220
Discursive tradition, 184–188
Divine, 143, 149, 151
Divine Grace, 48
Divine Revelation, 187, 189, 191, 197
Diwakar, R. R., 96, 98
Diya' al-Umari, Akram, 61, 63, 64
Dualisms, 229
Duality, 142

E
Eck, Diana, 227
Egypt, 156–158
Ekayāna, 30
Evangelical/evangelical, 43–56
Exclusivism, 28–35, 37–40

Exemplarist, 75–87
Exemplarity, 85–87

F
Al-Farabi, 190–193
Feminist Alliance, 11
Fereshteh, 133–135
Fihi ma fihi, 139–151
Fīqh, 116, 188, 216
First Saudi State, 173, 174, 180
Fiṭrah, 112
Foreigner, 156–161, 163, 164
Forty Hadith of Nawawī, 107–121
Foucault, Michel, 208, 209, 218
Freedom of faith, 62, 64, 69–71

G
Ğāhiliyūn, 171
Gandhi, Mahatma Mohandas K., 93–106
Gandhian nonviolence, 95–97, 99, 100
Ger, 158
God as primarily gracious, 52
God's self-communication, 109–111, 118
Grace, 107–121
Gulen, Fethullah, 131, 132

H
The Hadith, 107–121, 185, 186
Hadith collections, 108, 115, 117
Halacha, 4, 11, 19
Hamites, 128
Happiness, 190–192
Ḥasan, 115
Haskalah, 8
Hebrew Scriptures, 159
Hermeneutical, 220
Hizmet Movement, 129, 131, 132, 138
Hospitality, 139–151
Huá, 77
Hui, 78
Human freedom, 108, 110–111, 113, 117, 119–121
Hypocrites, 65, 66, 169

Index

I
Ibn Taymiyya, Shaykh Taqī al-Dīn, 168
Ijtihād, 194, 221, 222
Imamate, 216
Immigrants, 155, 156, 158, 160, 163, 164
Incarnation, 230, 232
Inclusive evangelicalism, 43–56
Inclusivism, 27–40
Infelicities, 86, 87
Infidel, 148–150
Inner self, 147
Islamic governance, 184, 199
Islamic Law, 71
Islamophobia, 203
Isnād, 115, 117
ITIM, 22, 23

J
Jadal, 187, 188
Jama'at, 67
Japhethites, 128
Jim Crow, 95, 96, 100
Johnson, Mordecai, 95, 98
Judaeanism, 125
Junzi, 79, 80, 86

K
Kalām, 188
Kalelkar, Kaka, 96, 98
Kamochah, 13
Kasb, 113
Khatābah, 187, 188
King, Martin Luther Jr., 93–106
Al-Kitab, 60
Klal Yisrael, 5
The Koan, 231–232

L
Legitimacy, 184, 185, 187, 191, 192, 194–196
Lohia, Ram Manohar, 96
Lotus Sūtra, 27–40
Love, 142–144, 148, 149
Lover of God, 142

Loyalty and Disavowal, 168–181
Luther, Martin, 45–46, 49–56

M
Madhaib, 114
Madinah Pact, 59–72
Makkah, 64, 69
Mán, 77, 78, 80
Mañjuśrī, 31, 33
Maqsad Amm, 68
Martyrdom, 205, 206
Masechet Hagiga, 16, 18
Maslaha, 68
Mawdūʿ, 115
Mechayavim, 3
Mechuyavim, 23
Middle Ages, 125
Migrants, 155, 156, 164
Migration, 155–164
Min zhi yi, 79
Mitzvot, 3
MRP'ing, 40
Muhajir, 65
Muhammad Ibn Abd al-Wahhab, 168, 173
Muhammad, Mevlana Jalaluddin, 139
Mujtahids, 196
Mu'tazilites, 113
Mysticism, 146
Mystics, 139, 146–148
Myth of Muslims, 203, 211, 221

N
Nāga, 33–35
Namu myōhō renge kyō, 37, 40
Negation, 228, 230, 231, 234, 238
New Testament, 162, 163
Niyābat al-nubuwwah, 197
Nokhri, 124, 125, 157, 158
Nokhrim, 158
Nonviolence, 94–97, 99, 100, 102–105

O
Ohr Torah Stone (OTS), 7
Old Testament, 157

Oneness of God, 171
Ontology of gift, 53, 55, 56
Opposites-in-tension, 230
Orientalist, 186
Other, 93–106
Othering, 125, 127, 128, 130, 138

P
Palm Sunday sermon, 93–106
Paradigmatic characters, 76
Paradox, 225–238
Paradoxical truths, 228, 231, 238
Parents for Torah for All Children (PTACH), 19
Paroikos, 160
Particularism, 29
Paterfamilias, 162, 163
Pelagianism, 108–110
People for Orthodox Renaissance and Torah (PORAT), 7, 10
People of the Book, 169
Peturim, 3
Pluralism, 28, 29, 39, 185, 189, 197, 198, 227, 233, 235
Political thought, 184, 185, 188, 189, 193, 198–199
Political use of Islam, 202
Polyreligious, 106
Polytheists, 169–171, 173–175
Pope Benedict XVI, 204, 205
Prajñākūṭa, 33
Pre-modern Muslim Community, 183
Privileging, 81
Prophetic, 232–235
Prophetic forms of education, 233
Prophetic Madinah, 59
Prophetic tradition, 185–187, 194, 197, 198
Protestant, 44
Pseudo-Dionysius, 229, 230

Q
Qadr, 113
Qin ai, 82
Quan, 78

The Qur'an, 185, 186, 198

R
Rabbaniot, 7
Race, 46, 48, 55, 56, 126–129, 134
Rahner, Karl, 109
Rākṣasas, 34
Reason, 45, 52, 53, 56
Reformation, 45, 49
Refugees, 155, 156, 163, 164
Religious pluralism, 225, 227, 236
Ren ai, 82
Revelation, 109–112, 118
Rong, 77
Rumi, 139–151
Rustin, Bayard, 97, 98

S
Sadāparibhūta, 40
Sahifah, 60
Ṣaḥīḥ, 115
Salat, 148, 149
Salt March, 103
Salvation, 107–109, 111, 118
Śāriputra, 30–33, 39
Satori, 231
Satyagraha, 95
Second Saudi State, 173–174, 180
Secularization, 226
Seeds of Peace, 129–131
Self and other, 123–138
Semites, 127, 128
September 11, 2001, 203
Shadows, 150
Shariʿa, 184, 185, 188, 190, 194–199
Shariah, 67
Shemites, 127
Shia Muslims, 170
Shinshūkyō, 38
Shrouds, 150
Shu, 85
Siddiqui, Mona, 144, 145
Signified, 208, 209, 211, 212
Signifier, 208, 209, 212

Signs of the Unseen, 139, 146–151
Siona Benjamin, 133, 134, 136–138
Sixth Commandment, 124
Snakes, 209, 210
Social dimension, 108, 111, 113–114, 120–121
Social integration, 61, 66–68, 71, 72
Sotah, 9
Soul, 143, 144, 146–149
Sovereignty, 183–185, 189, 190, 192, 193, 195, 197, 198
Speciesism, 77, 78, 81–87
Spiritual humility, 129
Spirituality of hospitality, 139–151
Stereotypes, 108
Stranger/foreign, 124, 130
Sufi Muslims, 170
Sufi orders, 188, 189
Sunna, 114, 117
Sunni, 108, 113–115, 117, 119
Sūtra, 30–32, 35, 37

T
Talmud, 6, 16–18, 20, 21
Ṭawāġīt, 171–173
Ten Commandments, 44
Terrorism, 210, 212, 217, 222
Thoreau, 103
Tīrthika, 35
Torat Chayim, 7
Tower of Babel, 226
Tripartite framework, 233
True Israel, 125
Trump, Donald, 43, 45, 46, 51, 56, 202, 210
Tzedakah, 21

U
Ummah, 67–69, 185
Ummatan wahida, 67
Unique, 226, 236, 237
Universal salvation, 28
Upāya, 28, 30, 39

Uri L'Tzedek, 7
Usness, 131

V
Violent Muslims, 201–208, 213, 218–222
Viraja, 33

W
Wahhabi movement, 170, 172
Wahhabism, 168, 170–171, 174, 176, 177, 179, 180
Al-Walā' Wa-Al-Barā, 167–181
Wallach, John, 129, 130
War on Terror, 208, 210–212
Water of faith, 149
Watheeqah, 60
Western duality, 201
Wine goblet, 143, 144
Wisdom, 225, 228, 229, 233, 235, 238
Witchcraft, 125

X
Xenophobia, 155
Xenos, 160
Xi ai, 82
Xiaoren, 79

Y
Yachad, 20
Yeshivat Maharat, 11
Yi, 77–80
Yoatzot, 11

Z
Zar, 124, 157
Zhi, 78, 79
Zhongguo, 77
Zomet, 19

Printed in the United States
by Baker & Taylor Publisher Services